◘ SPARKED ◘

SPARKED

George Floyd, Racism, and the Progressive Illusion

Edited by
Walter R. Jacobs
Wendy Thompson Taiwo
and Amy August

MINNESOTA
HISTORICAL
SOCIETY PRESS

mnhspress.org

The Minnesota Historical Society Press is a member of the Association of University Presses.

Manufactured in the United States of America

10 9 8 7 6 5 4 3 2 1

♾ The paper used in this publication meets the minimum requirements of the American National Standard for Information Sciences—Permanence for Printed Library Materials, ANSI Z39.48-1984.

International Standard Book Number
ISBN: 978-1-68134-208-5 (paper)
ISBN: 978-1-68134-209-2 (e-book)

Library of Congress Control Number: 2021935185

This and other Minnesota Historical Society Press books are available from popular e-book vendors.

Contents

Preface

From Wonderful/Wretched Memories to Sparked Discussion of Racial Dynamics in Minnesota

Walter R. Jacobs

"We are all shocked and saddened by the tragic events in Minneapolis, Minnesota over the past few days. As human beings, many of us are overwhelmed by the complexity of the situation and the intense emotions it has created. As members of an institution that strives for social justice, we feel discouraged and outraged. And, as social scientists, we are wondering how our disciplines and our knowledge can contribute to solutions. I have three thoughts about steps we can take."

So began a May 29, 2020, email I sent to the College of Social Sciences at San José State University (SJSU), where I am the dean and a professor of sociology. The May 25, 2020, murder of George Floyd by a Minneapolis police officer and subsequent protests about police brutality and other injustices faced by Black people in the United States—protests both peaceful and violent—prompted many social scientists to ask, *What can we do to help repair the many fractures in American society that seem to be getting worse each day*? The first step, of course, is to educate ourselves about the issues, especially about the history and culture of the place at the epicenter of one of the most recent conflagrations sparked by the murder of yet another unarmed Black person.

My email to the college included a paragraph about my being on the faculty at the University of Minnesota, Twin Cities for fourteen years. In addition to checking in with friends and former colleagues who were still living in Minnesota, I had conversations with folks who'd left the area, and those chats inevitably included discussions about Minnesota's progressive reputation. One good friend and I discussed the January 8, 2020, article "When Minneapolis Segregated" from the *CityLab* website, which analyzes how racial housing covenants in Minneapolis blocked home sales to people of color from the early 1900s to an official end in 1948 (but with unofficial enforcement for many years afterward), establishing patterns of inequality that persist to this day. The article notes, "Despite its reputation for prosperity and progressive politics, Minneapolis now has the lowest rate of homeownership among African American households of any U.S. city." My friend informed me about the work of the University of Minnesota's Mapping Prejudice project, which provides extensive analyses of the operation of racial covenants in the Twin Cities.

A conversation with Wendy Thompson Taiwo (assistant professor of African American studies at SJSU) about our experiences as African Americans living and working in the Twin Cities was very momentous. Wendy noted that her time in Minnesota was "wonderful and wretched for Black folks like us." That struck a nerve with me, as my time was also filled with both amazing and awful moments. After mulling over our conversation for a few days, I thought: *As a component of educating others about the fraught racial landscape of the Twin Cities, why don't I collect some stories about the good, the bad, and the ugly of life from college and university faculty members who were former residents of Minnesota but now have some distance to critically reflect on their experiences*? I contacted the editors of The Society Pages website, Doug Hartmann and Chris Uggen, and we decided to publish a special series of personal essays, "Wonderful/ Wretched Memories of Racial Dynamics in the Twin Cities, Minnesota." The series includes a reflection from Wendy and three essays from me.

Over the summer of 2020 I asked social scientists with ties to Minnesota to discuss their memories of racial dynamics in the Twin Cities, specifically about their own experiences regarding the wonderful and wretched components of life in the area. The essays addressed questions such as

Who lives in Minnesota? How does this racial composition shape the state's racial climate?

Are the specific type of racism and the racial dynamics of the Twin Cities different than in other parts of Minnesota?

What is so wonderful about Minnesota?

Amy August is now an assistant professor of sociology at SJSU, but in the summer of 2020 she was concluding her PhD studies at the University of Minnesota, Twin Cities. She and I edited the submissions, and they were posted on The Society Pages between June 8 and August 31, 2020. That October, Doug and Chris reached out to me about the possibility of converting the special series into a book. I loved the idea and suggested that Amy and Wendy could be coeditors given their contributions to The Society Pages series. Chris and Doug then pitched the idea to the director of the Minnesota Historical Society Press, Josh Leventhal. After a series of conversations, *Sparked: George Floyd, Racism, and the Progressive Illusion* was born.

Sparked: George Floyd, Racism, and the Progressive Illusion reprints many of the original "Wonderful/Wretched Memories of Racial Dynamics in the Twin Cities, Minnesota" essays in the first section of the book. The second section is a collection of personal essays by academics who currently live in Minnesota. These new essays are written by BIPOC authors, with a particular emphasis on Black voices. A few of the new essays were prompted—sparked!—by something the author read in one of the original "Wonderful/Wretched" series essays. For instance, Yohuru Williams's "Some Abstract Place: Reflections on 'Black Life and Death in Minnesota'" was inspired by Wendy's essay, "Black Life and Death in Minnesota." Other essays in the second section distill themes from the authors' own lives and work. The two main sections are preceded by an introductory chapter from Amy, "Coloring In the Progressive Illusion: An Introduction to Racial Dynamics in Minnesota," and Wendy, Amy, and I collaborate on a brief conclusion to the book, "Where Will We Be on May 25, 2022?," referring to the second anniversary of George Floyd's murder.

In the introduction to *A Good Time for the Truth: Race in Minnesota*, editor Sun Yung Shin argues,

> Race is certainly not always the most important dimension of our identities, but in Minnesota, and in the United States, it is undeniably important. Too often, in a split second, it can become a life-or-death matter. It can determine much of our destinies, our movements, our opportunities, our vulnerabilities. It has determined who has been taken from their families and sent to assimilationist and abusive boarding schools, who has been allowed to work and for how long, who has been allowed to live in certain neighborhoods, who is stopped and frisked, who has access to financing and opportunity and good education and safety. The structures built in the past live with us, just as systems we build now will exist after us.

Racism continues to divide us as a nation as we have too often failed, collectively, to address the issues of the past and to seek truth in the present. Many readers may notice that Americans are having more, and more urgent, conversations—and many highly visible public demonstrations—about race in this country, as there is a renewed critical mass of citizens and groups and leaders who are unafraid to speak the truth about these disparities and about the very real suffering of and harsh punishments meted out to certain communities and groups.

Shin notes that the essays in *A Good Time for the Truth* "are offered as contributions to that conversation. They are intended to enlarge our understanding of, and deepen our connections to, one another." *Sparked: George Floyd, Racism, and the Progressive Illusion* continues and intensifies that conversation; in the five years since *A Good Time for the Truth* was published, white supremacists have been emboldened and the state-sanctioned murders of Black and brown people have escalated. Our hope is that the essays in this volume will spark conversations among friends and family about race, racism, and racial inequality in Minnesota and beyond, and that they spark progressive action and radical change. As Jasmine Mitchell notes in her "Gesturing Toward Tenuous Inclusion" essay in this volume, "Minnesota nice comforts and illusionary progressiveness reside upon the ignoring of White racial terrorism and fears of Blackness, of brown immigrants, and of resistance to White supremacy." The thirty-six essays in *Sparked: George Floyd, Racism, and the Progressive Illusion* can help us confront the causes of anti-Blackness, racial inequality, and systematic violence and expand anti-racist efforts to create a more just, equitable, and democratic society.

Coloring In the Progressive Illusion
An Introduction to Racial Dynamics in Minnesota

Amy August

Not unlike the fictional rural enclave Lake Wobegon, "where all the women are strong, all the men are good-looking, and all the children are above average," Minnesota itself has the reputation of being more literate, progressive, and civic-minded than other states. *U.S. News & World Report* consistently includes Minnesota among the three best states and the Minneapolis–St. Paul metro in the top twenty-five best places to live. These rankings paint a rosy picture of the Twin Cities as a cosmopolitan utopia. "Having attracted residents from countries like Mexico, India, Laos and Somalia," according to the magazine's assessment, the Cities are replete with "a range of worship options, including a great number of churches, synagogues and mosques," not to mention a host of other opportunities for Minnesotans to enjoy the food, art, and music of these groups. Further contributing to this progressive, civic-minded image are the words of our elected leaders. As Representative Ilhan Omar tweeted following her election to Congress in November 2018, "Here in Minnesota, we don't only welcome refugees and immigrants; we send them to Washington." And as former senator Al Franken explains, "I grew up in Minnesota, where we treasure our tradition of civic engagement—and our record of having the nation's highest voter participation."[1]

On its surface, Minnesota's reputation as a welcoming, civic-minded place holds up. Relative to other populous metro areas in the United States, the Twin Cities offer good jobs, affordable housing, accessible health care, and a high quality of life. Relative to other states, taxes are high in Minnesota because citizens vote to invest public dollars in infrastructure and natural resources, parks and recreation, and the arts, further advancing the state's progressive image. Based on newspaper circulation, educational attainment, number of bookstores, and internet, library, and periodical publishing resources, Minneapolis consistently ranks among the top three cities nationwide in literacy, and St. Paul is usually not far behind. According to Steven Schier, a retired Carleton College political science professor, these trends hearken back to Minnesota's Scandinavian and German immigrant communities, "who were 'moralistic and public regarding' and tended to agree with the notion that government had a role to play when it's in the best interest of everyone."[2]

Indeed, in the aggregate, these figures look good. But underlying this big picture is what economist Samuel L. Myers Jr. describes later in this volume as the "Minnesota Paradox": not only does the state bear substantial inequalities in the structural conditions of Minnesota's many racial groups, it is also a place where "Minnesota nice" and the brutal killing of George Floyd can exist in unexamined juxtaposition. It is precisely this paradox that leads Yohuru Williams, in his powerful reflection on Black life and death, to quote Minneapolis NAACP president Leslie Redmond's characterization of Minnesota as a "White Wakanda"—idyllic for white people but full of contradiction and danger for Black folks. Nonetheless, the state's progressive image is easy to dismantle.

Minnesota's Racial and Ethnic Demographics

Before we unpack these disparities, it is helpful to consider Minnesota's demographic makeup. As of 2020, Minnesota's population is 79.1 percent non-Hispanic white, 6.8 percent Black, 5.6 percent Hispanic, 5.1 percent Asian, 2.3 percent two or more races, and 1.1 percent American Indian. But this demographic snapshot masks a more complicated racial history. As recently as 1970, Minnesota's population was 98.2 percent white. Beginning in the mid-1970s, a number of Hmong, Vietnamese, and Karen immigrants and refugees from Southeast Asia began to settle in Minnesota in the aftermath of the Vietnam War. By the 1990s, Minnesota also became a favored destination for Somali immigrants fleeing political turmoil in their homeland. Moreover, the racial and ethnic makeup of the state is rapidly changing. In the five-year period from 2013 to 2018, the white population grew by only 1 percent, compared to an increase of 18 percent in the population of Minnesotans of color. The Minnesota State Demographic Center projects that people of color will constitute more than one-third of the state's residents by 2053. In this way, Minnesota is not all that different from the country at large; the question is how the state will adapt to this demographic shift and how it will put its progressive reputation into policy and action.[3]

Racial Disparities in Housing

Due in part to this rapid diversification and the influx of immigrants, Minnesota has been hailed as a sort of progressive utopia, but a closer look at housing patterns and ownership data calls this reputation into question. In a city with a population that is more than 60 percent white, 87.2 percent of the owned houses in Minneapolis are owned by white people, whereas only 5.2 percent are owned by Black people. (Nationally, whites own 82.5 percent of owned houses and Blacks 8.2 percent.) Looked at from another angle, Minnesota is a state in which 74.5 percent of whites own homes but only 24.8 percent of Black people do. According to the Urban Institute, Minnesota's 50 percent homeownership gap is the largest in the United States. At the other end of the socioeconomic ladder, Black people also fare worse: compared to white residents, Black Minnesotans are fourteen times more likely to experience homelessness.[4]

According to the Mapping Prejudice project at the University of Minnesota, a research project charting racist, restrictive covenants in housing deeds in the Twin Cities metro area, this pattern of housing disparities owes a great deal to historical redlining and to the destruction of the Rondo neighborhood in St. Paul to make way for the construction of the I-94 highway, as well as the disruption of historically Black neighborhoods in south Minneapolis with the building of I-35. Not only do properties in Minneapolis that carried these restrictive covenants in the past still have lower rates of ownership by African Americans today, but those properties also have lower proportions of African American residents overall, and on average they carry 50 percent higher values.

Racial Disparities in Wealth and Income

Though Minnesotans enjoy a low cost of living relative to other states, those costs are nevertheless difficult to afford for some Minnesotans. Consider the racial disparities in median annual earnings: according to US Census data, in Minnesota, Black residents take home $20,763 compared to the median $42,322 earned by whites. (Nationwide, the median incomes are $24,509 for Blacks and $38,899 for whites, as of 2019.)

Moreover, Black Minnesotans are far more likely to suffer economic hardship than their white neighbors. In 2019, for instance, 26.8 percent of Black residents experienced poverty compared to only 6.7 percent of whites. In that same year, 6.1 percent of Black residents experienced unemployment compared to 2.6 percent of whites. In all these statistical measures, the disparity between Black and white is more extreme in Minnesota than the national averages.[5]

These socioeconomic disparities were present even before the COVID-19 pandemic singled out Minnesotans of color for the wreaking of disproportionate havoc. Individuals from communities of color both applied for and continued to need unemployment benefits at higher rates than white Minnesotans. By early December 2020, nearly 10 percent of Black workers had filed for multiple weeks of unemployment, compared to just 3 percent of white workers. Through early 2021, over 60 percent of Black workers and over 50 percent of indigenous workers had filed for unemployment benefits at some point during the pandemic. These disparities have only further exacerbated the racial wealth gap that has been present in Minnesota since long before the disastrous economic downturn of 2020.[6]

Racial Disparities in Education

Some of the most extreme racial disparities in Minnesota are evident in its educational system. Although Minnesota students' average test scores are significantly above the national average, there are huge racial disparities in achievement and attainment in the North Star State. Among a student population made up of 11.3 percent Black children and 64.8 percent white ones, 64.7 percent of Black students graduate high school, compared to 88 percent of their white peers. Black students also trail white students in math and reading, and Minnesota has the largest Black/white achievement gap in school test scores in the nation: only 26.5 percent of Black students meet the statewide goal for math achievement, compared to 62.9 percent of white students; and 34.0 percent of Black students meet the goal for reading achievement, compared to 66.6 percent of white students. These alarming disparities occur despite high constant attendance rates among Black students: 78.4 percent of Black or African American students consistently attend school, compared to 87.9 percent of their white classmates. These heartbreaking statistics reveal that Black students are coming to class every day and learning far less than their white classmates.[7]

Racial Disparities in Criminal Justice

Minnesota's criminal justice system is yet another area where residents of color receive unequal treatment and consequently experience differential outcomes. In Minnesota, 364 people are incarcerated for every 100,000 in the state. While the state's incarceration rate is about half the national average, Black Minnesotans are incarcerated at more than ten times the rate of whites. (The only racial group incarcerated at a higher rate than Blacks in Minnesota are Native Americans.) A comprehensive review by sociologist Chris Uggen and his colleagues shows that following incarceration, individuals experience poorer outcomes across a number of domains, including the labor market, health, family stability, and educational attainment. Minnesota also employs a system that sociologist Michelle Phelps and others refer to as "mass probation," in which a large number of convicted adults are put on probation rather than jailed, which allows the state to keep its incarceration numbers low.[8]

The patterns of racial inequality persist throughout the criminal justice system. Compared to white individuals, Black people in Minneapolis are 11.5 times more likely to be arrested for marijuana possession, 8.9 times more likely to be arrested for disorderly conduct, and 7.5 times more likely to be arrested for vagrancy. As a result, the percentage of Black Minnesotans convicted of felonies is also disproportionately high compared to the white population. Moreover, because sentencing guidelines take into account prior convictions, Black residents are more likely to receive prison sentences following a conviction, and their sentences tend to be harsher.[9]

A number of essays in this volume recount racialized interactions with the police and help us to understand why these patterns look so grim. So too do the facts we have learned about the killings of Jamar Clark, Philando Castile, Dolal Idd, and, of course, George Floyd.

Racial Disparities in Health Care

Despite the state's highly regarded health care system, racial health disparities in Minnesota include those of access as well as those of outcomes and treatment. Regarding access, in 2017, the proportion of Black Minnesotans who lacked health insurance was more than three times as high as that of white Minnesotans. People of color in Minnesota also fare worse than white Minnesotans from the effects of heart disease, stroke, drug overdose, and childbirth. During the 2011–17 time period,

Black mothers were 1.5 times more likely to die during pregnancy, delivery, and the year post-delivery than were white mothers. In her gripping essay in this volume, Wendy Thompson Taiwo addresses the differences in treatment and experiences that lead to such heinous disparities.[10]

COVID-19 has hit the Black community in Minnesota particularly hard. In the state, Black residents have had 1.5 times the number of cases, 4.7 times the number of hospitalizations, and 2.6 times the number of deaths from COVID-19 as have whites. However, recent analysis by sociologists and demographers at the University of Minnesota suggests that the rate of death is actually more than five times greater among African Americans than whites when adjusting for age-related factors and indirect causes. The Minnesota COVID-19 Response team explains this disparity as the product of Black Minnesotans' higher likelihood of exposure because they are more likely to be essential workers and less likely to have jobs that allow them to work from home. In particular, many Black workers are employed in the health care industry, especially as staff in congregate care and shelter facilities.[11]

Racial Differences in Lived Experiences in Minnesota

The widespread racial disparities that exist in Minnesota have profound implications for people's lived experiences. The Kids Involvement and Diversity Study, a project headed by sociologists Doug Hartmann and Teresa Swartz at the University of Minnesota, brought several such impacts to light. Through interviews with parents and children about how they choose and experience extracurricular activities, the researchers discovered that most preferred to have their children participate in racially diverse activities. However, white parents and parents of color had different reasons for this shared preference. Probing their rationales revealed that something insidious was afoot.[12]

Parents of color tended to offer explanations like the one shared by a Latina mom, who was raising an Afro-Latino son in north Minneapolis: "I wanted him to see how people that look like him live and how they can excel. You don't necessarily have to go live in a suburb to excel; you can do that here. You just need to have the right support system and people guiding you. . . . Here, he gets the opportunity to see so many different races and interact with everybody. You're not looked at as an outsider." That is, parents of color carefully chose spaces for their children that would foster development of a positive racial identity. They didn't take for granted that this would happen just anywhere. White parents, on the other hand, like a white father from Merriam Park in St. Paul, tended to see diverse activities as a way to prepare their children to cope successfully with future diversity: "They're gonna have to deal with all these people in life, unless they have . . . some isolated job, you know. And [by participating in activities with kids of different races], they're not afraid of other people—that's a big one. They don't have this fear, which happens a lot of times when you're white, you just have fear of what you don't know and what's different." White parents saw racism as a default that needed to be counteracted.

As Alex Manning argued in the *Du Bois Review*, "parents, especially Black parents and parents of color, guide their children into social environments that have a socialization purpose that goes beyond" the ends of concerted cultivation identified by Annette Lareau: a "valuable set of white-collar skills, including how to set priorities, manage an itinerary, shake hands with strangers, and work on a team." That is, parents of color have more work to do to prepare their children to navigate a racist world. Parents in the Twin Cities indicated that Minnesota was—and is—very much a part of that racist world despite whatever pretensions it may have to being the exception.[13]

The essays in this volume elaborate on the various ways the traumatic effects of George Floyd's killing—and the everyday injustices leading up to it—have rippled through Minnesota communities, inflicting many ancillary traumas and challenges. Beyond the immediate fear and disgust induced by the 8-minute, 46-second video, there are the ongoing concerns about BIPOC men being apprehended as suspects for crimes they didn't commit and that sometimes didn't even occur. The effects are evident in actual experiences of BIPOC men being accused of and apprehended for others' crimes, resulting in the collateral damage of lost time with friends and family, lost wages, lost jobs, and lost dignity. People of color are further confronted with the difficult quandary of deciding whether to seek police help in preventing conflicts from escalating, or instead allow altercations to continue without police intervention due to the possibility of a BIPOC man—and especially a Black man—dying at the hands of the police.

The ancillary traumas of George Floyd's killing extended beyond fears of direct encounters with the police. BIPOC Minnesotans also faced the difficult decision of whether to join the #BlackLivesMatter protests or to stay home during a pandemic that was disproportionately affecting communities of color, and they faced the gripping worry about the safety of loved ones who chose to venture out and participate in support of social justice protests. Add to these the concerns of mothers fearing for the safety of their Black and Brown sons, and the challenge of raising them to face a racist society with equanimity rather than resentment, and you have a beginner's guide to understanding the Minnesota experience for residents of color.

Police violence, while the source of many reprehensible social pathologies, is also the symptom of a much more insidious and pervasive disease. After all, incidents like the killing of George Floyd do not just happen at any place and any time. Rather, they occur in a certain type of social context that systematically disadvantages people of color and privileges their white neighbors. The state's interlocking and inequitable systems of housing, employment, education, health care, and criminal justice ensure that the odds are stacked against Black Minnesotans from the very get-go.

Amanda Gorman asked, in her poem at the January 20, 2021, presidential inauguration, "Where can we find light in this never-ending shade?" Somehow, despite the egregious disparities in resource allocation, treatment, and opportunity; despite the flagrant abuses of the power of the police against Minnesotans of color; and despite the recognition that this uneven playing field sets them up for unequal outcomes, Black Minnesotans have unceasingly persisted in creating elements of the wonderful. Consider the ebullient hip-hop of a diverse women's group described by Rachel Raimist in "My Beautiful, Broken Minnesota"; the work contributor Erin Sharkey does with Free Black Dirt, an "experimental arts collective of dopeness"; the street art memorializing George Floyd throughout Minneapolis (captured in a heartrending video, "All Roads Lead to 38th and Chicago," by Anna DalCortivo in the original "Wonderful/Wretched" series). These examples, these essays, and so many other sparks of light bring us closer to actualizing Gorman's challenge:

> When day comes we step out of the shade,
> aflame and unafraid
> The new dawn blooms as we free it.
> For there is always light,
> if only we're brave enough to see it.
> If only we're brave enough to be it.

We hope the essays that follow give you pause, open your eyes, make you see red, bring you to tears, and fill you with hope. Above all, we hope they rouse you to join the epic and unremitting battle against systemic oppression, racial inequality, and anti-Blackness.

The Organization of This Volume

The essays in this book are divided into two main sections. The first contains twelve essays from a summer 2020 series of The Society Pages website, "Wonderful/Wretched Memories of Racial Dynamics in the Twin Cities, Minnesota." (The preface to this book provides more information about that project and the evolution of *Sparked: George Floyd, Racism, and the Progressive Illusion*.) The second section of the book contains twenty-four essays solicited from contributors during the fall and winter of 2020. They provide readers with diverse perspectives on critical issues like policing, structural inequality, parenting, negotiating intersectionality, and community support, to name a few. We hope that the loose, thematic organization of the essays will spark further exploration of the parallels and similarities among the three dozen contributions in this book.

The twelve essays in section one, "Wonderful/Wretched Memories of Racial Dynamics in Minnesota," were written by academics who previously lived and worked in Minnesota but subsequently moved away. (Neeraj Rajasekar was a graduate student at the University of Minnesota when he penned his contribution.) They were invited to reflect on their own past experiences of the racial dynamics in the Twin Cities, in light of the killing of George Floyd and the revitalization of the #BlackLivesMatter movement.

The second section, "Sparked Reflections on Race and Racism in Minnesota," contains a set of essays by academics of color who currently live in and around the Twin Cities. Some of the contributions were written as responses to essays in the "Wonderful/Wretched" series, while others are new reflections on events and themes relating to racial dynamics in Minnesota. The section begins with Samuel L. Myers's "The Minnesota Paradox" and Taiyon J. Coleman's "What's Understood Don't Need to Be Explained: Sometimes Gifts Come in Ugly Packages." These essays discuss the many paradoxes of life in Minnesota. More specifically, they address the conundrum of Minnesota being thought of as a "nice" place to live while having some of the largest racial disparities in the nation.

Building on that theme of "Minnesota nice," we next feature David Todd Lawrence's essay, "Minnesota Nice White People." That is followed by Mi'Chael N. Wright's "It Shouldn't Be Me or You but Especially Not

Them: The Proximity of Black Death and Trauma" and Yohuru Williams's "Some Abstract Place: Reflections on 'Black Life and Death in Minnesota,'" the latter essay being a riff on Wendy Thompson Taiwo's piece from the "Wonderful/Wretched" series. Together, these essays explore the challenges of adjusting to life in Minnesota after moving there as an adult.

The next essays examine the criminal justice system, including encounters with law enforcement officials and calls to defund the police. Keith A. Mayes's "White Justice in Life and Death: Will George Floyd Receive Justice?" opens the section, followed by Erin Sharkey's "Crime and Imagination to Contend with It," Jason Marque Sole's "Woop-Woop! That's the Sound of da Beast," Amber Joy Powell's "A Reflection on Racism, Police Violence, and Abolition," and Terrion L. Williamson's "Remembering David Cornelius Smith." Sole's piece was sparked by the "Wonderful/Wretched" essay by Jerry and Sarah Shannon, "The Sound of the Police."

Shannon Gibney's "On the Precarity of 'Safety': A Black Mother Contemplates What It Means to Defund the Police" continues the conversation about law enforcement while exploring the challenges and opportunities in understanding the intersections of social identities. Similar themes are discussed in Ibrahim Hirsi's "Finding Myself in a Racialized World: A Personal Story of Being Black and Immigrant in Minnesota," Enid Logan's "May 29, 2020: We Are Not Okay," and M. Bianet Castellanos's "Brown Minnesota."

Jermaine Singleton's "Beyond Shadowboxing: Reflections on the Matrix of Race in the Post-Floyd Era of Racial Protest," Rose M. Brewer's "Minneapolis Rise Up 2020: Black Lives and Whiteness Unveiled," and Brian D. Lozenski's "The State Is Not Our Friend" are featured next. These essays provide social scientific context about inequities that are built into political, legal, and educational systems in Minnesota and the United States.

The essays that follow bring to life the collective action deployed by families, neighbors, and neighborhoods in response to unequal conditions and acts of violence. Among them are Gabriela Spears-Rico's "'End White Supremacy': From Black Lives Matter to the Toppling of the Columbus Statue: A Testimonio from San Pablo," Katrina Phillips's "'Beyond the Borders of the State': Being Native in Minnesota," and Brittany Lewis's "Rediscovering My Purpose: The Politics of Race, Access, and Change." Rounding out the set are Kate Beane's essay "George Floyd Was Murdered on Dakota Land" and Kong Pheng Pha's "Unsettled Mourning."

The concluding essays of section two take the form of poetic responses. The final two authors, Wendy Thompson Taiwo, in "All the Stars Point North," and Kale Bantigue Fajardo, in "Minneapolis to the Sea: Haibun in Memory of George Floyd," provide artistic interpretation of the social scientific themes explored throughout the volume.

The final chapter in the book is the editors' conclusion, entitled "Where Will We Be on May 25, 2022?," in which we share our thoughts on the progress we hope to see and the continuing challenges we expect to face a year after publication of this book.

In addition, you will find a list of recommended readings, containing all the works referenced or cited by authors in the two main sections of the book. We've also included a guide for readers, which provides in-depth discussion questions centered on the essays themselves. Thank you for joining us on an exploration of George Floyd, racism, and the progressive illusion of Minnesota.

Notes to Introduction

1. Al Franken, "Putting an End to Secret Campaign Contributions," *Huffington Post*, July 16, 2012, https://www.huffpost.com/entry/putting-an-end-to -secret_b_1676330.
2. Bierschbach, "Why Is Minnesota More Liberal than Its Neighboring States?"
3. Minnesota Compass, "All Minnesotans by Race and Ethnicity"; Gibson and Jung, "Historical Census Statistics on Population Totals by Race, 1790 to 1990, and by Hispanic Origin, 1970 to 1990, for the United States, Regions, Divisions, and States."

    The US Census Bureau projects that the nonwhite population will constitute a majority of the national population by 2045: Minnesota State Demographic Center, "Our Projections"; Vespa, Medina, and Armstrong, "Demographic Turning Points for the United States: Population Projections for 2020 to 2060."
4. McCargo and Strochak, "Mapping the Black Homeownership Gap"; "10 Trends in Housing in 2020," Minnesota Housing, October 2020.
5. The national poverty rate in the United States is 10.3 percent for whites and 21.2 percent for Blacks. In 2019, the unemployment rate was 7.7 percent for Blacks and 3.9 percent for whites: American Community Survey, US Census Bureau, 2019.
6. Minnesota COVID-19 Response, "Data by Race and Ethnicity."
7. Grunewald and Nash, "A Statewide Crisis: Minnesota's Education Achieve-ment Gaps," 8; "Who Are the Students? Demographics" and "How Well Are Students Doing? Graduation," both Minnesota Department of Education, Minnesota Report Card; Minnesota Department of Education, "2019 North Star Public File."

8. The national incarceration rate is 698 per 100,000. In Minnesota, the incarceration rate for whites is 216 per 100,000 residents, for Blacks it is 2,321 per 100,000, and for American Indians and Alaskan Natives it is 2,646: Prison Policy Initiative, "Minnesota Profile."

Wakefield and Uggen, "Incarceration and Stratification"; Phelps, "Mass Probation: Toward a More Robust Theory of State Variation in Punishment."

9. ACLU Minnesota, "ACLU Releases Data Showing Racial Disparities in Low Level Arrests in Minneapolis"; Frase, "What Explains Persistent Racial Disproportionality in Minnesota's Prison and Jail Populations?"

10. According to 2017 survey data, 4.2 percent of white Minnesotans were uninsured, compared to 13.9 percent of nonwhite respondents: Minnesota Department of Health, "Minnesota Health Access Survey." Minnesota Department of Health, "Maternal Morbidity and Mortality."

11. Wrigley-Field, Garcia, Leider, Robertson, and Wurtz, "Racial Disparities in COVID-19 and Excess Mortality in Minnesota."

12. Swartz, Manning, Hartmann, and Gulya, "Racial Variations in Understandings and Experiences of Organized Youth Activities."

13. Manning, "The Age of Concerted Cultivation"; Lareau, *Unequal Childhoods: Class, Race, and Family Life*, 39.

Works Cited in the Introduction

"10 Trends in Housing in 2020." Minnesota Housing, October 2020. https://www.mnhousing.gov/sites/np/plans.

ACLU Minnesota. "ACLU Releases Data Showing Racial Disparities in Low Level Arrests in Minneapolis." October 27, 2014. www.aclu-mn.org/en/press-releases/aclu-releases-data-showing-racial-disparities-low-level-arrests-minneapolis.

American Community Survey. "Per Capita Income in the Past 12 Months (in 2019 Inflation-Adjusted Dollars)." US Census Bureau, 2019.

———. "Selected Characteristics of People at Specified Levels of Poverty in the Past 12 Months." US Census Bureau, 2019.

Bierschbach, Briana. "Why Is Minnesota More Liberal than Its Neighboring States?" *Star Tribune* (Minneapolis), April 17, 2020.

Frase, Richard S. "What Explains Persistent Racial Disproportionality in Minnesota's Prison and Jail Populations?" *Crime and Justice* 38, no. 1 (2009): 201–80.

Gibson, Campbell, and Kay Jung. "Historical Census Statistics on Population Totals by Race, 1790 to 1990, and by Hispanic Origin, 1970 to 1990, for the United States, Regions, Divisions, and States." Population Division Working Paper No. 56. US Census Bureau, 2002. www.census.gov/content/dam/Census/library/working-papers/2002/demo/POP-twps0056.pdf.

Grunewald, Rob, and Anusha Nash. "A Statewide Crisis: Minnesota's Education Achievement Gaps." Federal Reserve Bank of Minneapolis, October 11,

2019. https://www.minneapolisfed.org/~/media/assets/pages/education
-acheivement-gaps/achievement-gaps-mn-report.pdf?la=en.

Lareau, Annette. *Unequal Childhoods: Class, Race, and Family Life*. Berkeley:
University of California Press, 2011.

Lass, William E. *Minnesota: A History*. 2nd ed. New York: W. W. Norton, 1998.

Manning, Alex. "The Age of Concerted Cultivation." *Du Bois Review* 16, no. 1
(2019): 5–35.

McCargo, Alanna, and Sarah Strochak. "Mapping the Black Homeownership
Gap." Urban Institute, February 26, 2018. www.urban.org/urban-wire/
mapping-black-homeownership-gap.

Minnesota Compass. "All Minnesotans by Race and Ethnicity." www
.mncompass.org/topics/demographics/race-ethnicity.

Minnesota COVID-19 Response. "COVID-19 Data by Race/Ethnicity." mn.gov/
covid19/data/data-by-race-ethnicity/index.jsp.

Minnesota Department of Education. "2019 North Star Public File." public
.education.mn.gov/MDEAnalytics/DataTopic.jsp?TOPICID=450.

———. "Minnesota Report Card." https://rc.education.mn.gov/.

Minnesota Department of Health. "Maternal Morbidity and Mortality."
August 1, 2019. www.health.state.mn.us/docs/communities/titlev/
maternalmorbmort.pdf.

———. "Minnesota Health Access Survey." www.health.state.mn.us/data/
economics/hasurvey/index.html.

Minnesota State Demographic Center. "Our Projections." mn.gov/admin/
demography/data-by-topic/population-data/our-projections/.

Missouri Economic Research and Information Center. "Cost of Living Data
Series." meric.mo.gov/data/cost-living-data-series.

Nichols, John. "Donald Trump Is Deliberately Distorting What Ilhan Omar
Says About America." *The Nation*, July 19, 2019. www.thenation.com/
article/archive/donald-trump-ilhan-omar/.

Phelps, Michelle S. "Mass Probation: Toward a More Robust Theory of State
Variation in Punishment." *Punishment & Society* 19, no. 1 (2017): 53–73.

Prison Policy Initiative. "Minnesota Profile." www.prisonpolicy.org/profiles/
MN.html.

Redmond, Leslie, interview by Michael Martin. "Minneapolis NAACP President on Why a City Ablaze Is 'A Long Time Coming.'" *All Things Considered*,
NPR, May 30, 2020. www.npr.org/2020/05/30/866204366minneapolis
-naacp-president-on-why-a-city-ablaze-is-a-long-time-coming.

Swartz, Teresa Toguchi, Alex Manning, Douglas Hartmann, and Lisa Gulya.
"Racial Variations in Understandings and Experiences of Organized Youth
Activities." Paper presented at the annual meeting of the American
Sociological Association, Montreal, Canada, August 2017.

Tausanovitch, Chris, and Christopher Warshaw. "Representation in Municipal
Government." *American Political Science Review* 108, no. 3 (2014): 605–41.

"U.S. News Best Places: Minneapolis–St. Paul, Minnesota." *U.S. News & World
Report*. realestate.usnews.com/places/minnesota/minneapolis-st-paul.

"U.S. News Best Places: Minnesota." *U.S. News & World Report*. www.usnews
.com/news/best-states/minnesota#state-rankings.

Vespa, Jonathan, Lauren Medina, and David M. Armstrong. "Demographic
Turning Points for the United States: Population Projections for 2020 to
2060." Current Population Reports, P25–1144, US Census Bureau, 2020.

Wakefield, Sara, and Christopher Uggen. "Incarceration and Stratification."
Annual Review of Sociology 36 (2010): 387–406.

"Wonderful and Wretched Memories of Racial Dynamics in the Twin Cities."
The Society Pages. thesocietypages.org/specials/wonderful-wretched
-memories-of-racial-dynamics-in-the-twin-cities-minnesota.

Wrigley-Field, Elizabeth, Sarah Garcia, Jonathon P. Leider, Christopher
Robertson, and Rebecca Wurtz. "Racial Disparities in COVID-19 and Excess
Mortality in Minnesota." *Socius* 6 (2020). DOI: 2378023120980918.

PART 1

Wonderful/Wretched Memories of Racial Dynamics in the Twin Cities

Blackasotan Identity Lanes

Walter R. Jacobs

For a little over a year—February 2016 to March 2017—the webzine *Blackasotan* published stories at the "intersection of place and race (among other things), [in order] to fill a gap and to encourage dialogue, thought, and action around the infinite manifestations of what it means to be Black in Minnesota." In June 2016, the site published my essay "30 Years a Minnesotan," in which I discussed my racialized experiences over three decades as a resident of or frequent visitor to Minneapolis and St. Paul, following the first eighteen years of my life during which I rarely left the southern United States. Those thirty years in Minnesota were very formative, as my regional identity switched from southerner to midwesterner. More specifically, I began to see myself as a Minnesotan. I still identify as a Minnesotan even though I last lived there in 2013 and have now spent five years in California, after two years in Wisconsin.

I first lived in the Twin Cities in the summer of 1986 while working as a college student intern at the 3M corporate campus in the St. Paul suburb of Maplewood. Just out of high school and before I started engineering classes at Georgia Tech, I immediately noticed a different racial order than the one I knew in the South. As I detailed in the first paragraph of my *Blackasotan* essay: "I grew up in mostly Black neighborhoods in the south, so spending three months in the predominantly White Minnesota Twin Cities was quite an adjustment. In fact, the first time I walked into a McDonald's my inner voice screamed, 'There are White kids working at McDonald's!' As the summer wore on, I was shocked to see White and Asian folks in public housing complexes, and was stunned when I could count the number of Cadillacs I saw on one hand."

Toward the end of the summer I had a nasty racist encounter—an elderly White woman screamed racial slurs at me while a friend and I were stopped at a traffic light in St. Paul—but my other experiences that summer and in the three subsequent summers between academic terms at Georgia Tech were overwhelmingly positive.

When I returned to Minnesota in 1999 to become an assistant professor of social sciences in the University of Minnesota's General College, I became a permanent resident of Minneapolis. I had a both large and multiracial group of friends from the past thirteen years of visits to the Twin Cities (and one weekend trip to a cabin in Nevis, Minnesota), plus I had become fast friends with several other new faculty in the college, so I existed in a very comfortable and privileged bubble. When I became the chair of the Department of African American & African Studies eight years later, however, I learned much more about the landscape of race in Minneapolis, where racial inequality is extreme. As summarized in a *Washington Post* article entitled "Racial Inequality in Minneapolis Is Among the Worst in the Nation," published on May 30, 2020, "the typical black family in Minneapolis earns less than half as much as the typical white family in any given year. And homeownership among black people is one-third the rate of white families. As a result, many black families have been effectively locked out of the prosperity that the city's overwhelmingly white population enjoys." My wife and I were well aware that we were one of the few Black families in Minneapolis's Prospect Park neighborhood, just east of the University of Minnesota's Minneapolis campus.

One of my first tasks as African American and African studies department chair was to start planning the department's fortieth anniversary events, beginning in the fall of 2008. I had known that the department was started when a small group of students took over the university's administration building in January 1969, but I was shocked to learn that there were fewer than a hundred Black students enrolled in the entire university at that time—out of a population of more than forty thousand students. Also, few of the Black students were from the Twin Cities. I'd be stupefied if any were from Prospect Park, as the city was then largely segregated, with Black families concentrated predominantly in north Minneapolis and in certain areas of south Minneapolis, near where George Floyd would be murdered decades later. Many African Americans today are still concentrated in those parts of town.

As a component of the fortieth anniversary activities, we started planning an on-campus living-learning community for African American men to help us change their especially low numbers on campus.

Named in honor of one of the leaders of the 1969 student occupation, Huntley House for African American Men opened in August 2012 with a goal of providing a sense of community and connectedness for African American males, and opportunities for personal and academic growth to ensure their success in college and beyond. The students regularly met with a resident advisor and a peer mentor, and engaged in both academic and social activities with faculty and other students. Huntley House is still in existence today and has been joined by the Charlotte's Home for Black Women living-learning community.

I haven't been in touch with members of Huntley House for a few years, but I know that many of the students who live there today are from the Twin Cities. I'd imagine that while Black Lives Matter protests rage close by their homes, some of the men might be feeling anguish over a choice to not go out into the streets to join them. They have a variety of reasons for staying inside, including not wanting to be exposed to COVID-19. If the campus were open, some of the students would also decline potential invitations to attempt to occupy administrative offices, as was done by members of their grandparents' generation fifty years ago. I would encourage them to keep a May 20, 2020, tweet by @Lindss_tastic in mind. She said, "Resistance is NOT a one lane highway. Maybe your lane is protesting, maybe your lane is organizing, maybe your lane is counseling, maybe your lane is art activism, maybe your lane is surviving the day. Do NOT feel guilty for not occupying every lane. We need all of them."

In the conclusion to my *Blackasotan* essay I note, "[life in] the land of 10,000 lakes helped me see that there were 10,000 ways to be Black." Indeed, there are also ten thousand ways to protest the inequality and discrimination Black people experience daily. Black Minnesotans—Blackasotans—have ten thousand lanes for creating Black identities that allow us to successfully navigate the complexities of life as Black people in America. There are ten thousand exciting paths that we can explore. Yes, we will encounter resistance on some of our journeys. For example, the "30 Years a Minnesotan" essay details an incident on the University of Minnesota's Minneapolis campus where my "authentic" Blackness was questioned when I prefaced directions to an African American couple with the "White" expression of "let's see." Ironically, the African American couple was traveling from north Minneapolis to Chicago Avenue, where George Floyd was murdered. Another example: the encounter I mentioned earlier about the St. Paul woman hurling racial insults at me remains to this day the most directly racist interaction I've had in the fifty-two years of my life. Indeed, resistance Black people encounter reminds us of wretched pasts or presents, but we should expand our explorations to seek more powerful futures. Let's go!

Oakland, CA
June 4, 2020

Walter R. Jacobs is a sociologist and the dean of the College of Social Sciences at San José State University. He is the author of the ethnography *Speaking the Lower Frequencies: Students and Media Literacy* and the memoir *Ghostbox* and is coeditor of *If Classrooms Matter: Progressive Visions of Educational Environments.*

A Letter to an Old Friend about Race

Darren Wheelock

Dear Minnesota,

The fact that George Floyd's murder took place in Minneapolis took on additional significance for me. I love you, Minnesota. I spent many summers fishing and swimming in your lakes surrounding Brainerd. I biked for countless hours in your neighborhoods, including Midway, Longfellow Park, Grand Avenue, Loring Park, Highland Park, Brackett Field Park, Near North, Powderhorn Park, Frogtown, Uptown, Dinkytown, and many others. I took the 21A bus up and down Marshall Avenue/ Lake Street more times than I can count. I graduated from Highland Park High School in St. Paul. I left you a while to travel but ultimately returned to attend the University of Minnesota as an undergraduate and then went on to complete my doctorate there, where I met my wife. Minnesota, we no longer share a home, but I consider myself Minnesotan to the bone.

That is why I say with confidence that you have significant issues with racism. To be sure, America struggles with race and racism, and I make no claims that Minnesota's race problem is qualitatively different or quantitively more prevalent than that of other states. I have heard accounts that Minnesota's racism is distinctive in that it is more subtle, less overt, and more coded. I do not know if that's true, but I do know I have seen, heard, and even been subject to its overt forms.

I had a physical education teacher for the first several years of my elementary education who was beloved by most of the other students. The gymnasium was eventually named for him after he retired. Whenever he would get upset with me, he threatened to ship me back to Korea.

A white substitute teacher in middle school held me after class and told me Asian people are not supposed to act boisterous or misbehave. He told me Asians are supposed to be quiet and obedient.

When I was thirteen or so, I was walking around one of the small shopping malls in downtown St. Paul with a white classmate. A group of white boys walked up to me and one spit in my face and told me he was going to "beat my ass" because he hated "chinks." My classmate watched and did nothing.

All during high school, white classmates and friends repeatedly begged me to act out scenes involving the Asian character from the movie *Sixteen Candles*.

These experiences scarred me deeply, and I still struggle with their impact as an adult. As the foundational book *Racial Formation in the United States* by Michael Omi and Howard Winant argues, however, not all racial animus is the same. I saw this as well. While I was threatened with being sent back to Korea, the lone black boy at my elementary school was ridiculed, shunned, and bullied. He didn't last more than a year before he left.

Then I bore witness to the criminal justice treatment of Black Americans in Minnesota.

I worked as a security guard while attending the University of Minnesota as an undergraduate. Most of my shifts entailed sitting at a kiosk in St. Paul's skyway system doing my homework. During one shift over a weekend, I saw two young black boys around twelve to fourteen years old walk by and head to an area that housed an escalator, which led to a bar and a building exit on the first floor. They disappeared from my view as they descended the escalator. About fifteen minutes later I saw them reappear in the skyway and walk back to my desk. They said they wanted to report "some crazy white guy" who started yelling at them, grabbing them, and physically hurting them. I was taken aback at first. I asked them to repeat their story, which at the time sounded outrageous.

We walked together to the escalator and went down to the bar. I asked the bartender if anyone here had assaulted these kids. A fortyish white guy stood up and walked over to me and told me everything was fine. Even though he was dressed in plain clothes, he brandished his badge and told me he was an off-duty officer. I noticed a beer where he had been sitting, and he appeared to be intoxicated. He told me that the kids had been sliding down the escalator, so he "taught them a lesson."

The bartender then joined in and said that kids like the ones next to me were always causing trouble and playing around on the escalator. I told them I didn't care what the kids did; no one should be putting their hands on them. I told the bartender that he should have called me if he needed to report something. Several other patrons at the bar, the bartender, and the off-duty officer (all of whom were white) started yelling at me and the kids and told the kids to leave and never come back.

The three of us were speechless as we walked back to my security desk. I apologized to the kids for not being able to help them, but I did let them know I would write up the incident in my daily log. As the kids left, I unsuccessfully tried to make sense of what had just happened. About thirty or forty minutes later, the boys came back with their father. He asked me what happened, and I told him. He asked me to call the police. I did and handed him the phone at my security desk. About an hour later, a lone black police officer arrived, and after we told him what happened, he took a long breath and said, "Look, I can report this to Internal Affairs if you want, but I can tell you now, nothing will happen and nothing will come of this."

The boys' father heaved his shoulders and shook his head, and the officer left. The boys, their father, and I stood in silence for several moments. He then told me he appreciated my help, took his two sons, and walked away. I will never forget that moment. I kept wondering, *What do fathers tell their sons in that situation? Are there words that can comfort two young boys who were assaulted by a white off-duty police officer who was likely intoxicated but also completely protected by his race and his badge? If so, what are they?*

Fast-forward to the present, and now I have a black son of my own. As a father, I have struggled to help him make sense of the past two weeks' events following the death of George Floyd. He's a smart, eleven-year-old kid, so he has some sense of what's happening, but whenever I try to talk to him about these issues, he resists. He does not want to talk about police violence against Black Americans. He does not want to hear what he needs to do if he should ever be stopped by the police (which may not help him anyway). He does not want to talk about racism. He does not want to talk about inequality. Why would he? These topics are painful and difficult. He wants to play video games, go biking, read his favorite book, and play with his friends. He wants to be a kid.

These talks are difficult for me as well. Can't I just let him be a kid? Can't I just pretend that when he steps outside, people will see him as a person instead of a threat? No, I can't. I would be grossly neglecting my parental responsibilities if I did. That is a luxury parents of black children do not get. The challenge I share with my wife is to initiate these critical yet difficult conversations that rob him of his innocence and childhood in a way that does not also make him hate and resent being black. At times, this seems like an impossible task, but for his sake, we must keep trying.

I would not go so far as to claim that there has been no progress on addressing racial inequality and injustice. My very life represents some level of progress. I am an adopted Korean American, married to an African American woman, with an adopted African American son. Scenes like Derek Chauvin kneeling on George Floyd's neck, however, remind us that we haven't made as much progress as is needed. As a father, I fear that my son will have to have these same difficult conversations with his black children.

Sincerely,
Me

Milwaukee, WI
June 7, 2020

Darren Wheelock is an associate professor in the Department of Social and Cultural Sciences at Marquette University. He is the director of graduate studies for the Criminal Justice Data Analytics Program. He is also the faculty liaison for the Educational Preparedness Program for currently and formerly incarcerated students at Marquette University.

Will Words Lead to Action?

Marcia Williams

I must admit that I didn't want to write this piece. It feels like I am giving away too much by sharing my experiences and emotions. I know that words have power, but black people have been writing our stories and sharing our truths for over four hundred years—and so much of that time our words have fallen on deaf ears. Constant accusations of "over-sensitivity," "making race an issue," or imposing "political correctness" onto "innocent" white folks gets old. It is also extremely painful. Black people are often accused of being angry, and we are. But underneath our anger is a pain so raw, so intense, and so constant that the only way to keep going is to "numb" ourselves to the many faces of racism that reveal themselves day to day. The numbing itself is exhausting, as is the process of deciding which racist comments/actions we will respond to and how, or whether to let them go.

If we are lucky, we have friends and family who provide a sanctuary to vent, to "feel," and to release enough of the pain to get up the next day and do it all over again. However, even that process has a heartbreaking component. For when sharing the trials and tribulations of the day, we see our parents and grandparents nodding their heads in understanding. They recount stories and feelings that echo our own. We realize that while much has changed since they were our age, so much has stayed the same, not because it had to but because white people were too invested in the status quo. I would like to think that the graphic and undeniable murder of George Floyd would be the catalyst we need for revolutionary change to the racial culture of America. But I fear that not many people would be willing to sacrifice their racial privilege, even those who are outraged at this act of police brutality and are now out in the streets protesting. Renouncing such privilege (and certainly relinquishing power) is fundamental to achieving racial equality, and while the protests may provide a glimmer of hope in the moment, it is too easy for white people to turn away and go back to a world where George Floyd's murder—much like Emmett Till's—becomes just another piece of American history that they can convince themselves we have moved past. Meanwhile, black folks are left behind with the Herculean task of trudging through the toxicity of racism—our reality dismissed, our words lost in the wind, and our bodies once again fodder for those who seek to eradicate us from the earth.

So here I sit, consumed with all that I have written above and struggling to figure out what in the hell I should write next. I suppose I can start with the fact that I was shocked that this murder happened in Minneapolis. I lived in Minnesota for a total of fifteen years, four in a little rural college town, and eleven in Minneapolis. I have never been under the delusion that racism was nonexistent in Minnesota (or anywhere for that matter), but the racism I witnessed during my years there was covert and of a nonphysical nature. Brutal, violent racism was thus very real but something "out there" in other places like LA, where Rodney King was beaten. I remember when the verdict came out and I participated in the protests and demands for change that characterized many post-secondary institutions at the time. Still, there was a cerebral, dissociative component to our protests—the kind that happens when you know about something but haven't experienced it yet. Like the difference between the time before you are called a nigger for the first time, and the immediate aftermath. Before that moment you have an abstract sense of injustice, but when called that word you feel like your entire body has been stomped into the ground.

My personal experiences living in Minnesota (and particularly in Minneapolis) were characterized by that cerebral component largely because I created a protective bubble around myself. First, I was a loner for the most part, and had a handful of friends whose political persuasions were similar to my own. Second, I did not drink, so I was never engrossed in the bar or club scene, and this further limited my social network. Third, I only worked in nonprofit institutions dedicated to social justice. So I took pains to make sure my daily life was as "racist-free" as possible and that most of my energy could be spent fighting alongside my colleagues against racism and other injustices. Eventually, I applied for and was accepted into the University of Minnesota's doctoral program in sociology. Certainly, the department was no utopia, but the discipline itself as well as its students and professors were more open to discussing issues of inequality and social justice than many other academic spaces, or social spaces in general. The program also introduced me to one of my life's greatest gifts: my husband, to whom I have now been married nearly seventeen years.

Thus, my graduate school career also afforded me a certain level of "protection" from the violent and nonviolent racism that so many others—especially black men—endure. The one experience shared by every single one of my black male friends (and acquaintances) is having been pulled over and harassed by the police because of his race. One was pulled over for driving a "nice car," another for being "in the wrong neighborhood," and yet another for daring to sit beside his white girlfriend in a parked car. He recounted how the police ran over to the car and asked his girlfriend if "she was okay" and pressured him to disclose his name. My friend was "lucky" in that his mother was a prominent attorney in the Minneapolis–St. Paul community. Once the police learned this information they returned to their car. Nevertheless, while walking away they were sure to let my friend know that they were "watching him." In essence, they were the predators, and he their prey. Their chief desire was not to serve and protect, but to hunt and consume. This is what the police did to George Floyd. They hunted him down, put their knee on his neck, and consumed his life by squeezing the very breath from his body.

So now the protests have begun, and along with them, riots. The instigators of the riots are largely thought to be white supremacists, but that little piece of information seems quite watered down, even among folks who are most sympathetic to those "looting and rioting." Many of the people who have turned a blind eye to the violence against black bodies for so long now either tell us to "focus our anger more constructively" or call us "animalistic and barbaric" for "looting" and "destroying." It is this very reaction that gives me so little faith that my beautiful black eleven-year-old son's experiences with the police will be any different than his predecessors'. Certainly, destroying buildings is not something one can endorse. But it is nothing compared to destroying lives—nothing.

Property can be rebuilt; those murdered cannot be brought back to life. Therefore, one would think that labels such as "animalistic" or "barbaric" would be placed on policemen who have ended black lives. But I have heard no such term used for the police officers who killed George Floyd. How can this be? Just two weeks ago a large group of white protestors marched into the Michigan State Capitol armed and screaming that the COVID-19 quarantine violated their constitutional rights, yet their behavior was not described as "barbaric," "thuggish," or even "violent." Further, how can we make sense of the self-discipline the police used to keep from acting aggressively toward these protestors when no such restraint is exercised while encountering unarmed black protestors?

The simple answer is that the accusations of "thuggishness," "barbarity," and "animalistic behavior" have little to do with the violent acts themselves. If they did, we would not have a holiday for Christopher Columbus, who appropriated what we now call America through the looting and genocide of Indigenous peoples. No, the critique is not about violence, it is about WHO is committing the violence and their RIGHT to do so—a right that, ironically, is granted on the perception of one's HUMANITY. According to American racial culture, whites are the most "human," thus their violence is "justified." This same racial culture frames blacks as "less human," and thus their RIGHT to fight back against their "superiors" does not exist. The Boston Tea Party would not have been hailed as an act of courage in the pursuit of liberty if conducted by free blacks; they would have been jailed for destruction of property. If the critiques against black protestors today were an authentic condemnation of violence, the United States would have no justification for the wars we fight under the veil of moral superiority, when our true intent is to loot and dominate others.

Whether brutality against black bodies takes place in Minneapolis, LA, New York City, or elsewhere, it will not stop unless we consciously and consistently challenge the white supremacy that is endemic to US culture. Until that happens, no act of violence against a black person, no matter how graphic or outrageous, will ever be enough to realize the equality we claim to seek. And it is only if and when that time comes that I, along with so many of my black brothers and sisters, will start believing that our words mean anything to anyone other than us. It is only then that essays like this one will seem to be more than a mere exercise in writing.

Milwaukee, WI
June 8, 2020

Marcia Williams is an adjunct assistant professor in the Department of Social and Cultural Sciences at Marquette University. She earned her PhD in sociology from the University of Minnesota, and her work challenges cultural deficit explanations of racial gaps in academic achievement for African American students.

My Beautiful, Broken Minnesota

Rachel Raimist

It was a deep freeze in January 2002 when I moved to Minneapolis with my five-year-old daughter, Tiana. I arrived as a PhD student in the University of Minnesota's Department of Gender, Women, and Sexuality Studies with the heart of a feminist, tired from the sexism, homophobia, and misogyny of what I call my former #RapLife. I worked interviewing rappers and artists for magazines, online platforms, and a clothing company while dreaming of making a DVD magazine of my own (I know: it was the early 2000s, and that seemed cool!). While working for a former "urban+skater+hip-hop" publication that was converted to a "men's magazine," my #RapLife ended. During a meeting to review the proofs of a photo shoot with the best woman snowboarder in the world, who wore only a skimpy fur bikini while contorted around a Siberian husky, I said, "Great, but can we see hot chicks at least do cool shit?" I quit the job, applied to the University of Minnesota, and got nervous because my only visit to the Midwest had been to Chicago. But I went, filled with hope that a PhD would give me a lens to understand the trauma I had endured.

I grew up in Upstate New York. My mother was Puerto Rican, and my father was Russian Jewish. In our mixed-race and mixed-faith family, we all sort of did our own thing. My oldest brothers went to Hebrew school and listened to white rock music, my middle brother played guitar in a jam band and loved every genre of music, and I went to Catholic school on Sundays.

I grew up with friends who were white, Italian, Jewish, Puerto Rican, Dominican, Black, and just about everything else—New York is truly a melting pot like that. My mother spoke Spanish but cooked hamburgers, hot dogs, and spaghetti because she felt it would be best to assimilate.

I didn't grow up speaking Spanish but learned broken Spanglish and classroom Spanish.

I lost both of my parents to cancer when I was twenty-three. They were diagnosed three weeks apart and died two months apart, when my daughter was a few months old. My daughter is Puerto Rican, Russian Jewish, Jamaican, Syrian, Indian, Chinese, and Cuban. When I enrolled her in kindergarten in Minneapolis, most of the other kids and the teachers were white, but their views seemed liberal and they were very welcoming. Her experiences in school were mostly positive, but her teachers were all white until she studied African and African American studies in college.

My son Joseph was born in Minneapolis. His father was from Oklahoma, the son of a Black farmer and grandson of a Cherokee chief from Oklahoma City. Joseph's father had many bumps with the law and a rough life in general. I will never forget the time the Minneapolis Police Department (MPD) sent its SWAT team to a domestic violence incident at our house. Instead of sending a peace officer to help assist Joseph's father with the duress caused by mental issues, they busted into my Northeast Minneapolis apartment with big guns blazing. They pointed them at me, at my daughter, and at the crib where my son was sleeping. They tore up our place but found nothing, just as I'd said after they stormed in. I don't share this story because my experience is unique or special, but precisely because it's not. We are just lucky that my white skin privilege afforded me the ability to get between the guns and my brown children and yell at the police. Or at least it did at the time, but I'm not sure I would yell again. The MPD has shown too many times that the lives of the Black and brown community are disposable. A new probe of the MPD's race relations over the past ten years, launched by Governor Tim Walz's administration in early June 2020, will show that, no doubt.

While I was a doctoral student in feminist studies at the University of Minnesota, other Latina scholars and I formed the "Kitchen Table Collective." These sisters helped me deal with a department full of power struggles, both hidden and overt. I once saw a faculty member of color throw a book at a white faculty member! The ivory tower is not always the warm and supportive place I thought it would be. It can be full of rage. In the Kitchen Table Collective we wrote our dissertations, gave each other support, and brunched. That is how we survived.

In addition to handling my formal classroom studies, I made documentaries. While filming different documentary projects in and around

Minneapolis, I learned of tensions between Black students and African students who were from Somalia, Ethiopia, and Eritrea. These students did not consider themselves Black, and certainly not Black Americans— they were Africans. There were many tensions, but arts projects helped to defuse them. A friend who is a rapper and community organizer, for example, led a workshop on painting self-portraits. He had each participant design a piece that they drafted on paper and outlined on a wall. Then they picked up aerosol cans and painted. I loved filming the participants' beautiful multicolored hands, streaked with a rainbow of paint. I realized that in Minneapolis the arts and creative expression outlets were an important part of building community, partnerships, and understanding.

My off campus activities also included the Twin Cities hip-hop community. I first met Desdamona, a white rapper from Iowa, at a film festival in Austin. She gave me her card, and I never forgot her name—like Shakespeare, but hip-hop. On my first visit to the University of Minnesota, I saw a flyer on a telephone pole that advertised a poetry reading she was hosting near campus. I went to it and was surprised when she called out my name, recognizing me many years after our first meeting. From there our project of organizing women in the hip-hop community was on.

Desdamona introduced me to the arts nonprofit organization Intermedia Arts, where she hosted an ongoing women-in-hip-hop event. There I met Maria Isa, a Puerto Rican Minnesotan who waves her flag for SotaRico. The community was filled with Muslim b-girls, white graffiti artists, Black poets, Native artists, indigenous photographers, Asian and Pacific Islander playwrights, immigrants, and truly just about everyone. Not to say that there weren't tensions and issues in our little hip-hop utopia, because there were, but together we put on the biggest event of women in hip-hop to date: "B-Girl Be: A Celebration of Women in Hip Hop."

After earning an MA in women's studies and a PhD in feminist studies, I moved to the Deep South to become an assistant professor at the University of Alabama. I also continued to make documentaries, ran the video crew at the Tuscaloosa Amphitheater, and codirected an arts organization, all while earning tenure and promotion to associate professor. Moving to Tuscaloosa made the racial tensions in Minneapolis seem less substantial. The weight of history in Alabama is still very heavy and ever present in daily life. I could write a book about that. William Faulkner's quote still rings true: in the Deep South, "The past is never dead. It's not even past."

But for now I'll close with a note about my home, because everywhere we have lived has helped to raise up and frame our racialized experiences. When people ask my kids and me where we are from, I say New York, my daughter says Los Angeles, and my son says Minneapolis. Joseph has beautiful memories of Minnesota and great pride in having been born a Minnesotan. But our family has survived many kinds of trauma, from microaggressions to too many instances of overt racism, like being called the N-word in public schools across this country. What we've learned on this journey is that our Midwest home of Minneapolis is just like most of America right now: beautiful, very broken, and full of pockets of hope.

Los Angeles, CA
June 6, 2020

Rachel Raimist is an associate professor of cinema and television and the academic director of Elon University in Los Angeles. She coedited *Home Girls Make Some Noise: Hip-Hop Feminism Anthology* and is a member of the scholar/activist Crunk Feminist Collective. Raimist is also an award-winning filmmaker who most recently directed episodes of the TV series *Nancy Drew*, *Roswell New Mexico*, and *Diary of a Future President*.

In This Country

Catherine Ceniza Choy

The binary *wonderful/wretched* aptly describes the racial dynamics I experienced in the Twin Cities, Minnesota. On one level, I recall my life in Minnesota with affection and gratitude. From 1998 to 2004, I was an assistant professor of American studies at the University of Minnesota, Twin Cities. It was my first tenure-track position. My husband also landed a tenure-track job in the Twin Cities. Academic couples struggle with finding permanent employment in the same place. We had hit the jackpot early in our careers.

Our two children were born in Minnesota. One of the most pleasant ways we settled into family life there was through weekend outings in the Twin Cities and the surrounding areas. Through our walks around Lake Harriet, visits to the Walker Art Center's Sculpture Garden and its awesome cherry-spoon sculpture, and fruit-picking excursions in Afton Apple Orchard, we were becoming the typical Minnesotan family.

Except that we weren't. I am Filipino American, and my husband is Korean and Chinese American. I could go into more detail about how both of us were born in the United States and how our family histories reflect a long-standing, multigenerational Asian American history. But in my mundane Minnesotan life, it didn't matter. During my time there, my nonwhite, Asian racial difference generated some of my most indelible experiences of feeling like an outsider and of not belonging.

At one of our family outings to a food festival, I found myself separated from my husband and baby while waiting in line to buy something to drink on that humid summer day. A man behind me accused me of cutting in line.

"We have rules *in this country*," he said to me.

I turned around to see his young white face sneering at me, his arm draped across the shoulders of his young, white, blonde girlfriend, who was laughing at me. I knew what he meant by *in this country*. The phrase conjures an ugly, centuries-old, white supremacist history with the act of coded speech. It draws the Orientalist line between "civilized" them and "uncivilized" you. It refers to the stereotype of Asians as perpetual foreigners, no matter how long Asian Americans have lived in, worked in, and died on behalf of *this country*.

I could have said or done something. Instead, I took a deep breath and let it go. Why? Because I was the only person of color in the crowd. I knew that others around us had heard what he said, yet I didn't see a sympathetic face anywhere near me. I concluded it was safer for me to calmly complete my purchase and move on.

Self-preservation matters, but moving on from experiences like these isn't so simple. They can haunt and hurt you by living inside of your head and your heart. When I reconnected with my husband, I told him what had happened. "One day," I said, "I'm going to write about this."

I put that writing aside after another wretched experience. It involved encountering racist advertising on massive billboards from the trendy new Minneapolis restaurant Chino Latino. Taglines such as "As exotic as food gets without using the dog" and "All the flavors without all the vaccines" were perched high on the busy intersections of Minneapolis's downtown and Uptown neighborhood for everyone to see.

When I spotted these billboards, I cringed in a moment of what W. E. B. Du Bois called *double consciousness*. A stream of oppressive racial and colonial images entered my mind: disease carrier, savage, dogeater. I wondered if that was how the people around me were seeing me.

That time, I wasn't going to let it go. I released my angst into an essay, "Salvaging the Savage," which was published in the anthology *Screaming Monkeys: Critiques of Asian American Images*, edited by M. Evelina Galang. The anthology's title derives from a 1998 restaurant review in a Milwaukee magazine that referred to a Filipino child as a "rambunctious little monkey." The anthology included many different works by various authors who were united in bringing attention to persistent racial and colonial inequalities. As James Baldwin noted, "History is not the past. It is the present."

My essay was "my scream." In it, I expressed this hope: "Through salvaging the savage, we learn a language with which to critique these representations, strip them of their innocence, and construct counter-narratives that challenge the imperialism and racism that inflict our daily lives."

I advocate for an anti-imperialist and anti-racist world primarily through my writing. One of the most wonderful things about my time in Minnesota is that the university, faculty colleagues, and students supported my research and writing. The presence of Korean American adoptees in my U of M classes and their belief that their history mattered to Asian American studies were the major sources of inspiration for my second book, *Global Families: A History of Asian International Adoption in America*.

While living in Minnesota, I also completed the writing for my first book, *Empire of Care: Nursing and Migration in Filipino American History*. *Empire of Care* explored how and why the "developing" country of the Philippines emerged in the late twentieth century to become the world's leading exporter of professional nursing care for highly developed countries. I argued that the origins of this contemporary labor migration stemmed from early-twentieth-century US colonization of the Philippines. US colonial nursing training in the Philippines followed American professional nursing trends and required Filipino nurses to learn the English language.

An outcome of this colonial history was the creation of a Filipino nurse labor force that was prepared to work in the United States. When critical nursing shortages and other health crises emerged in the post–World War II period, US health care institutions recruited nurses from the Philippines. Since the 1960s, over 150,000 Filipino nurses have worked in the United States.

We see this colonial legacy today in the most tragic way through Filipino nurses' deaths on the front lines of the COVID-19 pandemic. Like many Filipino Americans, I feel a deep sense of grief, but also anger. I'm sick and tired of the long history of Filipino nurses and other essential workers in the United States being treated as disposable.

Today Minnesotans might find themselves being taken care of by a Filipino nurse. As I wrote in the epilogue to *Empire of Care*, a group of Filipino nurses arrived in the Twin Cities in 2002 after several health care organizations hired more than one hundred of these skilled workers. The recruitment of Filipino nurses to care for midwestern populations illuminates how global and transnational forces continue to transform America's heartland.

I left Minneapolis in 2004 and now live in Berkeley, California. But is it ever really possible to leave a place when you carry with you all that was wonderful and wretched there? The grief and anger I felt as I learned about the killing of George Floyd are part of something much larger and deeper. We cannot simply say, *that took place over there, and it does not affect me here*. Black lives matter across any geographical border. My research and my own racial encounters confirm what I have known in my soul: our fates are inextricably linked. And they depend upon the recognition of Black humanity and dignity.

In the midst of so much existential panic, I find myself ruminating with urgency about how to build upon my previous research and also how to build a just society. How about you? How can we imagine our world anew in this country?

Berkeley, CA
June 14, 2020

Catherine Ceniza Choy is professor of ethnic studies at the University of California, Berkeley. She is the author of *Empire of Care: Nursing and Migration in Filipino American History* and *Global Families: A History of Asian International Adoption in America* and the coeditor of the anthology *Gendering the Trans-Pacific World*.

The Sound of the Police

Jerry Shannon and Sarah Shannon

On June 12, 2020, the Minneapolis City Council voted unanimously to disband the police department and replace it with another model, an extraordinary step. Like most white, suburban kids, we were raised to think of the police as first and foremost a source of public safety. Yet our actual experiences as a young couple in north Minneapolis caused us to question these assumptions.

Some context: Both of us grew up in the 'burbs during the 1980s (Jerry in the Chicago metro and Sarah in the Twin Cities), but we lived in Minneapolis from 2002 through 2013. We spent most of that time on the north side, which has a reputation for having the most crime and highest poverty rate in the city. We personally witnessed drive-by shootings, and four people were killed within two blocks of our house. We made *many* 911 calls and interacted with Minneapolis police on multiple occasions. As privileged white people, we never feared police violence personally, and we never felt threatened.

But here's what did happen.

Our first house was right off a main artery (Broadway Avenue), and the gas station on the corner was home to open-air drug dealing. Gunfire erupted regularly, sometimes multiple times per month. So we did what responsible citizens are supposed to do: we called the police. These calls had mixed results. Most of the time a police car would arrive, often thirty minutes to two hours after the call. Just a slow drive up, maybe questioning the guys on the corner. It did nothing to stop the actual dealing. The corner would be cleared for *maybe* ten minutes before commerce resumed.

What did work? Talking with our Black neighbors across the street, Hope and Linda, about strategies for dealing with the issue. Then contacting our city councilperson, who subsequently threatened the license of the gas station for harboring illicit business.

But this wasn't the only source of our interactions with the Minneapolis Police Department (MPD). During our time in this neighborhood, we were visited by well-armed MPD officers in addition to federal marshals and sheriff's deputies several times as they sought a relative of the former homeowner on a warrant sweep. Once when Sarah answered the door, the officer took a look at her and said, "I don't think you're who we're looking for." (Read: "What's a nice white lady like you doing in this neighborhood?")

Other incidents did not directly affect our household but certainly impacted our neighborhood quality of life. On one occasion, some nearby friends experienced interior damage to their house when police set off a flash-bang while serving a warrant. Another time, a domestic dispute next door got heated around 1:00 AM. Two police cars arrived and ordered everyone out via bullhorn. Officers entered the home and multiple gunshots were fired. We learned the next day that the police had shot the neighbor's pit bull. The eleven-year-old living in that house loved *Animal Planet* and had hopes of becoming a veterinarian.

One day on her way home from work, Sarah unwittingly drove into a highly coordinated bust on a house two blocks away. She watched as, almost in slow motion, police cars swung around the corner and blocked the end of the street in front of her while a SWAT team leapt from an unmarked van to her left. Her only choice was to throw the car in reverse and drive home another way. Sarah felt the danger of this situation, not because some fleeing felon might lurk on the other side of the door being rammed in, but rather because no apparent effort was made by the police to warn or otherwise exclude her from this violent scene.

In hopes of finding a quieter neighborhood, we eventually moved to a house about twenty blocks north but still in the city. Drug selling and frequent gunfire were less of a concern there, but on our first Halloween in our new home, someone threw a pumpkin through the window of the front door. More frightening still, a few months later someone kicked in the back door in the middle of the night and stole our purse and wallet. Two years after that, one of our cars was stolen from the street in front of our house.

With each incident, we called the police, who showed up, asked a few questions, and gave us a card with a case number. That was it. However, after the home invasion, they did tell us to get a dog and keep an eye on the (mostly Latinx) men reroofing our house who had the audacity to take a break in ninety-degree heat.

Sometimes, rather than a case number, police left us a bill. When our garage was broken into one day while we were away, a neighbor called the MPD, whose officers covered up the broken door with plywood and sent us an invoice for $200. Our stolen car eventually turned up parked in an illegal spot in St. Paul. We got it back after paying the $300 towing and storage fee. We learned that being victims of crime is expensive, and sometimes it's the police sending you the tab.

Perhaps one of the most serious incidents occurred when there was a shooting in a van stopped right outside our yard while our young kids were playing with neighborhood friends. Jerry, who was outside with the kids, talked with police on the scene while they picked up bullet casings and later was subpoenaed as a witness. The case was pled out, so we never faced the shooter(s) in court. We were merely left with the "what ifs" of stray bullets and stories of others in our neighborhood whose children such bullets didn't miss.

In all of these interactions, what stood out to us was the underwhelming response from police, even during or after very serious criminal events. This wasn't *CSI* or *Law & Order*. No fingerprints were dusted, no lineups arranged. Except for a few feel-good moments every National Night Out, their presence was always reactive and very frequently antagonistic to our neighbors of color. When we were direct victims of crime, our information was taken and we were told we'd get a call if something turned up. Sometimes advice was dispensed: get a dog, don't go out at night, watch the workers on your roof. This advising was done in a way that, for Jerry, emphasized shared positionality as (usually) white men. Looking back, it's hard to identify any specific ways that interactions with police increased our personal safety. What did make a difference: building relationships with our neighbors and working with our local representatives.

While we lived in north Minneapolis, we sometimes wondered what an alternative system would look like. One sunny afternoon, a man we didn't recognize stood on the corner diagonal from our house. He was rocking back and forth and held a cane in his hand. He clearly couldn't see and, when approached by neighbors, appeared disoriented. After a long while, someone called the only agency we thought could do something: the MPD. Not because this man was in any way a threat, but because no other community agency existed that might be of use. We collectively held our breath as the officers approached the man (who was also Black), and he was eventually peacefully taken away in the squad car.

While this last incident may look like a success—after all, no one ended up injured or arrested by the MPD—it shows the value of creating alternatives to policing like those that are being proposed in Minneapolis and elsewhere in the United States. Disbanding the police may sound radical, but it isn't a new idea. Scholars like Angela Davis and Ruth Wilson Gilmore have been writing about prison abolition (a closely related idea) for a long time. The June 6, 2020, article "Listen: Would Defunding the Police Make Us Safer?" in the *Atlantic*, summarizing some of the main ideas, has been shared a lot. It's not a process that will happen overnight, nor does it mean there's no role for law enforcement. Instead, these scholars and our experience suggest that community safety comes from focusing on real harms, making sure folks' basic needs are met, and providing community services that people can call without fear of intimidation, arrest, or violence.

Athens, GA
June 18, 2020

Jerry Shannon is an associate professor in the Departments of Geography and Financial Planning, Housing and Consumer Economics at the University of Georgia. He studies food accessibility and affordable housing, with a focus on participatory research methods.

Sarah Shannon is an associate professor in the Department of Sociology at the University of Georgia. She studies law, crime, and deviance, with a focus on systems of punishment and their effects on social life.

Jason Marque Sole's "Woop-Woop! That's the Sound of da Beast" was sparked by the Shannons' essay. See pages 110–13.

Black Life and Death in Minnesota

Wendy Thompson Taiwo

I actually lived in Minnesota twice. Once in the 2009–10 academic year for a postdoctoral fellowship at the University of Minnesota in Minneapolis. And again from 2014 to 2018 as a tenure-track assistant professor at Metropolitan State University in St. Paul, where I taught courses in Black studies. Born and raised in the San Francisco Bay Area, I returned home to a region championed for its diverse cities, but where Black life remains strained under massive tech wealth and ongoing Black displacement and deprivation, as private investors and municipal agencies upend historically Black neighborhoods, often with the assistance of the police. Watching from California as Minneapolis became the epicenter of Black uprising and protest following the murder of George Floyd at the hands of the Minneapolis Police Department, as well as the outcomes of Black organizing, activism, and community collaboration in the Twin Cities has led me to reflect on my time in Minnesota, a place that was both transformative and stifling for me and my family. There were supportive people and the potential to thrive, but these were not enough to anchor and feed us in an environment and during a time that was largely destructive and lethal for Black people.

During my time spent in Minnesota, the ways I taught, moved, and parented were shaped by the compounding events, systems, and deaths related to Black suffering and grief in and around the Twin Cities: hearing the aggrieved testimonies of Black students who had grown up under the passive-aggressive racist shroud of "Minnesota nice" (the supposed courteous, reserved, and mild-mannered behavior of white Minnesotans), experiencing the death of a beloved student followed by the killing of Philando Castile, and living through the birth of my son at the University of Minnesota Masonic Children's Hospital. That the accumulation of anti-Black violence was committed by white people, many of whom would consider themselves good people and allies, would lead me to expand my own racial identity and consciousness as a Black woman, scholar, and mother. Why did good white people need a Black person to be killed before deciding to take action, and why did most of their actions revolve around low-stakes anti-racist reading groups and listening sessions?

Below I offer three vignettes that provide a chronological account of events that occurred over two years while I lived in Minnesota from the vantage point of a California transplant, academic, and mother in the Twin Cities.

Losing a Student, April 2016

Prior to the murder of George Floyd by the Minneapolis Police Department, not many people outside of the Midwest knew about the condition of Black life in Minnesota. Perhaps it is because the state is so far north, blanketed half the year in snow, waiting to melt. Perhaps because for so long, the Black experience has been defined geographically and culturally by Black people from both coasts and the South. Or perhaps because they missed the footnote about Prince being from Minneapolis. Another footnote that is usually missed: Minnesota was home and hostage site for Dred Scott. Yes, the Dred Scott of the 1857 Supreme Court ruling in which Black people, free or enslaved, were found to not be eligible for US citizenship and thus unable to sue in federal court. Yet the story of Dred Scott, being about good white masters, long winters, and a desire for freedom that is continuously delayed, could not be anything but a Black Minnesota story: past, present, and future.

There are two ways of looking at the story of Dred Scott as a Minnesota story. First is by way of geography. Dred Scott was an enslaved Black man who was brought to Fort Snelling, a remote military outpost close to present-day St. Paul. Like Dred Scott and his wife, Harriet, the other Black people at the fort had been brought there as property. Long, brutal winters filled with ice and blizzards made survival tough and meant that escape was treacherous and nearly impossible. This was what slavery was like in the North, at Fort Snelling, where Dred and Harriet Scott were both Black and unfree.

The other way of seeing Dred Scott's story as a Minnesota story is in what it represents in our contemporary moment for Black people living in the Great White North: being one of the few Black people in a sea of whiteness in a northern territory where the protection of settler property rights is prioritized over Native sovereignty and Black life and secured via militarized and community policing. To engage in mundane, ordinary things like courtship, getting married, having children, and creating a home in the Great White North, but to always yearn for true freedom and autonomy, to be both unfree and given a little room to move, to be unchained but still constantly under white supervision. And to be kept waiting (or is it to keep oneself waiting?) until, old, sick, and facing the threat of a final violence, one is forced to act (or react).

For a long time, I was waiting for freedom. But during the spring 2016 semester at Metro State, I saw a glimpse of it when a student brought up Blackness, social death, and slavery in a way that I hadn't thought of. In *Lose Your Mother,* Saidiya Hartman argues that slavery has an afterlife: Black people have "skewed life chances, limited access to health and education, premature death, incarceration, and impoverishment." Slavery is why Black people continue to be marked as property and why, as Black Americans, we are "the afterlife of slavery," subjected to racialized violence from every institution and system that continues to exist and organize this nation. *Because we are still seen as slaves,* the student told the class, *we are being treated as such.* This he repeated until the white boys from places like Maplewood, Blaine, and Coon Rapids sat silent, raging, and shook, his words pointed and ready like a sharpened machete dancing around my blunt mentions of individual racism and white privilege. He handed us all the torch so that we could see that freedom required a bigger imagination, a wild hunger, but I was not ready and turned the class away, afraid of triggering our desire to destroy the slave patrols outside and the masters inside. *It is time for mutiny,* he continued. *They are still killing us because they see us as slaves.* Then, one late afternoon, someone, a woman, drove her car headfirst into the opposite lanes of traffic and killed him, taking away his presence and leaving behind an empty chair.

There is a terrible grief one feels when a student is lost. There is the initial outrage at still being expected to teach despite being wrecked and dead inside. But walking to class, the grief becomes all the more apparent. No longer is there snow, but winter clings heavily to the sky and you sweat under the many layers of clothing you have to wear while waiting for a bus later that evening that always runs late from the East Side. There is mourning all around you even though there is no public ceremony or eulogy delivered on campus. No homegoing among students on the slice of lawn between the library and the building you teach in, with its big picture windows overlooking downtown St. Paul. In the days that follow the accident, you will struggle to prepare your notes. The heartache will fill all of the space between your remarks on redlining and your slides on suburbanization and the Federal-Aid Highway Act of 1956 that led to the razing of communities and building of highways over houses and people. It will become a scar but not before the wound is reopened. Freedom, while presented again and again, will always be just out of reach.

Redlined to Death, July 2016

At the time of the murder of Philando Castile, I had watched numerous videos of Black men and boys being shot dead by the police. So when the video of his killing circulated, I chose not to watch it. But even without the footage, I felt like I had seen it before, with the news coverage describing the event scene by scene: the officer asking for license and registration becomes agitated after Castile tells him he has a gun; the officer panics and draws his gun and points it at the car before shooting Castile seven times at close range; Castile's girlfriend recording his murder, and her daughter comforting her in the presence of so much terror and death. This was supposed to have been a routine traffic stop like one of the many others that Castile had been subjected to in the past. But for Black motorists in the Twin Cities and elsewhere, a routine traffic stop can escalate at any time and turn fatal. Given the frequency at which police officers stop Black drivers, every time we enter our cars we are confronted with the possibility that we might be next. In St. Paul, police officers were found to have pulled over and ticketed Black drivers at a disproportionate rate compared to white drivers. Statistics were even higher in cities where there were few Black residents. This is what it means to be Black and seen as suspicious and responded to as a threat.

The addition of Philando Castile's name to the growing list of Black casualties of state-sanctioned violence and disposal is the reason why Black parents for generations have had to have "The Talk" with their sons and brothers and nephews, a conversation that usually begins with the first driving lesson and progresses in urgency after a teenager has received their first driver's license, about driving (or simply existing) while Black and what to do when they encounter the police. Put your hands where the officer can see them. Announce any contraband well before they pull your body out of your car. Lie prone on your face. Don't move. Don't run. Don't tell them anything. Remain calm and courteous in the face of an officer whose wild imagination keeps him perpetually triggered. Record the evidence of your detention, your beating, your tasing, your murder because body cam footage and the police chief's justification for the use of deadly force are indisputable defenses of every single officer's actions. Make sure there are Black witnesses watching because they will be the only ones to intervene in the performance of chase, capture, and punishment that we have all seen before.

But as much as Castile's murder was about restricting Black mobility on the open road, it was also rooted in the legacy of redlining and the dedication of law enforcement agents to continue to defend and protect the borders of Minnesota's wealthy white suburbs, such as the one in which Castile was killed. Many Black people in Minnesota are familiar with the roads through these suburbs, having driven on them to commute to work, get to shopping outlets, or take road trips to summer destinations. And while these trips are much less daunting than they were during the *Green Book* era, we are still sometimes routed through neighborhoods that are very purposefully racially exclusive and where we are visibly not welcome.

To be Black in America is to be considered a trespasser, a person who only conditionally belongs, and even then that belonging is dictated by white feelings and fears, and tolerated with white approval and permission. And for me, living in the Twin Cities where all the surrounding suburbs were white and therefore dangerous, I felt very much like a captive: unfree but given a little room to move.

Black Birthing in Minnesota, March 2017

There are certain things that you will definitely not remember while giving birth. The color of paint used on the walls in the room where you push for hours, trying to dislodge your second child from your womb, the boy you carried for nine months and agonized over because now you would be one of them: a mother of a Black son in America. You will not recall the way the sky looked outside at the exact moment that your baby is pulled from between your legs and carried to your chest, where he clings, still covered in filmy amniotic fluid, like a giant pale amphibian. And in a state of exhaustion and delirium, you will not remember the first thing you uttered after your baby was laid on your chest: Was it a word? A moan? His name? A cry?

What you will remember, though, is arriving six months pregnant for the tour of the birth center at the state-of-the-art children's hospital, a towering building looming over the Mississippi River, its face lined with iridescent paneling that radiates rainbow metallic colors like a soap bubble. You will remember walking through the pristine wards with the other expectant parents, none of them Black, and imagine delivering your baby there in comfortable reclining beds covered in crisp white sheets surrounded by warm nursery wall art. You will also remember the moment when you paused and looked at the photographs of the nurses lining the wall leading to the labor and delivery floor. They were all white women, and this became the first sign that things might not be okay. It was like a warning in a horror film, a foreshadowing of the violence you would later experience in your hospital gown and socks, on a cold night in March, as you prepared to deliver your son.

Then it happens, and amid the blur of labor you remember your husband dropping you off in the front of the hospital. "I'll park the car. I'm coming," are the last words he says before speeding off, leaving you standing there holding your daughter's hand. (There was no babysitter, and both your families live many states and continents away.) You show your ID to the Black female security guard at the front desk, who tells you the floor number you will be headed to and points you in the direction of the elevators. And after forever in that metal lift, you emerge, take three steps, and collapse on the maternity ward's admissions desk while two white women watch you lose control of your legs, as your young daughter, bewildered and powerless, is unable to comfort you. You remember their blank facial expressions and their robotic tone as they tell you to fill out the forms, and you write as fast as you can between contractions because it is clear that they will not call for help if you pass out on the floor.

You will not remember how you got into the delivery room, but you will remember the aggressive tone of the two white nurses who were assigned to your room, how they commanded you to sit up on the bed and sighed in frustration while they pulled the equipment toward your contorted body. You remember one of the nurses fumbling with the IV needle and snapping at you to sit up straight—*You need to sit up straight!*—and when you didn't because it was physically impossible to flatten your spine, she threatened you: "Until you sit up straight, I'm not going to call the anesthesiologist!" Only then, at the declaration that she controlled your pain, did you try to stretch out your arm so that she could jam the device into the back of your hand. By letting her do this, you believed your pain would be lessened. But when the anesthesiologist, a middle-aged white man with brown hair and a moustache, arrived, followed by a younger male assistant, and you were unable to flatten your body into a shape that pleased him, he shouted at you to sit still—*You need to sit still!*—otherwise you would not get the epidural, all while your baby twisted and writhed like a trapped fish in your birth canal.

It is no secret that the medical system in this country is inherently racist, especially having been built on exploitative research and predatory experimentation, and remains dangerous for Black people who are admitted into facilities where white doctors and nurses still deny the depths of our pain. But for a long time, I believed that having an advanced degree and an employer that provided good health insurance would protect me from poor care. However, numerous studies show that titles, insurance, and income can't protect us from the physiological manifestations of adverse childhood experiences or the stress born from racism that wears on our organs over our life spans. They are, in fact, ineffective talismans when it comes to vetting and warding off racist medical providers. In the 2002 *Phylon* journal article "Confronting Institutional Racism," Camara Phyllis Jones states that racial health disparities "are produced on at least three levels: Differential care within the health care system, differential access to health care, and difference in exposures and life opportunities that create different levels of health and disease." But for Black people, who tend to be the first and hardest hit by social disparities, there is usually a confluence of two or all three levels—insufficient care, limited access, and negative exposures and life opportunities—which leads to illness, suffering, humiliation, and sudden or premature death.

Looking back on the memory of my son's birth, in which I was trapped in a delivery room with white strangers responsible for caring for me while I was at my most vulnerable and in tremendous pain, it becomes apparent how a Black woman, fully insured, gainfully employed, and middle-class, could end up dying during childbirth in a state-of-the-art facility. And while it still fills me with anger to think about the violent way my son and I were forced to begin life as mother and child, it has led me to love both of my children even more fiercely.

In writing these vignettes, it is hard not to think about Black folks still living and trying to make it in Minnesota. They are the reason for economic and cultural vitality in numerous otherwise ordinary, forgettable cities. Black Minnesotans have made homes (and friends and magic and joy) in an often difficult and inhospitable landscape. They have lived through multiple high-profile police killings in recent years and continue to organize and thrive despite efforts to bury Black memory, gentrify Black communities, and displace Black people. They are the parts of Minnesota that will stay with me. Then there are the other parts of Minnesota, both wonderful and wretched, that I will also remember: how the best mid-century modern finds can be picked up at weekend estate sales for a bargain; how complete strangers will come together to dig a Metro Transit bus or your 2015 Toyota Camry out of a snowbank without you asking and without you owing anything; how there is nothing like the sonic experience of snow as it falls and mutes the sounds of the city, how it crunches deliciously beneath your feet; and how some of the nicest white people you will meet and work with—some of them participants in anti-racist book clubs with Black Lives Matter signs in their front yards—will still do their part in (re)producing and supporting anti-Black policies and practices that will directly harm Black folks in their cities and state. This is to say that while Black people can lead expansive lives in Minnesota, too often these lives are stifled and exhausted in a country that refuses to let us breathe.

Fremont, CA
June 24, 2020

Wendy Thompson Taiwo is an assistant professor of African American studies at San José State University. Her research and teaching interests include Black migration to the Bay Area, Black women and mothering, race and the built environment, and Black visual expressions of social status and class.

Two essays were sparked by Thompson Taiwo's essay. See "Minnesota Nice White People" by David Todd Lawrence on pages 84–88, and "Some Abstract Place: Reflections on 'Black Life and Death in Minnesota'" by Yohuru Williams on pages 95–100.

In Transit

Thomas X. Sarmiento

I moved to the Twin Cities from San Diego, California, in the summer of 2008 to pursue a PhD in American studies at the University of Minnesota. During my first two years in graduate school, I lived in Stevens Square, just south of downtown Minneapolis, in an old brick apartment building that faced I-94 and the convention center and that was around the corner from the now defunct African American Museum and Cultural Center. I remember driving around neighborhoods in south Minneapolis during recruitment weekend and falling in love with the urban charm of Stevens Square, which featured a park nestled among three-story brownstones. I chose to live there because of its affordability and its accessibility to several bus routes.

Some folx expressed concern for my safety in living in such a neighborhood. I immediately registered that concern as likely being connected to the neighborhood's history of drug use and crime and indirectly to its higher concentration of visibly Black residents in comparison to other neighborhoods such as the Wedge or Whittier, where more U of M grad students lived. However, I felt comfortable walking and going for runs around the neighborhood. I kept to myself, and others did the same. And while I became more alert after friends who happened to be White were mugged on their way home from the 19 Bar (Minneapolis's oldest gay bar) in adjacent Loring Park (though I do not recall the physical description of the assailant[s]), my sense of safety did not necessarily change; I tend to be anxious in public settings and aware of my surroundings, perhaps because I had been policed by White authority figures in schools and malls during my adolescence for looking like an "Asian gangster" (which in the 1990s meant an Asian person wearing baggy clothes).

As a transplant from Southern California, one of the things I loved about living in the Twin Cities was its public transportation system.

Riding the bus or the light rail meant I could save some money on gas, parking, and auto maintenance, not so trivial on a graduate student income; I also could use my commute time to catch up on endless reading for coursework and research. During the two years I lived in Stevens Square, I often took Metro Transit Local Bus Route 2 because it was a direct line to the U of M via Franklin Avenue and I did not have to transfer—a considerable detail, especially during the six months of Minnesota winter. Although it took only twenty minutes or so to get from my stop at Franklin and Third Avenue to the U, the ride still felt long, as we traversed Franklin before turning at Twenty-Sixth Avenue and riding up Riverside Avenue.

Through my daily commutes, I began to learn the racial and class geographies of Minneapolis. Between Nicollet and the light rail Blue Line, I noticed more Black, Indigenous, and Latinx passengers than there were between the Blue Line and the U. As a queer Filipinx first-generation graduate student, I appreciated riding with other people of color and not standing out for being non-White; but I also felt ambivalent because of our perceived class differences: whereas I was riding the bus en route to a doctoral degree and the social, cultural, and economic capital it provides, other passengers of color were riding the bus for purposes that presumably diverged from my upwardly mobile trajectory. Arriving at the U reminded me that I was entering a predominantly White space, a space not designed for people like me or most of the passengers on my daily commute. Nevertheless, riding the 2 along Franklin Avenue allowed me to recognize some of the city's unique diversity—from the halal market on the corner of Portland Avenue, to Maria's Café in the Ancient Traders Market, to the Minneapolis American Indian Center at Bloomington Avenue.

During my last two years of grad school, I lived in Whittier, which gave me walking access to Southeast Asian and Mexican restaurants along Nicollet's Eat Street as well as Limited Stop Bus Routes 113, 114, and 115, which I boarded and exited along Lyndale Avenue. I appreciated these express routes, which provided direct service to the U and cut my commute time by half or more. However, unlike my commutes along Franklin, I no longer had the opportunity to observe the city's more diverse streetscapes, as we bypassed them on I-94. Also, most of the passengers appeared White and were headed to the U, a Whiter space than the Minneapolis neighborhoods I lived in.

As I reflect on my time in the Twin Cities, a little over a month after the murder of George Floyd and the uprisings that ensued in areas I used to walk, run, ride, bike, and drive through, I am reminded that multiple worlds exist at the same time and in the same place. These worlds are racialized, as well as sexualized, gendered, classed, and abled. Riding various bus routes and the light rail, I experienced fleeting intimacies that prompted me to question my queer diasporic Filipinx embodied relation to others unlike me. As an Asian American pursuing an advanced degree, I fit somewhere in between the Twin Cities' racial matrix. This sense of being "not quite," which postcolonial theorist Homi Bhabha describes of the colonized, is a familiar feeling I have wrestled with as a queer man living in a heteronormative society, as the son of Filipinx immigrants whose homeland, the Philippines, bears the scars of Spanish, American, and Japanese colonialisms, and as an Asian American person whose experience of race often is erased in the Black-White paradigms that tend to dominate discussions of race in the United States.

The Twin Cities is where I solidified my political consciousness. My formal education at the U affirmed my belief in the power of knowledge to transform society; however, I also learned that I would have to put in the work to center marginalized voices, including my own. While my graduate program approached the "American" in its namesake from decolonial, critical race, and transnational perspectives, my seminar classmates from and beyond the program did not always reflect such embodied ways of knowing. As an Asian Americanist, and Filipinx Americanist more specifically, I often engaged with texts that seemed of little value to my peers, in addition to the texts I felt compelled to know in order to converse with them. Sometimes being the only Asian man was palpable in these classroom spaces.

Unlike the University of California, San Diego, where I completed my undergraduate degrees in critical gender studies and mechanical engineering, the University of Minnesota was (and remains) a predominantly White institution. Although I had more Black peers in grad school compared to my undergraduate years, I experienced a steep drop in the number of Asian American peers and became part of a numerical racial minority at the U. (The U of M had 338 Black and 684 Asian American graduate students [three and six percent, respectively, of the grad population] during my last year of grad school, 2013–14. UC San Diego had 273 Black and 8,238 Asian American undergraduate students [one and 41 percent, respectively, of the undergrad population] during my last year of undergrad, 2004–5.) Even though I knew I had every right to occupy university spaces, as one of the 12 percent of grad students of color, I often questioned whether I belonged in academe. This is the psychic life of race.

No one directed overt racism toward me; rather, the structures of higher education created the conditions for someone like me to be grateful simply to inhabit the fringe. And as someone who researches the communities of which they are a part, the charge of "me-search" devalued my work; sadly, to this day, someone in the academy who has the power to advance my scholarship will say that my work is "illegible," which I have come to understand as "not part of the norm." However, the invaluable mentorship I received from queer and trans* faculty and faculty of color reveals there is more than one narrative of the U and the Twin Cities. (I place an asterisk after "trans" to signal the variety of gender identities and expressions that exceed cisgender ones, though this notation is not without controversy.)

Living in Minneapolis gave me a new perspective on race in the United States and inspired my dissertation on queer literary and cultural representations of Filipinxs in the Midwest, which I am transforming into my first book manuscript. This project argues that Filipinxs and other people of color appear as out of place in the Midwest because the region figures as the nation's heartland, and that narrative is premised on White supremacy and settler colonialism. If I never stepped outside my California comfort zone and braved the unknown middle, I would not be the scholar I am today, nor would I know how to navigate predominantly White spaces and still find ways to queer and Filipinize them.

In transit, from south Minneapolis to the U, I witnessed the uneven racial dynamics of the Twin Cities. Attending grad school in Minnesota also was a period of transition into adulthood. And as I write with some critical and physical distance from that formative moment in my life, amid local, regional, national, and global racial reckonings and an ongoing pandemic that has generated a resurgence of anti-Asian sentiment and action, I recognize that we, as a society, are in transition—that our current world is not enough, that it has never been enough for some, but that it also does not have to be this way. I am hopeful for a world when and where Black lives will truly matter, and the intersectional coalitions already underway give us glimpses of that world yet to come.

Manhattan, KS
July 5, 2020

Thomas X. Sarmiento is assistant professor of English and affiliated faculty of gender, women, and sexuality studies at Kansas State University. He specializes in diasporic Filipinx American literature and culture, cultural representations of the Midwest, and queer theories. His research appears in *Amerasia Journal*, *MELUS*, and *Women, Gender, and Families of Color*.

Everybody's Going Uptown

Rodolfo Aguilar

Upon my arrival in Minneapolis, my friends put me on to the sounds of the beloved musician Prince. I had heard his music growing up but put little attention to it, as I was more immersed in hip-hop, G-funk, Mexican corridos, and salsa. I fell in love with his music as an adult. When I listen to Prince's catalog today, I cannot help but reminisce of my youthful days in the Twin Cities as a young grad student. Recently, I find myself frequently listening to the "Uptown" number from his *Dirty Mind* LP. The song appears on many of my curated playlists, inspiring me on my daily runs and exercise routines. Yet the song brings new significance to me not only as I reflect on my time living in south Minneapolis but also as I process the killing of George Floyd at the hands of Minneapolis police officers on Memorial Day of 2020.

Prince presented "Uptown" to be a rather inclusive space where people of color and Whites could party and hook up with little judgment. He proclaimed in this specific song, "White, Black, Puerto Rican, everybody just a-freakin' / Good times were rolling." I recall spending many days in Minneapolis's Uptown neighborhood digging for music at Cheapo Records, meeting friends for evening drinks, and spinning vinyl at various establishments like Muddy Waters and Nightingale. These memories of Uptown will always remain pleasant in my mind. Yet I also remember a stratified Uptown, where everyone was *supposedly* going, but the area serviced a predominantly affluent White consumer, with businesses placing their majority White staffs front and center. Immigrants and racialized minorities also labor in Uptown but are often tucked away in kitchens as cooks and dishwashers. Out of sight! I became acquainted with many service industry workers in Uptown; they were lovely and attended to my food and beverage requests when I DJed in different establishments (often my fellow DJs and I were the only visible people of color in these bars and restaurants, spinning Black and Latinx music). I often had to walk into kitchens to borrow restaurants' sound equipment for my sets. It was in these small moments that I met many Latinx workers, hidden out of public view, greeting them in Spanish with a "qvo" (what's up) or a genuine "hola."

I did not move to Minneapolis with intentions of becoming a part-time DJ. I moved to Minnesota in 2007, after being born and raised in Chicago, to pursue a PhD in American studies at the University of Minnesota. I found myself in a predominantly white space, very much like Uptown and its establishments, while at "the U." Whenever I visited the library, I would browse the floors housing the bound MA and PhD theses, hoping to find ones written by former Latinx grad students. I found my grad program academically rewarding as I sharpened my scholarly tools to analyze race, migration, political economy, class, and empire. My peers in the program were bright and in solidarity with workers' rights, immigrant rights, Indigenous peoples' struggles, African American and Black struggles (the Black Lives Matter movement came in the later years of my studies), and queer struggles. We pushed the field of American studies in unique ways by producing scholarship denouncing American empire, American exceptionalism, racism, anti-immigrant rhetoric, and anti-intellectualism. Yet something still felt out of place for me during my time at the University of Minnesota. I constantly dealt with imposter syndrome as a first-generation grad student of color. I recall sitting in several seminars, struggling to stay afloat with the readings, having a difficult time making sense of the scholarly theories, while many of my peers entered the program fluent in Foucault and Spivak. I needed to play catch-up and fast. I was not prepared for what graduate school had in store for me even though I had participated in the McNair Scholars Program and conducted undergraduate research during my time at the University of Illinois at Chicago.

My previous life experience and undergraduate education could not prepare me for making sense of the racial dynamics of Minneapolis either. I had to learn how the city was mapped out racially through experiences, not only through scholarship. Uptown, for example, was and continues to be a very White space in Minneapolis. It was also the place many of my grad student peers secured housing. So I found myself spending lots of time there, traveling from my apartment in the nearby Loring Park neighborhood (another predominantly White space). My friends and I often tried to find refuge at watering holes and other establishments when celebrating milestones and while routinely venting about the social structures that placed trauma in our lives and those of our families.

One night, I attended my friend's celebration after he successfully defended his prelims (the exams PhD students must complete in order to advance in their doctoral program) at the VFW hall in Uptown. The place was dingy and dark. The bulk of the patrons were working-class White and Black people in their mid- to late forties. I remember one older White woman came to speak to my group after an incident where a Black woman publicly shamed a male patron for sexist behavior. The White women sided with the Black female against the guilty patron during the altercation. She received praises from our group for doing so. When she came to speak to our party, she provided details about her upbringing as a working-class White ethnic woman in a northeastern city. At one point, the conversation took a turn for the worst. She blurted, "Fuck Ecuadorians," and moments later said, "They forgot about us [White folks]." We were all taken aback at her comments. My friends looked at me to see if I felt attacked by the woman's anti-Latino remarks. Knowing that I am a Chicano male, my friends wanted to ensure my personal safety and kindly asked if we should take the party elsewhere. I politely said I was fine and suggested we stay put at the VFW. I could not help but feel a real sense of being out of place. I wanted to disappear. I did not think about scholarly texts at that moment. My mind was in complete shock that this woman felt comfortable enough to express her discontent against a particular ethnic Latinx group. Looking back at this incident, I realize her comments attacked Ecuadorians, but she also attacked Latinx immigrants, African refugees, and Hmong refugees who had made Minnesota their homes.

I reflect on the incident now using a scholarly lens with the help of key texts like Leo Chavez's seminal book *The Latino Threat* and David Roediger's *Working Toward Whiteness* to better contextualize how this woman's discontent with immigrants was filled with xenophobia and nativism—the same xenophobia and nativism that fuels much of current popular conservativism, including the brand embodied by the forty-fifth president of the United States. The sentiment behind her remark "they forgot about us" resurfaced in January 2020 in Minnesota when the Beltrami County Board of Commissioners voted to prohibit refugees from resettling in their jurisdiction. These words also reminded me how the City of Lakes, which welcomes immigrants and hosts an annual May Day parade filled with youthful progressive activists, is still home to individuals and groups invested in preserving the status quo where police officers could kill Black men with excessive force and local residents could resent immigrants. This woman's words stung me—a child of one immigrant parent and a second-generation Chicana mother—that night, and they continue to sting today.

I guess Prince was right: "Everybody's going Uptown," including young White partygoers, youth of color, immigrant workers, grad students, military vets, and anti-immigrant locals. I just hope we create an Uptown like the one imagined in Prince's song, where immigrants, people of color, queer youth, progressive Whites, Indigenous peoples, and refugees can all partake in the "good times."

The George Floyd uprising gave Black communities and people of color the outlet to articulate a sense of discontent against years of systemic racism in the Twin Cities. It also provided spaces for many residents to reimagine and now rebuild the city in unique ways. If we look past the rubble from the burnt-down big-box stores, we will see community members making Minneapolis home and helping others do the same by providing food, financial assistance, and spaces for creativity. This is the Minneapolis I want to imagine now that I am physically distant from the city. It is the city where I spent the bulk of my twenties, made lifelong friendships, and met my future wife at First Avenue. I also earned an advanced degree from the University of Minnesota, which has allowed me the opportunity to enter the faculty ranks, currently as an assistant professor of Latinx studies and American studies at Kennesaw State University. Minneapolis will always be home (second to Chicago). My only hope is that current residents make room for more people who look like me and have similar immigrant backstories.

Marietta, GA
July 15, 2020

Rodolfo Aguilar is assistant professor of Latin American/Latinx studies and American studies in the Interdisciplinary Studies Department at Kennesaw State University. His scholarly interests include US Latino studies, popular music, American studies, immigration, and midwestern Latina/o communities. Aguilar's scholarship appears in publications such as *Aztlán: A Journal of Chicano Studies*.

Luna Lovers

Mario Alberto Obando

The sound and harmony that pulsates heavily in my heart and reminds me of my three years of life in Minneapolis is "Luna Lovers" by Las Cafeteras. My beautiful friends Reina and Danny, who became my chosen family while my spirit trudged slowly over the salty ice of the Twin Cities, would play this melody every night to bring peace and sweet dreams to their beautiful infant Diego Tlatoani. On nights when my dear friend Soham and I would visit Reina and Danny's cozy and warm apartment to hang out with our newest nephew, "Luna Lovers" was always on repeat and would soak the airwaves of our whispering *platicas*.

The echoes of the melody and lyrics still warm my soul whenever I am as sad and depressed as I was in Minneapolis. "Won't you walk with me luna through the dark / won't you take my hand, help me understand / take my hand, walk me through your land." The song's opening lines capture Diego, Danny, Reina, and Soham's familial comfort of friends from Los Angeles caring for one another in the unfamiliar and violent terrain of the Midwest—"So the story goes that my heart met yours / you touched my soul, it's you I adore / it's your beauty where I feel most free / it's you and me and it's plain to see." It is no coincidence, then, that through their friendship I found my life partner, Letty, once I moved back to Los Angeles, and it is therefore no coincidence that my story about my life in Minneapolis is more than just sorrow; it is a story of friendships.

The line "won't you walk with me luna through the dark" reminds me of when my friends and I were kicked out of Target Field by security simply for having cheered for Los Angeles Dodgers right fielder Yasiel Puig in Spanish. Excited to wear our Dodgers jerseys and cheer for our favorite player, we were ecstatic to yell "*vamos* Puig" and "*lo queremos mucho* Puig." A white woman in front of us turned around and told us that "we don't speak that here" and kept telling us "to shut the fuck up." Her partner ran to security, and without ever hearing our side of the story, the security guards "escorted" us out of the park. A violent reminder that there was no place for brown folks being proud in the corporate terrain of white Minneapolis feminism. If it wasn't for my friends sharing a drink with me and ordering chicken wings after and us consoling each other, I would not have been able to appreciate the *luna* through the dark that night.

The line "won't you take my hand, help me understand" reminds me of my first, and sadly one of my few, queer nightclub experiences in downtown Minneapolis. If it wasn't for my roommate Soham's solace and kindness after a white cisgender queer man bumped into me and let me know that he wouldn't dare be caught with someone who wears Nike Cortez sneakers to a gay bar, my homesickness for a brown space of queerness and community would have driven me way further into the numbing of a bottle. It was Soham's racialized solidarity that supported me when at school another graduate student of color had the audacity to grab the collar of my shirt to check the tag of my sweater that they seemed to gush over and state quite sternly and directly to my soul that "oh, must be from Walmart . . . gross." If it wasn't for my friends "taking me by the hand to help me understand" by going to dinner with me, sharing a meal, and processing the racialized classism, I would not have been able to dig myself out of the hole of numerous people telling me to stop wearing hoodies (in the middle of polar vortex weather) and substitute them with more presentable attire for a department event to make "good impressions" and appeal to whiteness. If it wasn't for my friends, I would not have processed with support and love the violence in the tongue of another white graduate student exclaiming that "Mondays were Maid Mondays back where he went to school" because that's when the brown women came in to clean up after frat parties. Who else but my friends could have grounded me in the worth of my mother's housekeeping labor?

The lines "and I'm asking you to stand / stand by my side (by my side) / and come along with me down the river singing the song" grounded me in the countless conversations I would have with Terrel, a wonderful friend I met in Minnesota, about music, community, activism, and love adjacent to, across from, and at the banks of the frozen and/or flowing Mississippi River. His reassurance of the value and power of comparative racialized politics in our conversations at the bowling alleys at Memory Lanes, in the studio for *Radio Pocho*, or over spicy wings at Smalley's in Stillwater always transformed the tensions I was feeling in the teaching and activism I was doing on campus. In activist spaces, self-proclaimed white "radicals" would begrudge the "unwillingness" of activists of color to prioritize solely a class analysis of the violence that saturated the Twin Cities and thereby aimed to stifle our queer- and feminist-of-color ruptures. It was Terrel's kind listening and loving laugh that transcended any of that nonsense.

Our "unwillingness," of course, was a refusal to center whiteness in our organizing, teaching, and everyday life, especially Marxism's prototype of revolution—which in Minnesota often gets misplaced in the ideal of the white midwestern farmer, while ignoring the energies and labors of the Black communities who fled Jim Crow, the recent immigrant farmworkers from Mexico and Central America, or the Black Muslim Somali community, much less the Ojibwe and Dakota people whose land this myth claims a stake over. In meetings with University of Minnesota president Eric Kaler for the Whose Diversity? activist collective at the U, where we would demand the university end its contract with the Minneapolis Police Department after repeated targeting, surveillance, and violence against communities of color and he would repeatedly say, "be patient, change is slow, be patient, change is slow," I would just leave. As history would show repeatedly with the countless murders of Black people, the ongoing genocide of Indigenous communities and sacred land, the never-ending war on terror and anti-Muslim racism, the anti-immigrant violence against Latinx communities, and the perpetual murder of queer and trans* people of color, a one-dimensional class analysis and a white liberal progressive temporality of "slow change" are part of the fissure and fusion of white supremacy's wrath on us. Yet I say this with no hesitation: my friends saved my spirit from the eternal violence with nights of ceviche at the apartment I shared with Soham, by taking the I-35W highway to protest the killing of unarmed Black people, and in continuing our studies with cups of coffee at the countless coffee shops we loved—especially Studio 2 in southwest Minneapolis.

When I moved to Minneapolis in the summer of 2013, I chose to live in Whittier because I grew up in Whittier, California. A symbolic act to find home away from home. Yet these two spaces, which ironically are named after anti-slavery abolitionist poet John Greenleaf Whittier, hold an overflowing of racial and ableist violence and haunting in their situatedness in Los Angeles and Minneapolis. The interconnectedness of these spaces and the significance of friendship solidified when Black Lives Matter protesters joined together in my hometown of Whittier to honor the life of George Floyd, which conjured the memory of a childhood friend of mine, Jonathan Salcido, who was murdered by the Whittier Police Department in 2017. Though he and I had lost touch over the years, the murder of a childhood friend, someone with whom I had sleepovers at friends' houses and who lived with schizophrenia, was heartbreaking and to this day is difficult to process and fathom. News reports still call Jonathan's murder simply a "death" even though cops asphyxiated him and beat him so badly that they also caused severe head trauma.

I consider activism and protest acts of intimate friendship and chosen local and global family. The weeks that the memories of George Floyd and Jonathan Salcido were conjured led me to envision a better world. A world where police killings and the murders of queer and trans* as well as differently abled black and brown folks, whether it be in places I have lived or in spaces I send my love and spirit to, like Palestine, like Kashmir, like Yemen, like Somalia, and to my Muslim brothers and sisters in internment camps in China and my Latinx beloved in detention centers across the United States, all these places where people of color are suffering are abolished. This envisioning has me meditating and praying for George and Jonathan to meet in the celestial space that transcends the violence of this hell on earth and find solace with the intention that my friends and I in spirit and in protest have so conjured. May their meeting and wisdom transcend this material plane of reality and grant us the spiritual terrain to honor their lives with justice in and beyond the state and allow this envisioning to become reality.

In my three years in Minneapolis and my four years since moving back to Los Angeles, I learned that I take my friends from the Twin Cities with me everywhere I go. A place where friends were made, and perhaps, as the song goes, "maybe we can be more than friends" and tell each other "words of truth and mystery," keep each other "inside this memory / where the grass is green and the sky is high" and never "say goodbye," so that "we will fly luna through the sky" because "aaa aaaa I love you / (I do I do I do I do I do I love you)."

Whittier, CA
July 15, 2020

Mario Alberto Obando is assistant professor of Chicana/o studies at California State University, Fullerton (CSUF). He finds joy in teaching the brilliant and magical queer and feminist interventions in critical ethnic studies in his courses and is also the faculty adviser to the student organization Central Americans for Empowerment (C.A.F.E) at CSUF.

Gesturing Toward Tenuous Inclusion

Jasmine Mitchell

A gust of frigid winter air swirled onto my face as I stepped out of the plane door and into the Minneapolis–St. Paul airport (MSP) for the first time. MSP was all too quiet. I was used to bustling John F. Kennedy airport in New York City, with its mélange of languages, attire, and physical appearances as business travelers, tourists, and families jockeyed to get to their gates. But, step after step, I saw a sea of White. Quickening my pace, I looked around instinctually for glimpses of anyone with a darker skin tone. As a mixed Black woman, this was certainly not my first time in predominantly White spaces. However, I wasn't expecting to stand out at an international airport. After acceptance into the University of Minnesota doctoral program in American studies, I had arrived in Minneapolis for a prospective student visit. At first I thought, *there is no way I am coming here despite the department's reputation with cutting-edge race and gender research.* It wasn't just the cold. I liked ice-skating and cross-country skiing, after all. My preconceived notions of Minnesota narrowed my mindset to a slow cooker cuisine, Mall of America, flannel-attired White land. But I would soon give Minnesota a chance. The University of Minnesota American studies department's Mas(s) Color group for graduate students of color members and student coordinators were unbelievably responsive and honest. The MacArthur Fellowship program offered an opportunity to learn alongside other graduate students and faculty in assorted fields working on social change in the Global South. I thought at worst these would be havens, and Minnesota is a blue state after all.

At the same time, I cared a lot about having a community away from academia. I had applied only to graduate schools located in big cities. I also thought, *well, if I'm getting a doctorate in American studies, I need to learn about the rest of the United States aside from the coasts.* I knew that the American Indian Movement started in Minneapolis. I figured since Prince was from here and Janet Jackson lived here for a while, there must be more to check out. But I began to realize that I had erased BIPOC communities from Minnesota narratives and imagery. The first step entailed a road trip from NYC to Minneapolis. With Paul Bunyan statues, beautiful lakes, and lots of stares at gas stations, would Minneapolis be an oasis?

Driving into Uptown, my new home, I passed crowds in front of Chino Latino, a trendy restaurant marketing "hot zone street food" with the logo of a masculine face fused with racially caricatured "Chino" and "Latino" top and bottom halves. This gesture toward a consumption of the "Other" characterized many of my later Minneapolis experiences. Growing up in an interracial family with an African American mother and a white father in 1980s Brooklyn, New York, I didn't know many other families like mine. But my appearance didn't stand out. If anything, I was assumed to be Nuyorican, a member of the Puerto Rican diaspora in New York City. In other parts of the city, I might be misidentified as Filipino. Although many of the neighborhoods are quite segregated, my place in diverse, multicultural New York City was never questioned. Here in Minneapolis, I often felt out of my place as Other. My racial ambiguity triggered discomfort masked as curiosity. The couched innocence of "Where are you from?" became more insistent when my answers shrouding racial categorization did not suffice. Follow-up questions of "No, I mean what country are you from?," "Where are your parents from?," and "You can't be American, what are you?" cascaded. Followed by, "Wow, that's an exotic look," or a worried-sounding "Oh," and then a quick scurrying away if I chose to announce my Black identity. In other corners, when asked by BIPOC members of the Twin Cities, the questions were not to police my place in Minnesota. Instead, the questions such as "Who are your people?" were often phrased as a means of connection.

Over and over again, Minnesotans praised Minneapolis for its progressiveness and inclusion. Yet this inclusion centered on who was deemed palatable and acceptable. Comments such as "We don't have much racism here because there aren't many African Americans" negates the continuing presence of African Americans, from the hauntings of Dred Scott to the segregation of neighborhoods such as north Minneapolis.

Bit by bit, I found welcoming Minnesotans and transplanted communities unbound by Minnesota standoffish friendliness. At multigenerational house parties imbued with salsa, samba, and hip-hop or at dinner gatherings, I would meet one person and often receive another added invitation with a nod to being "like one of us." In spaces and at performances such as Intermedia Arts, EQ at the Loft, Mixed Blood Theatre, Ananya Dance Theatre, and Penumbra Theatre, the immense solidarity for celebrating and supporting BIPOC performers was palpable. In many ways, I found that the racial dynamics of Minnesota generated a sense of shared fate, purpose, and support among BIPOC communities that I have not found in larger urban areas. This is not to say that there weren't tensions regarding alliance commitments, however.

The American studies department had many activist scholars, and I chose the department for its centering of race, gender, and sexuality, its decolonial lens, and its critical grappling with "America." The transnational focus alongside Indigenous perspectives, knowledge, and resistance especially fomented my understanding of racial formations, Blackness, and white supremacy in the Americas. But the semester I entered the department, Mas(s) Color was defunded. In other classes, I found White graduate students red in the face with clenched teeth and yelling at Black female professors over what was criticized as an overemphasis on race in the department. In some discussions in other departments, White students commented on my aggressive nature. In typical New York City fashion, I thought *aggressive* was a compliment and did not realize it was a supreme White, Minnesota nice, racialized insult. Some faculty members and students insisted that my research on mixed Blackness and racism was not relevant anymore because of Barack Obama's successful presidential campaign. Another faculty member suggested that I work with first-generation undergraduate students because I spoke English like a "native speaker." Thankfully, faculty members like that were in the minority. Overall, my advisors and faculty mentors were overwhelmingly supportive of my intellectual journeys.

Yet where were the Black graduate students? While I had attended predominantly White educational institutions in Massachusetts, there were already preexisting networks of Black students there. Eventually, in Rose Brewer's "Intellectual History of Race" course in the Africa and the African Diaspora studies graduate minor program, I met a few other African American students from other departments. "Why have we not met before and where have you been this whole time?" we exclaimed to each other. Sarah Janel Jackson generated the idea to start the University of Minnesota Black Graduate and Professional Students Association in 2008, and I soon came on board as vice president and then president. We wanted to create a sense of Black community at the university and support each other, combat isolation, and engage with the broader Twin Cities BIPOC communities.

Living in Minnesota was critical to my intellectual formation and sense of solidarity and community. I was lucky enough to find an assistant professor position in American studies at the State University of New York–Old Westbury and return to reside in New York City. New York City will always be my home, and its skyline still takes my breath away every single time, but the New York City I returned home to has become increasingly gentrified and stratified along racial and class lines. Minneapolis became one of my favorite world cities—the beautiful lakes and river with amazing arts, the affordability relative to New York City, the neighborhood communities. However, neither the murders of Philando Castile and George Floyd and countless others nor the violence inflicted upon protesters surprises me. The Minnesota nice comforts and illusionary progressiveness reside upon the ignoring of White racial terrorism and fears of Blackness, of brown immigrants, and of resistance to White supremacy. Residents of Minneapolis, like those of other cities including my hometown, pride themselves on liberalism and often define themselves as exceptional. Minneapolis is not exceptional but rather exemplifies the willingness to negate racism. The seeds of my book, *Imagining the Mulatta: Blackness in U.S. and Brazilian Media,* germinated in Minneapolis as I saw contradictions of illusionary racial progress, the denial of racism, and enduring legacies of slavery and colonization. Nonetheless, I remain inspired by the amazing movements that have sprung up since the tragic murders and the newfound solidarity between communities they have inspired. I hope Minneapolis will never be the same, that our nation will never be the same, that the world will never be the same.

New York, NY
July 14, 2020

Jasmine Mitchell is associate professor of American studies and media studies at the State University of New York–Old Westbury. Her scholarly specialties include race and gender representation in popular culture, African American and Afro-Brazilian studies, Black feminisms, and race and sports. She is the author of *Imagining the Mulatta: Blackness in U.S. and Brazilian Media.*

Learning the Scales of Music and Diversity in My Minneapolis

Neeraj Rajasekar

The "Wonderful/Wretched Memories of Racial Dynamics in the Twin Cities, Minnesota" special feature publishes stories of social scientists with ties to the Twin Cities of Minneapolis and St. Paul but who now live elsewhere. My family and I have lived in Minneapolis since 1994, but I was inspired to submit this essay to highlight a dynamic that has not yet been explored: the experiences of South Asians. I wasn't born in the United States, but everything else in my life from potty training onward happened here. Indeed, my midwestern accent with a hint of Minnesotan dialect (ya betcha!) has thrown many for a loop. We were far from the first people from India to live in the Twin Cities, and I've met many other second-gen Indian immigrants (nicknamed American-Born Confused Desis, aka "ABCDs") who are decades older than me. Yet, more than twenty-five years after we unpacked the boxes in our first apartment—a one-bedroom in Brooklyn Park—I still have encounters where people comment on how impressed they are by my English fluency; many of these people are well intentioned, and several are not.

"Where are you from?"

"Minneapolis."

"No, where are you really from?"

(*Rolls eyes*.) "India."

My family is from the Mylapore neighborhood of Chennai, the capital city of the state of Tamil Nadu, the southernmost state in the Republic of India, a country of over a billion people, fifty languages, and many different religions. To reduce that diversity to the one-word answer of "India" is a disservice, but a prudent maneuver in a world full of "Where are you from?" and the annoying follow-up question. After all, most people living in the United States do not have the experience to learn about the diversity of the Indian subcontinent and South Asian culture. Sometimes, when I'm feeling cheeky, I answer "Sri Lanka" or "Pakistan" instead.

Of course, the one-word answer of "Minneapolis" is in itself another disservice. What does it mean to be from Minneapolis when "Minneapolis" can span affluent suburbs such as Eden Prairie, Wayzata, and Eagan, or "Minneapolis" can mean "less affluent" neighborhoods such as Cedar-Riverside, Near North, and Phillips? Indeed, how can we squeeze the entirety of the Twin Cities into words like "Minneapolis" or "St. Paul"?

When my parents moved to Minneapolis, they were no strangers to being foreign internationals in a different land. Between the two of them, my parents had lived in Iran, England, Switzerland, and several other countries beforehand. Yet, when I was discussing thoughts about race with my parents as I planned this essay, something my mother said struck me: "It took us a little while to learn about race in this country and this city. It's not the same as elsewhere." After all, the culture here was not a foreign concept, given the international presence of all things American, from Michael Jackson to Kentucky Fried Chicken. The image of the United States in the early 1990s was that of a modern, cosmopolitan, self-proclaimed post-racist society; this was a defining narrative in American media, politics, and news, and my parents say this reputation had given them high expectations for tolerance and racial harmony in this advanced multicultural nation. But this certainly wasn't the case; discrimination, prejudice, and the differing conduct and interactions among varying racial groups soon became clear.

My mother, an internationally acclaimed Carnatic musician, quickly learned the scales of race and racism in the United States and the Twin Cities. Her instrument, the veena, is as large as a jazz bass. She has traveled around the world for her music, no thanks to the efforts of TSA agents. She recounted a story to me when she and her friend, a White cellist, were flying to California in the mid-2000s with their instruments. The TSA agents barely glanced at the cello, not even opening its case to check inside. But they unceremoniously dragged my mother's instrument from the box and threw it forcefully on the examination table. They made her take off the strings and separate the wood holding the sound chamber together so they could peer inside. They looked at the ornate symbols, patterns, and calligraphy upon the veena itself with disgust. My mother, used to this behavior, was upset but tried to put it out of her mind and focus on inspecting the veena for damage. Her friend was so horrified that she immediately drafted a letter to the airline staff demanding an apology and explanation, sending several letters over a few weeks, but she never received a response.

I have learned a lot about race as a result of my mother's music. Indeed, the social circle of musicians she knew was a diverse affair, including Robert Bly the celebrated poet, Marcus the White man who plays the Indian drum tabla, Hong the Chinese woman who plays an Asian lute called a pipa, Gary the Black leader of the world-class group Sounds of Blackness, David the Sephardic scholar and musician, Nicole the inspiring White, deaf actor, as well as Indian theater director Dipankar, and dancers Ranee, Rita, and Ananya, who hail from many different parts of India—this is just the tip of the iceberg.

Through meeting artists from around the world who represented the intersections of various cultures and experiences, my understanding grew. I gained an appreciation for foods, music, and arts outside my own group. As a young child I received the kinds of formative experiences that helped me respect people who didn't look like me. When I think back to the kids in high school who made fun of my race, my funny-sounding name, the "smelly" lunches my parents packed, and the "weird" clothes my people wear, I wonder if they ever had the same chance as I did to learn better.

Some of the most important parts of my learning about diversity and race came from insights from Black musicians in Minneapolis. Anthony, a nationally known, legendary Black jazz bassist, shared insightful and painful recollections of his experiences performing with my mom, tales that trickled to me as I got older and gained understanding. His family moved to Minneapolis when he was the same age that I was when my family moved to Minneapolis. They came from Oklahoma in the 1950s, whereas we came from Switzerland in the 1990s, but their story taught us a lot about race in the United States and Minneapolis. Anthony's family faced the racism and hostility of pre-civil-rights-era White America. As he describes, "Minnesota nice" wasn't nice to him or his family. Though his parents worked as servants and laborers in the Jim Crow South, they experienced new kinds of racial aggression and humiliation in Minnesota that they had not experienced in Oklahoma. The air of "you're-different-than-me" felt more palpable here, where Whiteness was an overarching default and minorities of any kind were an oddity. The only thing colder than the Minnesota winters was the frigid-at-best treatment Anthony's family received from their neighbors when they bought their first house in an all-White neighborhood. I had convinced myself that the bullies from my youth gave me the same insight into being a minority as all other minorities. Spending time with Anthony ("Anthony Uncle," as I called him then) was part of my broader awakening to the fact that people of color don't all share the same experience when dealing with Whiteness. His tales made my lunchroom bullies look like Mother Teresa. For perspective, consider that his family received so many violent threats that the attorney general ordered a protective detail and had to use wiretaps to trace the origin of the calls.

When we consider "race" through an academic lens, we can see that this little four-letter word captures many different sociological concepts and constructs in empirical data and research. Here I turn to C. W. Mills's famous "sociological imagination." The impacts of race and racism in history perfectly show the power and importance of social constructions; race is a concept that provides myriad opportunities to exercise and awaken the sociological imagination; the history of efforts, energies, and excellence of anti-racist scholars has been a foundational building block in forwarding critical social science as a vehicle of equity, change, and social good.

If I have to pick the earliest moment when my own sociological imagination was sparked, it comes from hazy memories of the multiethnic, multiracial apartment complex we first lived in during my preschool and early days of K–12. This neighborhood in Brooklyn Park would prove a thousand times more diverse than the sprawling White suburbs such as Wayzata, Eden Prairie, and Edina where we lived for the majority of my early education. White families, Chinese families, Hmong families, Vietnamese families, Mexican families, Nicaraguan families, Black families, and many more lived in these affordable apartments, and many were other immigrant families. Indeed, we were far from the only Indian family in the neighborhood as well. A veritable hodgepodge of diverse, five-year-old boys could be seen running around the apartment complex at any given moment, playing tag and Power Rangers.

I have a vague memory, corroborated by my parents' recounting of the story. Another Indian kindergartener and I were riding the bus to school. Every morning, a teacher would board the bus and call, "Breakfast students!" Some students would get off the bus and follow her. One day, my Indian friend and I joined that line of students; our youthful curiosity was dying to know what was going on there. We were led into the school cafeteria, where there were cinnamon rolls and cartons of milk. My friend and I weren't hungry; we threw away most of our serving. Little did we know, we were encroaching on the designated space for providing free or reduced-cost meals for low-income students.

Our families were not on the designated list, nor were any other Indian students. My friend and I received quite the scolding for our little adventure after the school called to report our mischief. I remember what stood out to me about the experience, though I didn't have the understanding as a five-year-old to put it into articulate words. In the language of a kindergartner, I noticed that my friend and I were the only other desi kids sitting with the "breakfast students." Looking back on this story today as a sociologist who studies race, this moment was one of my first in learning the scales of race in the United States. Despite the racial diversity on the bus ride to school, in the kindergarten classroom, and in the apartment complex during the many afternoons spent playing tag, the "breakfast students" were a nearly all-Black group, and notably *none* of the many other Indian immigrant families in the neighborhood had children enrolled in this presumably needs-based program.

In many ways, this anecdote captures the power of diversity to foster interracial understanding and cooperation, but it shows the shortcomings of diversity for pursuing true racial equity and structural change. This is a common theme in research about "diversity" discourse today. Research establishes that diversity is good. Diversity can breed intergroup friendships and understanding. Diversity can give us opportunities to learn about new cultures. Diversity can make organizations more creative and make groups more productive. Yet diversity is not a panacea for racism or the ticket to racial equality. In fact, another common theme in research about diversity discourse is that such language can be used in ways that celebrate race yet downplay racial inequality and deny the continued relevance of race and racism in the United States. I had a fun time playing with the neighborhood kids and developing a taste for tacos, chicken, and banh mi when their parents had us over for lunch. But at that age, I never once realized that some of the other kids would go on to face challenges I could never dream of. I never thought about why some of them ate breakfast at school.

Thus, though I have discussed "diversity" as a tool that can create more harmonious interracial understanding, diversity falls far short of fostering the critical, anti-racist energies that we need today in order to dismantle systems of White supremacy. Living in Minneapolis has taught me that we must leverage our diversity as solidarity. The hodgepodge of different ethnicities, cultures, and communities that defined my family's old apartment in Brooklyn Park characterizes the Twin Cities; for a relatively small urban area in comparison to major metropolitan hubs in the United States, Minneapolis still sports its fair share of ethnic and racial diversity. Yet it is amid this very diversity that George Floyd was murdered and Black lives have been harassed, terrorized, and ended at the hands of systemic state violence.

In the weeks following the protests for George Floyd, my mother and her music school, Naadha Rasa, organized funds for community relief and supporting peaceful protesters; when she took bags of food to the drop-off point, she saw a diverse group of people standing in the streets in support of the #BlackLivesMatter movement. She stayed and participated for a while; her work had always placed her in a position to foster interracial friendships and understanding, but today her instrument was not her veena but her support for the movement. Leveraging the diversity of music and art gives us the opportunity to learn the scales of race, but it is time to move further.

We must not only learn the scales of race; we must work to transform the score that these notes are written upon so that murky and jarring low notes become melodious and clear high notes. We must recognize systemic racism for what it is: an overarching, life-defining soundtrack, a theme song for the United States. For many people of color in this country living under the specter of systemic racism, a large part of their existence has been trying to convince media, politicians, academics, and their own friends that race still matters; this issue clearly persists today. Changing this tune will require all of us as a society, but doesn't the best music come when we put our heads together?

Minneapolis, MN
July 21, 2020

Neeraj Rajasekar is a PhD candidate in the Department of Sociology at the University of Minnesota. He studies the intersections of "diversity" discourses, race, and cultural beliefs. He is also the social media editor at The Society Pages open-access social science project.

PART 2

Sparked Reflections on Race and Racism in Minnesota

The Minnesota Paradox

Samuel L. Myers Jr.

On May 25, 2020, George Floyd, a forty-six-year-old Black man, was killed by a Minneapolis police officer during an arrest. The officer pressed his knee to Floyd's neck for 8 minutes, 46 seconds while Floyd was hand-cuffed face down in the street. Two other officers further restrained Floyd, and a fourth prevented onlookers from intervening.

In the wake of Floyd's death, widespread protests—both violent and nonviolent—occurred for several days in Minneapolis and St. Paul, caus-ing considerable property damage. The events in Minnesota sparked further action, as demonstrations took place in major cities across the United States and worldwide. For a Midwest state known for being "nice," it begs the question: How could this happen in Minnesota?

The answer can be found in what is called the "Minnesota Paradox."

Minnesota is one of the best places to live in America. It regularly produces some of the highest average scores in the nation on the SAT exams and boasts a disproportionate share of Rhodes Scholars and ad-missions to MIT and Harvard. The famed Mayo Clinic is an international leader in medical research and development of vaccines for critical dis-eases such as COVID-19. Housing prices are considerably below the na-tional median.

It nurtures a large and vibrant arts, theater, and music community and was home to both Prince and Judy Garland. Good schools. A robust regional transportation network. Major employers like 3M, Best Buy, Cargill, General Mills, Target, and US Bank contribute to a sustained and vigorous corporate giving culture where nonprofits are some of the best known in America.

Surprisingly, Minnesota is also putatively one of the worst places for Blacks to live. Measured by racial gaps in unemployment rates, wage and salary incomes, incarceration rates, arrest rates, homeownership rates, mortgage lending rates, test scores, reported child maltreatment rates, school disciplinary and suspension rates, and even drowning rates, African Americans are worse off in Minnesota than they are in virtually every other state in the nation.

The simultaneous existence of Minnesota as the best state to live in, but the worst state to live in for Blacks is the crux of the Minnesota Paradox.

Baked-in Racism

At one point in Minnesota's history—during the 1930s and 1940s—Black residents across the state had high homeownership rates and high academic achievement levels and made impressive contributions to the rest of the world. There were thriving Black-owned businesses, a vibrant community of fraternal and social organizations, and leaders in virtually every walk of life.

Unfortunately, the small number of Black households faced brutal redlining practices by real estate brokers and lenders, racial covenants, and limitations on what types of jobs they could hold. Urban planners, with the support of elected officials, destroyed historic Black neighborhoods like St. Paul's Rondo community after World War II to make way for Interstate 94.

The cities' police departments substituted explicit racial profiling with scientific management of racially disparate arrests. The state and city governments' child welfare and public housing policies resulted in heavy concentrations of poor minorities in a few isolated census tracts.

In short, racially discriminatory policies became institutionalized and "baked in" to the fabric of Minnesota life. When racism becomes institutionalized, you do not need individual racists for structural racism to systematically disadvantage people of color.

Costs of Calling Out Racism

There is no racism in Minnesota because there are no racists, according to conventional wisdom among many whites. Scholars and academics who allege that the cause of observed racial disparities is racism or racial discrimination can face intense ridicule. In my profession and within the conservative brand of economics championed by the University of Minnesota's economics department and its allies at the Federal Reserve Bank of Minneapolis, racial discrimination cannot exist in the long run in competitive markets. Evidence to the contrary is criticized as being marred by "omitted variable" bias, where the omitted variables include such unobservables as innate ability, motivation, intelligence, culture, family structure, or other putative correlates of race.

Meanwhile, Black academics are accused of what critical race theorist Derrick Bell calls *special pleading* and face the ironic charge of being racist or anti-white when they allege racism. In my nearly thirty years of teaching economics and policy analysis at the University of Minnesota, I have discovered the significantly worse sin a Black man can commit: accuse a white colleague of being a racist. This sin is worse than accusations of homophobia, sexism, classism, or ableism.

I once served on the admissions committee for our graduate program. The admissions director used an algorithm to determine the relative rankings of applicants to the program. Grade point averages, GRE scores, and *Peterson's Guide* rankings of the undergraduate institutions were combined into an index, and the students were ranked.

I pointed out that *Peterson's Guide*—at least at that time—placed almost *all* historically Black colleges and universities at the bottom or near the bottom of the rankings. I pointed out that including these scores in the index for ranking students had a disparate impact. I don't think I actually called the admissions director a racist. If I remember correctly, she asked, "Are you calling me a racist?" And I may have said, "If the shoe fits."

In any event, the admissions director reported my "racist and threatening" behavior to the dean, and I received a warning about my own racism and accusations. It is precisely because of that incident in Minnesota that I recognize the personal risks associated with raising legitimate questions about racism, whether individual or systemic. I discuss the incident in more detail in my article "Why Diversity Is a Smokescreen for Affirmative Action," in *Change: The Magazine of Higher Learning*.

Outside Influence

By the 1990s, good liberal whites were outraged by what appeared to be the widening racial gaps in social and economic outcomes. In a characteristically Minnesotan manner, political leaders blamed rising numbers of violent murders, mounting welfare caseloads, and deteriorating school performance in the Black community on migrants from Chicago, Detroit, and Gary, Indiana. These issues were the problems of the dispossessed of other urban cores. This was not Minnesota. This was outside influence.

The "outside influence" thesis reinforced negative views toward the new migrants among many whites, especially white public welfare managers, law enforcement officials, school officials, and housing authorities.

The result was the perpetuation of institutions of racism and racial discrimination wherein disparities were normalized within Minnesota's structure of life.

The denial of the internal roots of racial disparities is seen in response to the violence and looting in the aftermath of the murder of George Floyd. State and local officials invoked allegations of "outside influence" to justify law enforcement's militarization in the face of mounting protests.

Whether the outside agitators were white nationalists from Montana determined to start a race war or Black hoodlums from Chicago opportunistically making the eight-hour drive to stock up on Johnnie Walker Red is unknown. Either way, it eases the narrative to locate the perpetrators among the outsiders.

Lesson to Learn

The alternative explanation—similar to findings in the September 2018 *Russell Sage Foundation Journal of the Social Sciences* retrospective on the 1967–68 riots in the United States—is that defeated and oppressed people who have nothing to lose will often join in the melee of destruction and violence regardless of how the civil disorders originated. The lesson that Minnesota leaders must learn is that unless and until we acknowledge and remedy the internal roots of the racial disparities in our midst, we run the risks of future disorders.

The violence, looting, and destruction have meaning to African American residents because they are a reflection of the rage and anger built up within us for decades. Explaining the uprising as an external one orchestrated by white nationalists, anarchists, or international forces exacerbates the chaos and undermines the legitimacy of the protest in the court of white public opinion.

North Oaks, MN
January 15, 2021

Samuel L. Myers Jr. is director of the Roy Wilkins Center for Human Relations and Social Justice at the Hubert H. Humphrey School of Public Affairs, University of Minnesota. He is an MIT-trained economist who publishes widely on racial inequality. His latest book (with Inhyuck "Steve" Ha) is *Race Neutrality: Rationalizing Remedies to Racial Inequality.*

What's Understood Don't Need to Be Explained

Sometimes Gifts Come in Ugly Packages

Taiyon J. Coleman

I've seen the future and it will be.
  —Prince, "The Future"

It was on a Tuesday, just two weeks into the fall 2017 semester, when Brent P. Ahlers, a White male security guard, was shot and wounded while patrolling a heavily wooded part of the St. Catherine University grounds. It was two months and a year past the shooting death of Philando Castile by a St. Anthony policeman and the start of my second year as one of the few full-time African American tenure-track faculty members in the entire university. As I sat in my early-twentieth-century, high-ceilinged campus office, romantically gazing out my large picture window, I wondered if it was the same security guard who mistook me and my Tanzanian American husband for janitors a little over a year ago as we excitedly worked late into the night to move me into my new office.

WCCO and the Minneapolis *Star Tribune* reported that Ahlers told St. Paul police that he encountered a Black man around 9:25 at night. Ahlers told the police that he confronted a Black male wearing "a navy-blue sweatshirt" and with "a short afro," and that the Black man shot him in the shoulder, ran through the trees, jumped over a six-foot-plus fence, and then disappeared.

After hearing the story, I did the mental self-check that most institutionally traumatized Black people in America who are always seen as naturally suspect do.

Am I Black? Yes.

Do I wear a short Afro? Yes.

Do I own a gun? No.

Was I in the campus woods on Tuesday? No.

Do I own a navy-blue sweatshirt? I wear a nice navy-blue top some-times, but I'm sure it can't be mistaken for a navy-blue sweatshirt. Right?

Can I scale and jump a six-foot-plus fence? Hell no!

Will they think it was me? Only time will tell.

In response to Ahlers's initial report, the *New York Daily News* re-ported that "55 officers, a Minnesota State Patrol helicopter, and four K-9 units" responded to the crime scene to apprehend one person. The university was put on lockdown while law enforcement officials searched for the "hostile shooter" until an all clear was given. All the while, the historic and highly racially segregated St. Paul neighborhoods of High-land Park and Macalester-Groveland and their various businesses and schools were on high alert. According to a CBS Minnesota report, the shooting incident "had residents . . . fearful that a suspect was on the loose and [they] . . . could be victimized at any moment" by a Black man running and hiding in neighborhoods that, as Minnesota Compass re-cords, are over 79 percent White and 90 percent White, respectively, as a direct legacy of racial covenants.

By half past midnight, the St. Paul Police said that Ahlers was at a local hospital with non-life-threatening injuries, and according to the *Star Tribune* "no one had been arrested, but there was an active search for the suspect." It was an expected, micro (Minnesota) and macro (na-tional) narrative. A foreign unlawful Black body perpetuates violence, makes life unsafe for lawful White bodies, and that Black body must be caught and stopped by any means necessary—that is, deadly local and state law enforcement.

No one, publicly, seemed to question the narrative for at least the first twenty-four hours. As Rachel Siegel reported in the September 15, 2017, edition of the *Washington Post*, almost three and half hours after the event the St. Paul Police released tweets that said: "search has concluded; no suspect located; investigation ongoing." Internally, the police were already doubting the security guard's story, and as a result, they never released an official statement that the suspect was a Black male. However, "audio from police scanner traffic posted by MN Police Clips was widely shared on social media." That audio included identifiers such as the fabricated suspect's race, navy-blue sweatshirt, and Afro. The official St. Paul Police tweets never specifically stated that there was no threat from a Black male assailant or that a Black male assailant did not exist.

I thanked God that my husband was not in the neighborhood that night, coming to pick me up from the university or going to the Kowal-ski's grocery store that we frequent in St. Paul. Imagine what could have happened to any Black person unlucky enough to be anywhere in that neighborhood during those initial hours after "the shooting" had been reported.

The following day, students and community members were, understandably, shaken and needed to be calmed and counseled. The entire school met in the campus chapel with the university administrators for support and answers. As the chapel overflowed, I, like many faculty, staff, and administrators, gave up my seat on the church pew for students and took my place standing along the back wall of the sanctuary with my colleagues. As we watched and listened to university officials deftly field questions from frightened and concerned students, they answered that "sometimes gifts come wrapped in ugly packages."

"Taiyon, don't crucify yourself on a small cross" is what a well-meaning White male supervisor and mentor once told me when I sought him out for advice on how to handle an inequitable workplace experience I was having. I was being low-key bullied by a White male employee who was my counterpart but seemed to have an ongoing problem with my having more education and consequently earning a higher salary than him, although we held the same job title.

I know.

I should have known better.

I wanted to believe.

I wanted to believe that my education could really work and keep me safe from institutional racial injustice.

"Your education is the one thing they can never take away from you," my momma constantly preached to me and my siblings growing up on Chicago's South Side. She neglected to talk to us about the things that they *could* take away.

The job with the White boss was my attempt at achieving the American Dream through employment assimilation, so I had accepted a career where the dress code required female employees to wear pantyhose. I don't think at the time my boss knew that I was a first-generation college-educated and a fifth-generation Black Catholic woman in resistance and recovery. I answered his deadpan crucifixion statement in response to my complaints of racial discrimination and sexual harassment with belly-felt hilarious loud laughter that moved into quiet nervousness and a reflection that permeated my entire body. It's a feeling that comes when you know that what you just experienced has marked your whole person, physical and spiritual, like annual growth rings marking a tree.

My White boss's advice at the time assumed that my workplace crucifixion was inevitable, yet he implied that I had a choice in how I would sacrifice my Black life for others. He was saying, "Yes, Taiyon, what is happening to you in the workplace is not fair, it is wrong, but let this one go. You will have bigger fish to fry" (another Catholic reference), meaning that some inequity and injustice is acceptable, maybe necessary for success and daily life in our societies, cultures, and institutions.

Was he saying that my direct experiences of racism, sexism, and other forms of oppression as a Black woman are necessary in order to maintain workplace (read: institutional, social) peace and order?

I left that White boss supervisor meeting feeling that one day there would be an injustice so big that I would pick up a really big cross for it, do the right thing, and eventually die.

Death on a cross for whose benefit?

Is this the gift?

Who's the recipient?

One lump or two?

I felt like the 1950s cartoon character Pete Puma when Bugs Bunny invites him for tea and asks him how many lumps he wants. Pete Puma is trusting and assumes that his host, Bugs Bunny, is offering him sugar to sweeten his tea. Instead, Pete Puma ends up being beaten in the head.

I left that job and returned to classroom teaching.

Many scholars believe that the tradition of gift giving started with the three kings who brought gifts to honor the birth of Christ. In the article "The History and Complexities of Gift Giving," Kristin Grant writes that it is based on culture, but most agree that gift giving is reciprocal and involves indebtedness. Ahlers lying about a Black man shooting him to avoid the consequences of his illegal actions was a *gift* to himself and simultaneously a *gift* to the construction and perpetuation of Whiteness and White supremacy, as Black in the United States is *always guilty* and *never free*, and White in the United States is *always right* and *full of liberty*. As a result, the cultural and institutional perpetuation of the racial stereotype of Black men as dangerous and violent becomes *a cross* and subsequent *gift* that just keeps on giving in St. Paul, greater Minnesota, and the larger American society as a necessary tradition since their onset.

In his book *Slavery and Social Death*, Orlando Patterson asserts that racialized slavery within the United States of America helped to define and shape what freedom meant to a new, young nation by possessing people (enslaved Black Africans and their descendants) who did not have freedom. Was the enslavement of Black Africans and their subsequent cross—that is, their racialization, oppression, torture, and killing in America—an ugly package gift wrapped for White Americans in order to define US citizenship, freedom, and Whiteness, which takes priority over Black life? In this paradigm, how might one consider the inevitable (read: necessary) oppression of Black people in academia and other US institutions that historically determine and measure the quality of life, freedom, and equity in the United States of America?

There is a better way to remove the obscuring illusion of institutionalized White supremacy to see the reality of Black people in America. We should accept that some Americans consciously and/or subconsciously have been socialized to believe that the direct or indirect social and/or literal death of Black people is central and necessary to their individual, financial, and national success and identity. In an 1820 letter about the conflicts of slavery and states' rights, Thomas Jefferson wrote to John Holmes that "justice is in one scale, and self-preservation in the other" when considering the then and now future dialectic of American democracy. Even Dan Patrick, lieutenant governor of Texas, as reported by Justine Coleman in *The Hill* on April 22, 2020, said "there are more important things than living and that's saving this country for my children and grandchildren and saving this country for all of us" when asked about shutting down his state to reduce the spread of the deadly COVID-19 virus.

Considering that the deaths in America have exceeded 400,000 as of January 2021 and Black, Latinx, and Native Americans are twice as likely or more to die from COVID-19 than their White counterparts, it is highly problematic that the majority of Americans still don't see racial disparities in health care and life outcomes. What Lieutenant Governor Patrick was really saying: The lives of my children and grandchildren are more important than the lives, safety, and health of Black, Latinx, and Native people. And letting Black, Latinx, and Native American people die (killing them) saves this country for *us*, not them. If Black and Brown people have to die of COVID-19 in order for me to generate revenue and save a way of life within a capitalist economy at all costs, then so be it. The cost is always the death of the Black and Brown body, and that body is the gift. So many White people in America from Thomas Jefferson to Dan Patrick and Minneapolis police officer Derek Chauvin are willing to take and accept that gift.

In order for American Whiteness and a White way of life to exist and be sustained, Black people, like George Floyd, must be literally and/or figuratively choked to death. Black children must drink lead-tainted water, breathe mold from within segregated homes, and receive a substandard public education that tracks them into incarceration like sheep to slaughter. Black women must be strong, brilliant, and overqualified and work twice as hard just to receive no credit and less pay. They dispro-portionately remain in generational poverty, have a lower life expectancy than their White counterparts, are more likely to die from hypertension and other preventable diseases caused and exacerbated by sexism and racism, and on top of all of this, are told they are intimidating, difficult, and hard to work with because they (we) dare try to thrive and sur-vive. Black men can't run and walk openly in neighborhoods, they can't kneel during the national anthem, they can't use a twenty-dollar bill at the neighborhood corner store, but they are always suspected felons who can be choked to death for holding a loose cigarette, incarcerated without trial for three years on suspicion of stealing a backpack before committing suicide, and shot point-blank in the park for being a twelve-year-old boy and wanting to play with a plastic toy that looks like a gun.

And if you can't find an actual real Black person to kill, you can always just magically make one up.

The paradox of Minnesota being a "nice" place to live while having some of the largest racial disparities in the nation is actually an American paradox, as racial disparities today in the United States are worse than they were before the civil rights era. If the police state executions of Jamar Clark, Philando Castile, David Smith, Terrance Franklin, Travis Jordan, George Floyd, and Dolal Idd in Minnesota are any evidence, it seems the fears that Jefferson wrote about in 1820 were prophetical and material. Minnesotans like many Americans are still choosing Whiteness and the institutionalized social and literal death of Black people as the ritualized sacrifice that sustains them and maintains a *certain way (quality) of Ameri-can life*. And they continue choosing their own self-preservation over jus-tice, with the result being the real gift that keeps on giving, wrapped in ugly packages of oppressed Black life and death, no matter the gender or age, contorted and obscured as freedom celebrating liberty.

In the Catholic tradition, Jesus's gift to humankind was that he died on the cross for the sins of man, and he even asked his Father, God, to "forgive them for they know not what they do," after they betrayed and tortured Him. His death was very ugly, so the story goes, yet it is taught and celebrated as a gift to humankind.

Lord knows, it couldn't be me. Yet Sandra Bland said the same thing, and look what happened to her.

In the chapel, I was one of the few Black bodies in the space. I was so busy being compassionate toward the fear and anxiety of my students and other community members that I didn't think about their fear of Black bodies, especially my own Black body in St. Paul, Minnesota. I should have been just an associate professor in the English department. But after receiving that cross from Ahlers's lie, a gift that placed me on the periphery of the spectating crowd looking at the aftermath of a social lynching, I was just another witness to another ritualized murder of a Black body swinging from an institutional tree. How easily the situation can turn when you are the marginalized Black body in White-dominant spaces and institutions whose data in employment, student enrollment and matriculation, and experiences of BIPOC members mirror a larger system of racial, class, and gender apartheid.

I left the chapel before the program ended and spent the rest of the day grading papers in my office. Thursday morning, it was reported that Ahlers had actually shot himself, had completely fabricated the Black male suspect, and had been arrested by St. Paul Police without incident. Ahlers was convicted on one count of misdemeanor for falsely reporting a crime to police, fired from the university, and sentenced to one year of probation during which he was required to attend a "Black men's" group, with actual real Black men.

I know.

What are real Black men?

Real Black men are men that White people can easily imagine and still kill.

As the sun set, I looked out my office window over my plants and into the trees. Their swaying green leaves reminded me that this wasn't the first time and it wouldn't be the last time that Black bodies produced by White imagination would die like they did in poet Cornelius Eady's *Brutal Imagination*. I thought about how American racial narratives are so cruel and tyrannical that the actual Black body does not need to be present in order for the killing to occur.

In Minnesota, it just takes eight (8) minutes and forty-six (46) seconds to wrap that package.

Minneapolis, MN
January 16, 2021

Taiyon J. Coleman is a poet, essayist, and educator. Her collection of critical essays is forthcoming from University of Minnesota Press in 2022. She is associate professor of English literature and women's studies at St. Catherine University in St. Paul, Minnesota, and she also teaches writing part-time at Minneapolis College.

Minnesota Nice White People

David Todd Lawrence

> *This essay references the "Black Life and Death in Minnesota" essay by Wendy Thompson Taiwo on pages 41–48. Readers may want to read Thompson Taiwo's essay first.*

Some of the nicest white people you will meet and work with—some of them participants in anti-racist book clubs with Black Lives Matter signs in their front yards—will still do their part in (re)producing and supporting anti-Black policies and practices that will directly harm Black folks in their cities and state.

—Wendy Thompson Taiwo, "Black Life and Death in Minnesota"

I've lived in the Twin Cities since the fall of 2003, when I moved here with my partner to take a position at the University of St. Thomas, a midsize, private, Catholic university located near the Mississippi River in a wealthy neighborhood in St. Paul. I was a thirty-year-old, Black, newly minted PhD who grew up in rural southwestern Missouri and had made the journey to Kansas City for college. After spending six years in grad school in relatively small Columbia, Missouri, I was eager to return to a metropolitan area. The Twin Cities that I saw and experienced during my visits intrigued me—it was *so nice*. Sure, it was cold too, but it was *nice*. It reminded me of my grandpa's old Buick: it wasn't flashy, but it was roomy, comfortable, dependable, and clean. I was hooked.

We rented a duplex in the Midway neighborhood of St. Paul, an old, established, working-class neighborhood halfway between the downtowns of Minneapolis and St. Paul. It was filled with small, hundred-year-old bungalows—perhaps the official house of the Cities—with tall trees lining the streets. Our neighbors, like folks we encountered all over town, greeted us without hesitation. When it snowed, everyone would help dig each other's cars out of drifts and would instantly jump out at an intersection to help push a stuck vehicle. One day not long after we were settled, I sat stopped in my car at a traffic light on one of the busier streets in the neighborhood. As I waited for the light to turn green, I caught a movement to my right and turned to see what it was. A police car had pulled up next to me and the officer, a white man, was gesturing for me to roll down my passenger-side window. Hesitantly, I did. He leaned his head toward my car and put his arm out the window to point at the rear of my 1996 Toyota Camry.

"You've got a taillight out," he said. "Better get that fixed."

A little startled, I replied, "Oh, okay—thanks."

"Have a good one," he said, pulling away as the light turned green.

I sat there for a moment, surprised. While I hadn't been frightened by the encounter, I was taken aback by the way the officer had spoken to me. He addressed me nicely without taking the opportunity to demonstrate his authority over me. I hadn't experienced his advice as a threat. It actually seemed like he was simply offering me a little help. Having grown up in small towns in the rural Midwest, I found this to be a bit of a shock. As a young Black man, I had had my encounters with the police. Small-town police always seemed to want to prove something. And though I had never been the victim of violence at the hands of the police, I was used to being lectured, harassed, and mocked by them. I certainly had never ever been offered a piece of friendly advice. I thought to myself, *What kind of place is this?*

I had a similar feeling of disorientation when I visited one of the Cities' upscale grocery markets for the first time. On walking into this particular establishment, just off of one of St. Paul's most exclusive streets, I was awestruck by all the displays of luxury items I had never seen before. Then an employee (it seemed that there were ten employees for every one customer)—a white woman—walked up to me and asked, "Can I help you, sir?" Her question was sincere. It wasn't tinged in that way Black and brown people know really means, *Are you in the wrong place?* I stammered, finally replying, "No, I'm just looking," a response more suited to a Macy's. I immediately thought to myself, *Do I belong here? What is this place?*

The Twin Cities is like that. It is confusingly nice. It is disarmingly nice. It is *Minnesota nice*—so nice that it can seem like some kind of paradise. *Everyone* is nice. *Everything* is nice. Everything that people say sounds nice too. But just like at that luxury store I visited, nice doesn't come for free. There's a price to be paid, and someone has to pay it.

Over time I met and talked to more people around town—Black folks in particular. They were familiar with the experience I was having, and they had a bit of advice for me. They explained that the Cities weren't as nice as they appeared on the surface. Folks told me I needed to be careful, that I had to watch myself, that what white people said to me might not be reliable, and that appearances weren't always what they seemed. These folks had experienced and understood what I would come to figure out: "nice" doesn't necessarily mean "good," and niceness has a limit and is an essential element for constructing boundaries that allow "nice white people" to feel good about themselves and their communities without interrogating their racial privilege. I came to understand that niceness was really a kind of imperceptible camouflage that allowed social violence against BIPOC folks to take place without anyone having to take responsibility for it.

It is now well known that the Twin Cities are one of the worst metropolitan areas for Black people to live in the United States. Their income, employment, housing, education, and health disparities place Minneapolis and St. Paul near the bottom of every ranking for racial inequality in the United States. Many white Minnesotans are aware of this fact but don't really understand what it means. They live in the world of "Minnesota nice." The Twin Cities are so segregated that many white residents never have to witness the challenges that BIPOC residents and particularly Black folks face on a daily basis. They can live their lives considering these issues in the abstract, driving into the cities in the morning and home to the suburbs at night, only absently pondering what it is they could do about problems they rarely, if ever, see with their own eyes.

These nice white people are, as James Baldwin calls them in *The Fire Next Time*, "innocent." They live in an innocent country and in innocent cities with other innocent white people. The innocence that Baldwin describes is seemingly innocuous but functions to impede the moral development necessary for social transformation and racial justice. If one is and has always been innocent, then once has nothing to atone for, nothing to change about oneself. But as Baldwin so powerfully declares, "It is not permissible that the authors of destruction should also be innocent. It is the innocence which constitutes the crime." Baldwin understood that white people experience their innocence not as a condition but as an ontological state—a state of being that both insulates them from their own history *and* assumes their superiority to Black people.

It is this corruptive innocence that animates Minnesota nice and defines Minnesota nice white people. Their innocence allows them both to experience the crimes of injustice at a distance and to see themselves as disconnected from those crimes ("It happens in the South, not here"). Indeed, this innocence allows their implication in those crimes to remain invisible and imperceptible to them such that the solutions to the problems we all face as a community together are understood in terms of a service that could be done or a gift that might be given. I am reminded of Claudia Rankine's description of a question posed to her by a white man at a reading, which became the impetus for her play, *The White Card*. The man asked her what he could do *for her* and was angered when her response was to turn the question back on him. The question itself, as Rankine explains, is a kind of "age-old defensive shield against identifying with acts of racism at the hands of liberal, well-meaning white people" that allows the person who asks it to simultaneously seek the moral reward of offering help without bearing the burden of responsibility or implication.

When I talk about Minnesota nice and nice white people, I am talking about the way white folks here are oblivious to their own power and desire. Equity and racial justice aren't now, nor have they ever been, about being nice. They are about transforming systems that continue to operate regardless of how nice individual people are or what they offer to do for an individual Black person. I wasn't wrong about the Twin Cities. People are nice—very nice. But perhaps this niceness is what "constitutes the crime" in that it conceals the benefits of oppression and inequity. The police officer I encountered was certainly nice in offering that advice to me, but does it matter that one officer is nice when the police department systematically kills Black people with impunity?

I'm finishing this essay days after a mob of thousands of mostly white people overran the DC Capitol Police and invaded the US Capitol, ransacking it. After violently overpowering police and security, they calmly strolled around the building with no fear that they would be stopped or arrested, much less beaten or shot. They paraded with stolen souvenirs, sat on the Senate dais, and leisurely smoked dope in the halls of Congress. After some time, they were escorted out of the building and off the grounds mostly unharmed. I am not the first to observe that this event was a clear and explicit enactment of white supremacy. These were people who understood themselves as owners simply coming to take possession of their goods—goods that were theirs by right the moment they were born.

Watching from across the country, many were shocked and horrified by what they were seeing. They exclaimed in articles and tweets and videos that this "is not who we are!" I imagine that many nice white people here in the Twin Cities were thinking and saying that too, and that they were also thinking to themselves: *We aren't like that here.* The truth is, this is exactly who we are and always have been. It is also the truth that there are people like that here in Minnesota, as there are people like that everywhere in the United States. More importantly, the danger BIPOC, and particularly Black, people face here in the Twin Cities is not posed by the people who committed those explicit acts of violence against a "sacred" symbol of democracy. Rather, as Wendy Thompson Taiwo explains in the above epigraph, a serious threat is posed by Minnesota nice white people who don't understand themselves to be part of the problem.

In his recent book about James Baldwin, *Begin Again*, Eddie Glaude explains how the ontological condition that Baldwin called "innocence" both informs and is animated by what he calls "The Lie." He identifies it as "the mechanism that allows, and has always allowed, America to avoid facing the truth about its unjust treatment of black people and how it deforms the soul of the country . . . [it] cuts deep into the American psyche. It secures our national innocence in the face of the ugliness and evil we have done." In the same way that the sacking of the Capitol didn't come out of nowhere and isn't a unique moment of white supremacy in American history, the murder of George Floyd is not an aberration in the history of the Twin Cities. The officer who killed George Floyd acted with the same expectation of impunity as those who ransacked the Capitol. These are not simply the acts of individual people; they are the logical products of normalized white supremacy. Niceness is not an antidote to white supremacy. It is only a performative mirage, a mechanism of self-comfort that allows nice white people to convince themselves of their innocence over and over again.

While nice white people maintain their innocence, BIPOC people pay the price.

St. Paul, MN
January 10, 2021

David Todd Lawrence is associate professor of English and American culture and difference at the University of St. Thomas. His writing has appeared in the *Journal of American Folklore, Southern Folklore, Open Rivers,* and *The New Territory.* He is cocreator of the George Floyd and Anti-Racist Street Art Database and codirector of the Urban Art Mapping Project.

It Shouldn't Be Me or You but Especially Not Them

The Proximity of Black Death and Trauma

Mi'Chael N. Wright

W. E. B. Du Bois, one of the great American sociologists, dedicated his life to analyzing the lived experience of African Americans through historical and societal lenses. Addressing the duality of Blackness as an identity and an experience that is unique to Black Americans, Du Bois's concept of double consciousness reveals the extent to which Black and white people in the United States live in two very different worlds. In *The Souls of Black Folk*, he described double consciousness as "always looking at one's self through the eyes of others, of measuring one's soul by the tape of a world that looks on in amused contempt and pity. One ever feels his two-ness, an American, a Negro; two souls, two thoughts, two unreconciled strivings; two warring ideals in one dark body, whose dogged strength alone keeps it from being torn asunder." The constant back and forth of finding where one belongs, where one feels accepted, and where one feels safe is a part of navigating the experience of being Black in the United States. For me, the experience of double consciousness was heightened in Minnesota and oftentimes happened in subtle ways.

When I first moved to Minneapolis to attend graduate school, I went to the university bookstore to shop—you know, that thing students cannot wait to do: get a notebook, pen, or lanyard—in preparation for beginning a new school year. It was a rite of passage for me, and it felt especially important because I was entering the first year of my PhD program in sociology. As I looked at the coffee mugs, an older white woman smiled kindly and asked, "Oh, what sport do you play?" Honestly confused, I asked her what she was talking about. I was wearing a black shirt and jeans—what would give her the impression that I played any sport? She repeated, with full authority, "I *said*, what sport do you play for the U?" Now fully aware of the question and the intention behind it, I replied, "I don't. I am a graduate student getting my PhD." I watched the surprise set in on her face as she replied, "Oh, oh, oh, oh. Isn't that lovely?" She walked away not giving it a second thought, but I have not forgotten that moment as it was one of my first encounters with people in Minnesota. It wasn't the first time in my life that someone asked me if I was a student or an athlete, but the shock and feeling all seemed so new.

Four years ago, if someone would have told me that I, a Black lesbian, would be living in Minneapolis in 2020, I would have looked at them like they had two heads. Born and raised in Southern California, I never thought Minneapolis, Minnesota, would be somewhere I would end up living. I mean, I am a West Coast kid through and through. Yet I applied to and got accepted into the University of Minnesota, and that changed my life. If I am being honest, I was shocked when I first got to the Twin Cities. I had not expected to see as many people of color as I did. It also crossed my mind that Philando Castile was murdered thirty minutes away from where I was living. I was conscious of that fact as well as my Blackness, which was always in the back of my head. Maybe it was the Trump 2020 flags I saw on several cars driving on the freeway, or even the MAGA shirts and hats in the grocery store. Either way, I felt like I always stood out.

Throughout my life, I hadn't had many direct interactions with the police other than a ticket or two. And while this did not change much in Minnesota, I felt that my proximity to the police increased. When encountering campus police in the university's hallways or subterranean tunnels, I found myself trying to avoid them in order to evade any potential interaction. Conscious of the world we live in, I avoided going through those tunnels late at night and always made sure I had my campus ID on me when walking by myself. I knew in theory that it was not fair nor right to have to live this way—in fear—but we (Black people) do what we can just to make it another day.

In February 2020, my computer was stolen from my car. After locating it with the "Find My" app, I called the police and asked them what I should do. They said they would send officers, who eventually came after two and a half hours. The first thing the officers asked was whether I was sure that the computer was not in my car. After one of the officers went inside of a building where they suspected it was, the other officer continued to look inside my car to "see if the computer was in the back seat." I was unsure of what to expect during the investigation, but I knew I should not have been accused of stealing my own computer. These experiences, however minor and shared by many other Black people, add to the very real feelings of distress and unease Black people have when dealing with police officers. The entire time the officers were searching for my computer, I remember feeling terrified because one loud comment or wrong move and my family would have found out about my death through the news.

When life-altering events happen, do you remember what you were doing, wearing, or even thinking? These memories remain so clear and so vivid that it is almost scary. The moment becomes ingrained in your mind: the day you had your first real heartbreak or realized that you were different from those around you. You remember these experiences, the emotions you felt, every detail of that exact moment that changed your life and who you are as a person. Can you remember where you were or what you were doing when George Floyd was murdered? Do you remember what you were doing when the uprising started? Do you remember how you felt when George Floyd's face and murder were all over your screen? What were you doing? Where Were You on May 25, 2020?

Where was I? I was just starting to pack up things in my apartment. I was getting ready to move out after a three-month COVID-19 delay put my March relocation plans on hold. It seemed like just a regular day for the most part. You know, the kind where packing up one's possessions amounts to organized chaos with boxes and clothes and shoes everywhere, and nowhere to eat, sit, or stand. It was a lot, but things were happening quickly, and I was excited to move. On the night of May 25, I remember falling asleep to *The Boondocks* series on Hulu before being woken up at 1:30 AM by a text from my partner. Because my partner worked late hours, we normally would send a couple of texts back and forth in the early hours of the morning, and then I would go back to sleep. This time, I didn't fall asleep right away and instead checked Twitter, Instagram, and Facebook.

When I opened up Facebook, there it was. Another unarmed Black man harassed by the police. I clicked on the video and initially watched and heard what looked and sounded like chaos. Honestly, there was so much going on that I almost did not realize what was happening. But there it was again: a police officer being overtly violent to a Black man. As I watched the officer kneel on George Floyd's neck, I could hear other voices in the video crying, screaming, and yelling. I remember getting off Facebook because I did not want to watch this before going back to sleep. I had no idea that George Floyd's murder had happened fifteen minutes away from where I lived.

Although our attention to police violence is at an all-time high, we are never really prepared for the impact of our proximity to Black annihilation. The level of intense pressure, the feeling of trauma and fatigue on your heart, and the hyperawareness you feel when you realize how close you are to another Black person's murder by police and racist vigilantes is one of the heaviest things I have ever experienced. When we watch these tragedies on the news, it always seems as though it will not happen so close to home. When it does happen, as painful as it feels, it's still distant and "far away." For me, it did not feel that way this time. It was here, happening down the street. I know police-involved murders happen, I know that it can happen to me or someone I love, but I have normalized the pain and suffering, having watched it happen to someone else over and over through my television. The dehumanization of Black people in this country has become so common that it hurts, but the story and outcomes are expected. Yet, even as we know these injustices happen anywhere and everywhere, it hits just a little bit different when it happens close to you. As the day went on, the air around me felt like it was getting thicker, and just thinking about George Floyd's murder made my skin warm. Then, as the sun went down and the day began to vanish, the fear of being Black and in the streets demanding justice for the murder of one of our own got stronger.

At around 6:30 PM on May 26, 2020, I remember being in full tears, hyperventilating, and feeling stuck. People were creating Facebook groups to organize meeting spots to ensure that there were enough bodies to pack the streets and fight, but I just felt stuck. Stuck in fear and shock. I remember having an internal debate about where I would be and what I would do: *At this moment, I feel terrified to be out of the house. Police kill people here and people are angry. Black people are in danger tonight, tomorrow, and the days after. I feel terrified to be out tonight; I mean, **police kill Black people here!*** I had received countless texts that day from people checking in on me and asking how close I was to the site of George Floyd's murder. My mom and my granny had been calling me throughout the day in a panic, telling me that they had been keeping up with the news and wanted to check on me. I got a text from my old boss that said, "If you must be there, be there. But please be safe. We need you to live to tell the tale." I found myself feeling guilty. How could I be so worried about my safety when someone was murdered on the street? How could I sit at home and watch CNN pan through the different streets that I regularly drove on? How could I stay at home when so many other Black people were out demanding change? Although in that moment I did not know George Floyd would change the world, I knew that his murder and these memories would change my life forever.

It is unfortunate if you think about it. It is so unbelievably unfortunate that we are not *shocked* when police kill Black and Brown people. We are disappointed and angered about it, yes, but surprised? Not so much. We have gotten so numb to these experiences that we expect cases to end in despair even when they shouldn't. I remember being hopeful for Breonna Taylor, yet a feeling in my gut and my heart told me not to hold my breath. My heart was beating like a little drum watching the Kentucky attorney general read the decision. I remember feeling sick, nauseated, when he said that only one officer was charged, with three counts of wanton endangerment for endangering Taylor's neighbors with his shots. No charges for Breonna's life or even her possessions, but for a few bullet holes in her neighbor's apartment wall; another painful memory was ingrained in my head. This is the world we live in. It is dark and scary, but we are living. George Floyd is not. Breonna Taylor is not.

You know, if we are being completely honest, I never thought it would be me. I never thought I would be so close to yet another police murder. I never thought I would experience the closing of freeways and streets because Black people have had enough. I never thought I would be standing in the middle of George Floyd Square. I never thought I would see the National Guard setting up base camp at a police station. I never thought it would be me. Maybe I am naive or hopeful, but I genuinely never thought it would be me. This should not be happening to anyone, to Black people. I shouldn't be writing this, and you shouldn't be reading it. Black people should not still be strongly pulled in two directions, where we are American but not really American. Double consciousness should not be so widespread. This should not be happening.

It shouldn't be me. It shouldn't be you. But more importantly, it especially should have never been Rayshard Brooks (at age 27), Daniel Prude (41), Atatiana Jefferson (28), Stephon Clark (22), Aura Rosser (40), Botham Jean (26), Philando Castile (32), Sandra Bland (28), Alton

Sterling (37), Mike Brown (18), Michelle Cusseaux (50), Eric Garner (43), Rekia Boyd (22), Freddie Gray (25), Miriam Carey (34), Akai Gurley (28), Tony McDade (38), Tamir Rice (12), Kathryn Johnston (96), Aiyana Stanley-Jones (7), Nina Pop (28), Jonny Gammage (31), Amadou Diallo (23), Ahmaud Arbery (25), Kiwi Herring (30) . . .

It should have never been Breonna Taylor (26) . . .

It should have never been George Floyd (46) . . .

#AllBlackLivesMatter

Minneapolis, MN
January 11, 2021

Mi'Chael N. Wright is a PhD student in the Department of Sociology at the University of Minnesota, Twin Cities. Her primary research focuses on media, mental health, and identity development. She is specifically interested in how digital communities, which can be simultaneously encouraging and hostile, constitute the identity development and mental health of Black and Brown adolescent girls.

Some Abstract Place

Reflections on "Black Life and Death in Minnesota"

Yohuru Williams

This essay responds to the "Black Life and Death in Minnesota" essay by Wendy Thompson Taiwo on pages 41–48. Readers may want to read Thompson Taiwo's essay first.

In the aftermath of George Floyd's murder, the "Wonderful/Wretched" series moved me. The thoughtful and provocative collection of essays offered much-needed insight to me as a still relatively new, three-year-old transplant to the Twin Cities. While the entire collection proved helpful in understanding the complex backdrop of the Floyd murder, none was more impactful than Wendy Thompson Taiwo's "Black Life and Death in Minnesota." I recall first being struck by the title; then, reading the essay made me reflect on my own journey to and experience in Minnesota. Thompson Taiwo powerfully perceives that "To be Black in America is to be considered a trespasser, a person who only conditionally belongs, and even then that belonging is dictated by white feelings and fears, and tolerated with white approval and permission." Thompson Taiwo's powerful DuBoisian reflection affected me in multiple unexpected ways.

Growing up in Connecticut, I was keenly aware of the often subtle but nonetheless toxic, dehumanizing effects of White supremacy masquerading behind a veneer of progressive politics. However, it remained fully visible in the stifling effects of de facto segregation in housing, education, and employment. Not surprisingly, these same issues were painfully evident in Minnesota upon my arrival, but also not unexpected.

And while I certainly felt the familiar distancing and alienation from the white community, an experience I have known my whole life, I oddly also felt alienated from the Black community—something that was new and foreign to me. In other places I lived and worked, there was an immediate embrace and acceptance that I had grown accustomed to experiencing on arrival. But in Minnesota, the atmosphere was cautious and guarded—not at all unfriendly, but decidedly distant. Initially, I wrote it off to just being the new kid, but on several occasions I experienced it as a firm barrier, at least in some quarters, and it worried me.

I came to Minnesota with the hopes that the Twin Cities could serve as a laboratory for a new collaboration between the campus and community on a range of concerns, including addressing issues of racial inequality. But wounds run deep here. The walls people from many different backgrounds erect to guard against those injuries, while not impenetrable, are difficult to scale. It was, perhaps, my fatigue from attempting to climb those walls, which I rightly or wrongly read as resistance, that led me to apply for a position as a dean back in New York City. At least there I knew the terrain and the fault lines—not to mention the culture.

I was in the process of finalizing my exodus from Minnesota when George Floyd was killed. In the midst of my own grief and concern, I experienced a shift.

The murder of George Floyd seemed to finally tear down those walls within the Black community. In the days and weeks after his killing, I felt a unity and acceptance that previously had eluded me. The shared experience of this trauma as a Black Minnesotan finally affirmed my place here and my status as a dues-paying member of the Black community through a personal understanding of the twoness of being Black in Minnesota. The dues, of course, derived from the experience of the unique contours of Minnesota's midwestern style of apartheid.

This, of course, is the rub, because I desperately wanted to and continue to want to believe in what Walt Jacobs refers to as "a willingness by progressive Minnesotans to think about race in new ways, so the path forward is not as steep as in other places." But to accomplish this Minnesota will have to overcome the real barriers that exist to people of color. These impediments reinforce former Minneapolis NAACP president Leslie Redmond's description of the state as a "White Wakanda"—a place that is a utopia for white people and a place of contradiction and danger for Black folks.

This is certainly not a new phenomenon. In August 1973, the cover of *Time* magazine featured a photograph of a smiling Governor Wendell Anderson admiring a freshly caught northern pike with the headline,

"The Good Life in Minnesota." The accompanying article celebrated Minnesota as a "state that works," for its success despite the Watergate scandal, the continuing war in Vietnam, and the stifling inflation ravaging other states, as a place where the good life was to be had.

As journalist Dave Kenney observed on the fortieth anniversary of the article's publication, "Many Minnesotans took *Time*'s affirmation as proof that their state was in fact a special place. The image of Anderson and his fish assumed iconic status."

While George Floyd was not the first Black man to be killed by police, the video and images of his death at the hands of Minneapolis police officer Derek Chauvin have become their own infamous symbols of the state—not a glowing model of progress but the epicenter of a national reckoning with police brutality and racial injustice.

I moved to Minnesota from Bridgeport, Connecticut, in June 2017 with, I must admit, a good deal of trepidation. It wasn't merely the tales of frigid winters or the icy politeness of Minnesota nice that fueled my concerns; it was the specter of two high-profile police shootings, of Jamar Clark and Philando Castile, that unsettled me. While Minnesota is far from exceptional in the realm of police violence against people of color, I admit to being haunted by the video of the killing of Philando Castile. Nearly a year before, on July 6, 2016, Castile was cruelly gunned down in the front seat of his car in full sight of his four-year-old daughter and streamed live to the world by his girlfriend in the passenger seat. While the unprovoked police violence was familiar enough, Minnesota at that time seemed a world away, no place I would ever visit, let alone live. So I mourned the loss of Philando Castile from the abstract space of another world.

This abstractness was not from a lack of connection to the issue. Only a few weeks before my departure, a fifteen-year-old boy was shot and killed by police in Bridgeport for joyriding not far from the community college where I delivered a speech demanding justice in the case of Trayvon Martin, who had been shot and killed by a self-appointed neighborhood watch captain in Sanford, Florida, in 2012. My activism resulted in work in Ferguson, Missouri, with the National Alliance of Faith and Justice in the aftermath of the police shooting of Michael Brown in 2014 and participation in various protests, not to mention writing about other acts of police violence. But Minnesota may as well have been another country.

Having lived and/or worked in New York, Connecticut, New Jersey, Delaware, Pennsylvania, and Washington, DC, I knew the flow of those spaces, the routines and the racial landscape. I assumed, as any Black person must blindly assume, that I knew how to avoid Castile's fate in the local context of my own tortured encounters and relations with police, the scars of which also run deep. The prospect of moving to Minnesota required me to think through my survival strategy. I did that subconsciously from the same abstract space.

I was thus pleasantly surprised after my first few weeks in the Twin Cities to attain a sense of the peace and wonder so many described as essential to their love of the North Star State. My first walk through Hidden Falls Regional Park in St. Paul, only steps from the banks of the mighty Mississippi River, reinforced my sense of relief, though not fully. As I came to know my new home, the number of Black Lives Matter signs that peppered the lawns of affluent neighborhoods struck me. They were at once both an affirmation and a denial of Black life. They reassured and mocked at the same time. Of course, Black Lives Matter, but only in abstract ways, viewed from a world apart, a place of distance and privileged safety. The well-intentioned white people in these affluent neighborhoods who put out signs to display their support for the lives of Black people could never intimately know the fear of what it is to be Black in America.

The signs said one thing, but the Minnesota judicial system communicated something else. Only weeks before I arrived in Minnesota in May 2017, a jury acquitted the St. Anthony police officer, Jeronimo Yanez, responsible for Castile's death. Despite the incontrovertible evidence of the cell phone video that in my mind removed any pretext of justifiable use of force, they let him go. This occupied my mind daily during the first few weeks in the city as I made the short commute from the university to my home, partly out of a sense of my own worry and anxiety, but mostly out of concern for my son.

Mason was due to join me in Minnesota in August as a second-year university student. I worried for him. I harbored the general worry of any parent sending their child off to school as well as the special worry of Black parents. We fear the dangers that face a son "fitting the description": young, Black, and in the right place at the wrong time. I had given him "The Talk," the gruesome rite of passage for Black children on how to conduct themselves with police and hostile white people, many years before in Connecticut when he was a preteen. I gave him a much more urgent and unedited refresher in New Jersey, shortly after he received his driver's license. But now driving the streets of our new home, I wondered whether he would be able to learn the landscape and jettison the pseudo sense of security that sometimes settles in between brutal reminders of the potential danger that awaits in seemingly minor encounters with police. I wanted him to remain alert not from an abstract place but as a matter of survival. And this is the sad reality, both in Minnesota and America: this alertness is a matter of survival.

Then, on the evening of July 15, 2017, a forty-year-old white woman, Justine Ruszczyk Damond, was shot and killed by Somali police officer Mohamed Noor in Minneapolis. The case was immediately racialized. The usual swell of support for police, especially in the White community, shifted to Damond. The comments on social media, in particular, called out the hypocrisy. The cries of "Blue Lives Matter" in the wake of police killings of Black people gave way to a tide of racially fueled assaults on Noor.

At his sentencing hearing in June 2019, Noor's defense attorney Thomas Plunkett asked for leniency. "A prison sentence," he argued, "only punishes Mr. Noor for a culture that he didn't create and, by all accounts, a culture that he would have liked to see change himself. . . . What really caused this [tragedy] is the fear that continues to permeate our society. The police are afraid of the people, the people are afraid of the police."

Given the racial implications of the Noor trial, Plunkett's appeal seemed both reasonable and hopelessly unacceptable. A life had been taken, after all. In the context of the killing of so many Black and Brown people going unpunished, Noor's guilty verdict seemed especially harsh, and not only in terms of its inconsistency. It exacerbated the nagging questions about race, religion, and immigration that informed the pretrial publicity.

On the day of the decision, I found myself revisiting the verdict in the Castile case. I felt a renewed sense of grief and sadness—no longer from an abstract place of anger and frustration, but now one of deep resentment.

Also expressing unhappiness at the Yanez ruling, prosecutor John Choi nevertheless called for acceptance. "I understand this verdict brings a lot of hurt and pain and deep seeded frustration to a lot of people in this community," he explained. "But we have to accept this verdict." He insisted it was the product of a "fair and impartial" process. That may very well be true, but it is also true that we must accept the other verdict rendered on Minnesota and America by the likes of Jamar Clark, Philando Castile, and George Floyd. Black life remains cheap in a nation, as the Reverend Dr. Martin Luther King once observed, "poisoned to its soul with racism."

We have to correct this. We must not only fix the process but also truly affirm our commitment to life. We must do so not from an abstract place but from a place of true meaning. We can't pick and choose when to be moved by the violence. It cannot be relative to our own sense of comfort or its proximity to our homes, menacing the lives of our sons, our daughters, or others in our community. It must become a critical part of our sense of collective responsibility for the community and world in which we live. We must address the depth of racism in America—that's what makes one a member of the only community that should count: the human community.

St. Paul, MN
January 3, 2020

Yohuru Williams is Distinguished University Chair and professor of history and founding director of the Racial Justice Initiative at the University of St. Thomas in St. Paul, Minnesota.

White Justice in Life and Death
Will George Floyd Receive Justice?

Keith A. Mayes

> *This essay was first published as "Justice Always Eludes Us in Minneapolis. Will George Floyd's Case Be Different?" in the* Washington Post *on June 3, 2020. The author penned a short epilogue for this volume.*

The shooting of Justine Damond, a white woman, and the prosecution and conviction of Mohamed Noor, a black police officer, was a historic moment in Minneapolis. On July 15, 2017, at 11:41 PM, Noor, a Somali American, and his white partner, Matthew Harrity, were called to the scene of a possible assault. Their police cruiser quietly inched down a dark alley when suddenly an object hit the car, and a person later identified as Justine Damond appeared at Harrity's window. Mistaking the situation as an ambush, both officers drew their service weapons, and Noor fired a single shot from the passenger seat, striking Damond in the stomach. She died moments later. After an eight-month investigation, Noor was charged with third-degree murder and second-degree manslaughter. He was convicted and is currently serving a twelve-and-a-half-year prison sentence.

Last Monday, Minneapolis police detained George Floyd, a forty-six-year-old African American man, on suspicion of forgery. Less than fifteen minutes later, Floyd lay in the street dead, the result of Officer Derek Chauvin pressing his knee into Floyd's neck while he lay handcuffed and prone for almost nine minutes. If it weren't for Darnella Frazier, a teenage onlooker whose phone video went viral, Chauvin and the three other officers would still be policing the streets of south Minneapolis.

The juxtaposition of these two cases is important for understanding the mood and tenor in the Twin Cities in the past week. A black man became the first police officer convicted for police misconduct in the city's history. Noor's conviction was a game changer—and, less than two years later, it's a deal breaker. As demonstrators call for the arrest of the four officers involved in Floyd's death, some can be heard shouting, "Free Mohamed Noor." The irony has been lost on local and state officials: after years of white police violence against black bodies without requisite justice, why is the only police officer behind bars black?

Some will say the cases are different, or that Chauvin, who has been arrested, may receive the same fate as Noor. But consider the Philando Castile case. On July 6, 2016, thirty-two-year-old Castile, along with his girlfriend Diamond Reynolds and her four-year-old daughter, was pulled over in a suburb just north of St. Paul. Castile announced, properly, that there was a licensed firearm in the car, after which Officer Jeronimo Yanez shot Castile seven times, with five bullets hitting him in the chest. Yanez had asked Castile for his license, but later claimed Castile was reaching for the gun instead of the requested identification. Yanez was charged with second-degree manslaughter and two counts of dangerous discharge of a firearm, and like every other police officer in Twin Cities history but one, he was found not guilty. In a strange world that exists between hope and fate, this was the one we were waiting for. That is why the community was thunderstruck by the verdict.

The aftermath of these incidents brought the usual well-wishes and condolences to the families, with occasional commentary about changing the nature of police training. But what is lost on police officials and elected leaders is that a racially predictable way of seeking criminal justice results in the unequal distribution of social justice. Justice is not guaranteed because we live in a democracy; neither is justice neutral. Justice is only as good as the men and women rendering it. If justice is blind, as the cliché goes, then injustice has twenty-twenty vision, for it continues to track black bodies and deliver differential outcomes for blacks and whites: convictions for black folks and exonerations for whites and others.

White justice is a form of white entitlement. When white people are the victims of deadly violence, the expected outcome is the arrest and conviction of the perpetrator, despite the complexity of a legal case. When black people are the victims of deadly violence by police, the expected outcome is a hope in things seldom seen and experienced in the legal system—especially the arrest, prosecution, conviction, and sentencing of police officers. Black people rarely procure the latter two, even if they are lucky enough to receive the former two. Though Yanez was an officer of color, the benefit of his acquittal still accrued to white America because he represented state-sanctioned power, which has a white face. Noor's sentence is a victory for white America too, because he had to pay for the sin of mistakenly killing a white person.

The longer it takes to prosecute and convict the four officers directly involved in killing Floyd, the longer white America evades judgment. I fear the power structure is already working to bend Floyd's case away from justice.

I remember watching the media coverage of Damond's death and filing away some important curiosities. I distinctly remember Hennepin County Attorney Mike Freeman acting as both prosecutor and healer. I saw stories that humanized Damond, from her impending wedding to the vibrancy of her personality. I remember hearing repeatedly what Damond did for a living: she was a yoga instructor and a life coach. I saw pictures of her with her fiancé, friends, and family members here in Minneapolis and in Australia smiling and enjoying life as they knew it. At the tender age of forty years, Damond had so much to live for, the coverage went. And then I remember the trial—feeling that Noor did not stand a chance, that he would be convicted of one of the charges, not only because he was guilty but also because the men in blue in Minneapolis would not stand up against the rolling tide of whiteness as it sought justice. When the jury came back in a day with a guilty verdict, I remember how easy it was to convict this police officer. I almost forgot he was one.

Epilogue: January 4, 2021

Remembering and forgetting Noor's status as a Minneapolis police officer is situational, contextual, and racial. While on the streets of Minneapolis encountering different people during the George Floyd protests, I overheard one white person asking curiously, "Where is Justine Damond's protest?" At first I thought the question was rhetorical. It was plausible that, rather than searching for the reasons why a city- and nationwide galvanization on behalf of Damond did not follow her death, the inquiry may not have been designed to elicit an answer. For the white woman asking the question, the answer would be obvious not only to her friend standing next to her but also to anyone in the vicinity of hearing it. But on a second and longer reflection, I reached the conclusion the question was not rhetorical, so I began engaging her in conversation. She really could not understand the different community responses on behalf of Floyd and Damond. She believed that any police officer who killed indiscriminately and unjustifiably should face the condemnation of a city if not a nation. Not overly desiring to play my day role as a professor in that moment standing on East Lake Street in Minneapolis, I agreed, but I argued the most important variable was race, not the police officer, or the victim, or the nature of the "crime," or the way the person was murdered. White racial justice is a one-way street, operating as a form of white entitlement and white privilege that protects white perpetrators and white victims alike. History has taught us that justice attaches to white bodies and stays clear of black and brown ones. I also kindly told her she should check out a *Washington Post* op-ed article written by Keith Mayes, who said something similar.

Minneapolis, MN
January 4, 2021

Keith A. Mayes is a Horace T. Morse-Alumni Distinguished Teaching Professor in the Department of African American & African Studies at the University of Minnesota. He is the author of *Kwanzaa: Black Power and the Making of the African American Holiday Tradition*. Mayes is currently working on another book, *The Unteachables: Civil Rights, Disability Rights and the Politics of Black Special Education*.

Crime and Imagination to Contend with It

Erin Sharkey

On December 28, 2020, KARE 11 news interviewed a woman who described living through a traumatic experience: the night before, she had been the target of a carjacking in her Uptown Minneapolis neighborhood. The woman, who appeared to be white and middle-aged, described months of having previously imagined what it would be like if she was ambushed by armed assailants who forcibly removed her from her vehicle. She had played out scenarios in her head after learning about many recent incidents on the news. Despite believing that it was only a matter of time before it happened to her, she was caught off guard when the occasion did arise, and she described feeling like a sitting pigeon while she was getting into her white Honda Civic on Hennepin Avenue late at night.

With her fingers curled as if pointing a gun, she reenacted for the camera what had happened to her. All the while, images flashed across the screen: an officer aiming a gun at a vehicle, police lights flashing, a high-speed chase on the freeway, a clip of a red BMW flipped onto its roof, grainy surveillance camera images of someone stumbling away from an altercation, Minneapolis Police Department (MPD) officers and Hennepin County Sheriff's officers pointing and conversing between their vehicles. An infographic then appeared, informing viewers that there had been more than four hundred carjackings in Minneapolis in 2020, which was four times the rate in 2019. The segment ended with the woman sharing that the incident had made her very sad that she does not feel safe in a neighborhood she loves. And despite her love for the people who make up the Uptown neighborhood, it is no longer livable for her because of the fear she has of crime.

Pay attention to how imagination works when it comes to race relations. Listen to how we reveal how our imagination works when we talk about crime and safety.

When I was in high school in the mid-1990s, my parents would caution me to be vigilant on certain streets on the south side of Minneapolis. Our family attended a church there, and I suspect my mom was getting information from friends in her Bible study or during the church's social hour. Raised by my white mother and my white stepdad whom I've called dad since before I was in kindergarten, I was one of the few mixed-race girls in my grade at my school. In those days, we lived in a northern suburb, and the neighborhoods where carjackings occurred were not ours. The fear was distant; it was for somewhere we visited, not somewhere we lived.

In those years, Minneapolis was dubbed "Murderapolis" due to the record number of murders during that period. There were stories of drive-by shootings and kids getting jumped for their Starter jackets and Nike sneakers. Streets in the Powderhorn Park neighborhood were turned into one-ways or made into dead ends to discourage gang activity. The evening news featured stories of carjackings most nights. Yet, in my imagination, carjackings didn't happen where I lived.

Two weeks before the news segment about the Uptown carjacking in 2020, KARE 11 aired a story about the arrest of a group of youths in the Jordan neighborhood on the north side of Minneapolis by Hennepin County's Violent Offender Task Force as part of a larger sting resulting in forty felony arrests and the recovery of several stolen cars. This is the story that produced the video clip of the flipped-over red BMW that KARE 11 used in the Uptown carjacking story. This video also showed officers in tactical gear, brandishing long firearms with scopes on their barrels. The story noted that the young occupants had scattered from the upturned car, and one of the youths ended up in a nearby home.

The report did not say whether the youth had any relationship to the home but did show a group of Black people comforting one another on the front steps. The reporter then interviewed a Black man, who described himself as a peace activist and expressed frustration after watching the youths being taken away in the back of a squad car. In talking about his work, he remarked that despite his efforts in showing young people love and connecting them to jobs, some of the individuals refused the opportunities he offered. "Sadly, this is one of the outcomes," he supposed.

These kinds of news stories make use of our imagination by letting us fill in the blanks with contextual clues. Nowhere in the news story was the race of the carjackers identified, nor was that of the vehicles' owners. But the neighborhoods that were featured, the footage KARE 11 chose to run in order to highlight the story, and the individuals they chose to interview, all signaled something about the racial dynamics of the Twin Cities.

I teach creative writing in Minnesota prisons and an ethnic studies course on race and mass incarceration at a local university. The ethnic studies course is designed to begin with the Thirteenth Amendment of the US Constitution, which abolished slavery except as punishment for those convicted of a crime, and it ends with a debate about justice reform and the contemporary abolition movement. In this class, one of the first things I ask students to consider is what makes someone a criminal. Then I ask whether they think of themselves as criminals. Often students are shocked to be asked this question, though many admit to having broken the law in some way, like speeding, shoplifting, or drinking while underage. This exercise is designed to have them reflect on how they imagine themselves, which I then challenge by suggesting that maybe crime is a sign of a society's failure to provide for its people and satisfy unmet needs or deal with conflict before it escalates, rather than evidence of simple personal moral failure.

The first year I taught this course, many students were shocked by the idea of abolishing the police and prison system. But this semester the course felt different from the start. A student emailed me the first week to ask when we were going to discuss the "defund the police" movement. Another identified as an abolitionist in their introductory letter to the class. I could tell that in the wake of George Floyd's murder, the students were thinking about what was possible. The uprising was expanding their capacity to imagine.

In June, a majority of members of the Minneapolis City Council pledged to defund and dismantle the police force in a public announcement in Powderhorn Park, just blocks from where George Floyd was asphyxiated under the knee of a Minneapolis police officer. Despite their promise, little change was made by the fall, and the MPD was not defunded. The issue was revisited on December 2, 2020, in the city council budget process, which culminated in a more than seven-hour-long public meeting and hearing.

Because of the statewide restrictions imposed on in-person gatherings due to COVID-19, the hearing took place virtually and was broadcast live on YouTube. Callers were required to register beforehand, and each person was invited to offer ninety seconds of testimony about the budget. Four hundred thirty speakers were registered. And other than its length, this meeting had the feeling of a radio call-in show.

Community organizing efforts were evident as individuals began to offer their testimonials, with one side arguing for the mayor's proposed budget (which featured a modest cut of 7.4 percent—$8 million—to MPD's budget). This group provided evidence of what they described as rampant crime, unsafe conditions, and lawlessness. The opposing group argued for what they called the People's Budget, created by the organizers behind the Defund the Police campaign. This group proposed a larger cut, taking $53 million from the police budget and allocating it to address issues like homelessness and to direct funds to services like a mobile mental health response team.

Callers signaled their identities by indicating in their statements which ward they lived in, how long they had lived there, their employment status, whether they were business owners or not, and whether English was their primary language. These signals suggested something about the racial makeup of the groups as well. Because of the disparities in our city and its distinction as one of the worst places in the country to be Black, stating where you live, how long you've been a homeowner, and what job you have says a lot about your racial identity.

Early on, a speaker said that she learned survival skills while living in South Africa and never imagined using those skills in Minneapolis. I guessed that she was white. Another speaker who said she lived downtown called members of the council "a posse of snake oil salesmen . . . selling an unproven plan using deception." I guessed that she was white as well, especially when she added to her statement that north side community leaders were pleading for more police. Many talked about being scared to walk their dogs. A few called the city "the wild west." I thought they were all white. One caller said that he owned the only home on the National Register of Historic Places on the north side and that the house had suffered a gunshot wound, marring a prime example of Prairie architecture. Despite the fact that the north side is primarily a Black community, I guessed that he was white as well.

Carjackings played a significant role in the budget hearings. Comprising one of the most organized groups were residents from the Tangletown neighborhood of southwest Minneapolis, in the Eleventh Ward. A particular carjacking was mentioned dozens of times in the hearings. Caught on surveillance video, this incident was particularly violent: the driver of the car, on the way to work as a housekeeper, was shot by her attackers in front of her employer's home.

Over an hour into the testimony, a caller suggested that this rise in crime might be attributed to the pandemic and the stress that came from unemployment, isolation, and the fear of contracting the virus. This resident reminded the audience that Minneapolis police had not yet been defunded and that their inability to deal with crime wasn't because they didn't have the funds but because the institution of policing was not designed to be used to address the wide range of community issues they were tasked with handling.

Some residents offering testimony in support of the mayor's budget indicated that they were people of color, like a caller who self-identified as a minority, a Mexican American, and Hispanic. He said that he felt his perspective was unheard and emphasized that while crime disproportionately affects communities of color, the accusations of racism in policing were a joke. Other residents reminded listeners that the city has its first Black police chief, Medaria Arradondo, and that he deserved support to reform the force.

Many people who I presumed were white spoke in favor of the People's Budget while signaling other things about their identities: their sexuality, their level of education, their neighborhoods, their jobs, and their interest in climate justice. These signals were meant to indicate what kind of white people they were: progressive or liberal ones. In addition to the many people I knew from the community, I speculated that many callers who advocated for the People's Budget were Black, Indigenous, and/or people of color. This assumption came from their signals too.

When crime happens in communities far away, it occupies a certain place in your imagination. The fear or dread might grow when the risk moves closer to you, your home, your children, or your nightly dog-walking route. I'd argue that race impacts our imaginations the same way. Those folks who don't have to live with certain kinds of fear often ascribe their freedom from danger to their hard work, their good neighbors, or their good intentions, rather than their privilege. To contend with mounting challenges in public safety, we need a radical imagination that addresses the root causes of the disparities we face, one that requires that we reevaluate our long-held assumptions and interrogates the ways our comforts come at the cost of communities with less privilege.

Minneapolis, MN
January 15, 2021

Erin Sharkey teaches at Metropolitan State University in St. Paul. She is the cofounder of an arts collective called Free Black Dirt. Currently she is editing *A Darker Wilderness*, a forthcoming anthology of Black nature writing for Milkweed Editions, and she is working in concert with other Black organizers to respond to COVID-19 and lead in this moment of uprising.

Woop-Woop! That's the Sound of da Beast

Jason Marque Sole

This essay responds to "The Sound of the Police" essay by Jerry Shannon and Sarah Shannon on pages 37–40. Readers may want to read the Shannons' essay first. Also, note that the titles of both essays refer to the song "Sound of da Police" by KRS-One.

I migrated from Chicago to Minneapolis in 1997. The war on drugs was in full swing, and it felt like the walls were closing in on me. Oftentimes, when scholars research the Great Migration and focus on the mass exodus of black southerners to the North, they tend to focus on larger streams and larger cities, overlooking the number of Black folks who moved to smaller metropolises like the Twin Cities for refuge. I was a confused eighteen-year-old when I chose Minneapolis as my home. One of my high school friends from Paul Laurence Dunbar High School had family in Minneapolis and St. Paul.

I had a high school diploma, and by all accounts I had had a successful academic journey. However, whenever we heard da police sirens, none of our accomplishments seemed to matter. *Woop-woop*! It was so often the case that my friends and I would hear the police cars advancing and know that trouble was on the way. Didn't matter what we were doing. Unlike many white folks, as described in Jerry and Sarah Shannon's "The Sound of the Police" essay, I never grew up with the perception of the police as a source of safety, because whenever there was a police presence situations escalated. An argument with a friend was always met with an officer threatening to take us to jail if we didn't back down. No resources. No alternatives. Just threats. The lip service in the daytime mixed with violence after dark felt like they had their public relations strategy laid out. They hated Black people unapologetically.

I moved to Twenty-Second Street and Aldrich Avenue in north Minneapolis, and within a week the place was raided. Because we were all Black with braids, the police claimed we fit the description of someone they were pursuing. They rammed the door and held us down at gunpoint. We were grateful they didn't just start blasting, but the damage to the house and to our reputation in the community seemed irreparable. I guess I should just be happy to walk away with my life. I wish Breonna Taylor was given the same grace. All seven of us were paraded out to the front yard in handcuffs and made to stay there for what seemed like an eternity. No arrests were made.

From there, my friends and I moved to St. Paul to lay low, but we never could seem to escape the long arm of the law. I was no saint, but the treatment always felt personal: snatching the tint off the windows, ripping out our stereos and speakers, sitting outside of our homes for hours to intimidate us. One of the most traumatic encounters happened the night an officer was brazen enough to throw my clothes in the snow and urinate on them. This was during the heyday of the Minneapolis Police Department's Metro Gang Strike Force, a unit that was hell-bent on destroying Black communities.

In the spring of 1998 I was living in north Minneapolis again when my life was changed forever. On March 28, I had just finished my shift at the Ramada Inn on White Bear Avenue in St. Paul. I told my supervisor and the other staff goodbye and assured them I would see them on my next shift later that night. Third shift was not my jam, but hey, it paid the bills. I was tired but had money and wanted to shine bright that sunny Saturday morning. My buddies enthusiastically asked if I wanted to have a barbecue, and although I wasn't rested enough, after a few hours of sleep I was off to kick it with the squad.

There were over twenty people, children included, eating food and dancing. It was an amazing day. I remember feeling hopeful, like the best was yet to come.

As I was sitting on the porch between two of my good friends, a tall, white officer started running down the street with his assault weapon cocked and aimed—at me. He held it to my face and shouted, "If you move, I'll blow your damn head off!" I immediately asked, "What is this about?" He demanded that I shut my mouth and cooperate or face a harsher punishment.

"Why do y'all always mess with Jay?" my friends asked more than a dozen times. The officers swiftly arrested one friend in front of her three-year-old daughter. I could sense that this was going to get ugly and contemplated running but didn't. The cop told three of us to walk with him to his vehicle, which was parked at the end of the block. He asked me to smile because the "witness" had complimented my teeth.

The cops then drove two of us to the local library and had us face the window so we could be "identified." After this, they drove us to Folwell Park. Same procedure: face the window for identification. It made no sense. Finally, they brought us to Hennepin County Jail and said we were being charged with making terroristic threats. We were held there for the weekend and released on Monday morning.

I missed two days of work and was fired as a result. The loss of my job was hard enough, but we also had to fight this phantom case for eight months before we were worn down to the point that we agreed to accept a "deal" for disorderly conduct. Tired of going to court, paying parking fees, and having this case hang over our heads, we took the misdemeanor charge just to be over with it.

No one ever said that we terrorized them. The assault weapon to my face was awfully traumatizing, though.

Privileged white folks have a hard time seeing the connection between modern-day policing, its slave patrol origins, and the Fugitive Slave Law that is still being used on Black men, women, and children today. Myon Burrell, Phillip Vance, Malo Gomez, and so many others with Black skin were essentially kidnapped by cops; many never made it back home.

Tycel Nelson should still be with us. Terrance Franklin should still be with us. Jamar Clark should still be with us. Philando Castile should still be with us. George Floyd should still be with us. Countless others should still be with us. The badge and gun may symbolize security for the privileged, but it symbolizes slavery for Black, Native, and Brown folks.

Advice like "just get a dog" or "don't go out at night" are easy and convenient security alternatives for many white folks, but for Black folks there are no safe places. We are killed in cars or on trains, in our own homes, in shopping centers, in parks, in jails. We get killed while exercising or vacationing. We get killed when we try to defend ourselves or when we don't "comply." The condescending and useless preventative advice we get is "don't be a thug."

Police and prisons only further exacerbate our subjugation. When I was shot in December 1998 as a bystander to an altercation a friend had, I wasn't seen as a victim. As I lay in a hospital bed, police kept saying, "Well, you must've done something!" But as the passenger in the vehicle, I had no control over the situation. Nevertheless, I was criminalized. Hospital staff and cops didn't think my life held much value.

After several more traumatic experiences, including jail and prison stints, I learned the laws of the land and became an activist and an academic. I studied criminal justice at Metropolitan State University, where I was the president of the African American Student Association, and I volunteered with Angela Davis when she came to Minneapolis in 2004. I became a Freedom School teacher and learned restorative justice. In 2009 I became an adjunct professor and national restorative justice trainer.

These experiences and my education convinced me that what is most important when it comes to justice is, as the Shannons point out, "building relationships with our neighbors and working with our local representatives." Building (and evolving) our relationships while holding local representatives accountable for their words and deeds can have real, positive impacts. Transformative justice works. Defunding the police and putting those resources in the hands of the most marginalized works. Creating space for survivors and formerly incarcerated juveniles and adults works.

My role as a criminal justice professor didn't stop me from stepping out of the classroom and into the uprising in Ferguson for Mike Brown or prevent me from standing in solidarity with the community during an eighteen-day occupation for the senseless killing of Jamar Clark. And because my relationships at the grassroots level mean more to me than any dollar amount, I left my role in the St. Paul Mayor's Office, where I worked from March 2018 to January 2019, when more money was allocated to one of the most murderous police departments in the state of Minnesota.

Guided by my morals and values, my journey has allowed me to be a humble servant working for social change. When we as a society decide that it is necessary and worthwhile to serve our people and meet their basic needs, we will no longer have to worry about the sound of da police. For they won't fulfill any needs of the community.

St. Paul, MN
February 28, 2021

Jason Marque Sole is a formerly incarcerated abolitionist. He has been a criminal justice educator for over eleven years and is currently an adjunct professor at Hamline University. In 2019 he received the John Legend "Can't Just Preach" award for his work to abolish prisons. In addition, Sole is the cofounder of the Humanize My Hoodie Movement.

A Reflection on Racism, Police Violence, and Abolition

Amber Joy Powell

Living in Minnesota turned me into an abolitionist. This transition toward abolition wasn't a quick one. Of course, growing up in Milwaukee, one of the nation's cities leading the mass incarceration of Black men, I knew the criminal legal system was rigged against Black Americans. From an early age, I understood that neither I nor my five brothers would receive the leniency often afforded to white children. My peers and I stood watch as countless Black women, men, and trans and gender nonbinary individuals lost their lives at the hands of police, with little to no accountability to the system that perpetrated their deaths. And as a sexual assault victim advocate and court observer, I witnessed firsthand how the system often revictimizes Black survivors. Still, even with all these explicit signs of system failure rooted in part in anti-Black racism and criminalization, I couldn't fathom a world without police, jails, or prisons. How else would we hold people accountable for the harm they caused?

When I moved to St. Paul, Minnesota, in the summer of 2015 as a PhD student in sociology, I understood the criminal legal system's failure through a reformist lens. Perhaps what we needed was more training, more awareness, more Black people working in the system to change disparities from within and improve Black lives. Yet, over the course of my next five years in Minnesota, I watched as these proposed policing reforms continuously failed Black communities. With each police killing, I became more convinced that the political reforms put in place to "protect" communities of color did little (if anything) to dismantle the harsh realities of criminalization, racism, sexism, and socioeconomic vulnerabilities. By the time I left Minneapolis at the height of the George Floyd protests, I realized that reforms simply could not redress years of racial trauma for Black Minnesotans. Over five years, my encounters with Minnesota police, my experiences as an advocate for those experiencing gender-based violence, and my participation in policing research transformed my understanding of what Black communities need to feel safe in Minneapolis.

What ultimately led to this new understanding of the role of police in public safety began in 2018 as I worked as a research assistant for Professor Michelle Phelps on a qualitative project that explored policing and police reforms in north Minneapolis. Despite Minneapolis's reputation at the time as a "progressive" city of policing reform, many residents of north Minneapolis, one of Minnesota's most racially segregated and under-resourced areas, remained distrustful of police, as was evident in the dozens of protests and community organizing efforts for several local residents who had died at the hands of police, including Jamar Clark and Philando Castile. Our objective for the project was to learn how neighborhood residents understood policing, their knowledge of new policing reforms, and how local incidents of police violence impacted their lives.

From 2018 to 2019, we interviewed 112 north Minneapolis residents. While I spoke with a handful of white residents, it was my conversations with Black community members that revealed what Tracey Meares calls "dual frustration." Under dual frustration, Black residents held concerns about both neighborhood and interpersonal violence, yet felt reluctant to call police for fear of experiencing further state-inflicted violence. Black residents also expressed how the media's and police department's characterization of north Minneapolis as a "high-crime" area reinforced anti-Black stigma and subsequent criminalization. While a few residents discussed abolitionist ideas, by and large Black residents in our sample desired better policing through procedural justice, implicit-bias training, and body-worn cameras. Black residents also criticized the lack of police accountability in cases where Black residents were killed. Yet, unbeknown to many of these residents, Minneapolis had begun adopting several of these policies through the National Initiative for Building Community Trust and Justice. Thus, the very proposals Black community members had recommended failed to actually translate into strong community-police ties. In documenting their truths, I developed cynicism regarding how to redress police violence in Black communities.

I grappled with where and with whom I could share these feelings.

Despite a welcoming community in the sociology department, as one of only a handful of African American students it was difficult to find spaces to talk openly (and unapologetically) about racism, violence, and white supremacy. I found refuge with other Black and Brown graduate students and activists from sociology, Chicano studies, geography, American studies, and women, gender, and sexuality studies who opened their homes, shared their experiences, and provided safe spaces for us to discuss our collective struggles. We talked about local police violence and the vicarious trauma that resulted from images of Black people being killed by police. It was in these spaces that I first heard about the need to abolish police and prisons.

Initially, I struggled with what abolition meant in everyday contexts. I met their sentiments with "What about sexual or domestic violence? We can't hold perpetrators accountable without police or prisons." Even as I was becoming increasingly critical and pessimistic about the proposed reforms that would supposedly transform Minneapolis policing, I was skeptical that an abolitionist alternative would fare better. I remain grateful to those friends and colleagues who were patient with me and continued to challenge me by providing reading materials and recommending conferences that planted the seed in my mind for reimagining public safety without police.

While I was largely shielded from police aggression in Minneapolis, the few encounters I did have further influenced my understanding of police. Less than two years after I moved to Minnesota for graduate school, my roommate and I watched through our living room window as a Black man struck a young Black woman and her friend during a heated altercation across the street. Of course I wanted to help these young women. Yet, when my roommate suggested we call the police, I told her, "Hell no! We are not calling the cops! They'll kill him!" It had been only a few months since the fatal shooting of Philando Castile by a St. Anthony police officer. Castile's death, along with those of countless other unarmed Black men and women between 2014 and 2016, weighed heavily on my mind. If we called the cops, I was certain that this man had little chance of walking away unharmed. The cops would justify any use of force, just like they had done with Philando Castile and Jamar Clark. I also couldn't be sure that any police presence would actually protect these young Black women, given the hostility survivors often encounter from law enforcement officials, who may see them as the aggressors. Thus, like so many Black women who find themselves reluctant to call police for interpersonal violence, I wasn't willing to take that risk.

Another neighbor did call the police. Within ten minutes, two white male cops arrived outside our apartment building. To my surprise, they quickly de-escalated the altercation. One cop carefully guided the young Black women to their apartment, while the other spoke calmly to the young man. What I assumed would escalate and result in yet another killing by Minneapolis police ended swiftly and quietly. In the months following, I continued to reflect on that night. For a while, I remained hopeful that perhaps *some* police could be trusted. *Maybe they're not all bad. What if more acted like those cops? Wouldn't that resolve some of the tension?*

Still, my training as a sociologist and my lived experience as a Black woman reminded me that policing has always been embedded in the systematic criminalization of marginalized communities. This discriminatory treatment places an undue burden on Black women. Generations of Black feminist advocacy by scholars like Elaine Brown, Beth Richie, Kimberlé Crenshaw, and Mariame Kaba argue that our experiences of gender-based violence as Black women cannot be understood solely through the lens of racism but must also be understood through its intersection with other structures of marginalization, including sexism and classism. Thus, when we experience—or, in my case, witness—interpersonal violence perpetrated by Black men, we also fear that police will use racist tropes of Black men as "criminals" and "monsters" to inflict further harm.

I remembered how quickly Jamar Clark's criminal record and his alleged domestic dispute with a woman friend became the subject of scrutiny to defend the police. Knowing these incidents can later be used to justify police violence against Black men, many Black women feel reluctant to call the police. Perhaps we'll share a sigh of relief when police don't use aggression, yet Black women shouldn't have to feel grateful or surprised for every nonfatal police encounter. This unpredictability and fear of police violence defines the frustration many Black Minneapolis residents feel.

It is precisely those moments that do result in Black death that reaffirm feelings of distrust toward police. The evening of George Floyd's murder I began receiving notifications on my Twitter timeline about yet another murder of a Black man by Minneapolis police. For the first fourteen hours after Floyd's death was caught on camera, I refused to watch the video. I was already reeling from the deaths of Breonna Taylor and Ahmaud Arbery. I didn't have the energy to stomach another Black death at that moment. Yet, as the video went viral on social media and local protests broke out, I decided I needed to watch what Floyd went through in his final moments. Watching Floyd call out for his mother and beg for his life as an officer choked him to death felt like bearing witness to the countless images of public lynchings I had seen growing up. Only these weren't old black-and-white images in history class or some docuseries about the early 1900s. This lynching happened in 2020, less than three miles from where I lived. I felt sick, angry, hurt, and disgusted. No, none of this was new. By that time, I had seen several cases where police killed Minneapolis residents. Just a few months earlier, our research team had sat in a room with the Minneapolis police chief and several members of his staff, all of whom expressed interest in changing the culture of the department. I had appreciated what the police chief and his team were trying to accomplish. Yet, in the wake of a moment in which a police officer held Floyd's neck down and refused to let others help him as he called out for his life, it all felt like empty talk.

I grappled with what I could do next. I wanted to protest, demand accountability, and participate in cleanups around the city following the uprisings. At the same time, however, we faced the harsh reality of COVID-19. In those early months, there were still a lot of unknowns about transmission. I knew that being in close proximity to hundreds— if not thousands—of people increased my risk of contracting the virus, even if I wore a mask. Initial reports suggested that African Americans held significantly higher risk of contracting the virus, being hospitalized, and losing our lives. And while I contemplated taking that risk to help hold these officers accountable, having immunocompromised parents and siblings whom I would visit in the following weeks kept me home, though reluctantly. Other Black peers felt the same, caught between our commitment to police accountability and the potentially deadly risks of a global pandemic. This entrapment between two potentially deadly realities—police violence and COVID-19—reaffirmed our need for institutions that prioritize Black people's safety, health, and well-being. I finally got it: I began to understand abolitionist advocacy. It wasn't about addressing state violence, but rather a broader political commitment and movement toward creating a world that not only held communities accountable to one another but also provided the material resources necessary to sustain community peace without relying on the criminal legal system.

In the days and weeks that followed Floyd's death, I encountered a slew of comments about how Black Americans should stop focusing on police brutality and focus on "Black-on-Black crime." They dismissed our calls to "defund the police" as ridiculous and unrealistic. But what these commentors fail to recognize is that our fight against police violence has always included the broader struggle to build safe communities. When we demand accountability and say "Black Lives Matter," we are reaffirming the desire to build safe communities for Black people to live in. Yet, if the main institution responsible for public safety (i.e., the police) criminalizes, abuses, and in the most egregious cases kills members of the communities it vows to protect, those same communities become cynical and maintain their distrust of an institution whose very history began with Black subjugation. Our fight to end police violence is *always* connected to the desire to address crime and build safe communities more broadly. As an abolitionist, I echo the voices of many organizers and activists who believe that one way forward is to equip ourselves with the tools needed to both prevent and respond to community and interpersonal violence. But we also acknowledge that Black Minnesotans are not a monolith. There seems to be a general recognition that the system has failed us, yet many remain reluctant to embrace an ideology like abolition that they see as jeopardizing public safety. Moving forward, abolitionist calls toward defunding police, decarceration, abolishing cash bail, and other political efforts must be rooted in community engagement that also seeks to build alternatives for Black residents' public safety.

Milwaukee, WI
January 15, 2021

Amber Joy Powell is a PhD candidate in the Department of Sociology at the University of Minnesota. She is also a former Sexual Assault Survivor Advocate volunteer. Her work uses critical legal and critical race feminist theory to examine how law, punishment, and violence intersect in the lives of Black and Brown communities.

Remembering David Cornelius Smith

Terrion L. Williamson

An earlier version of this essay was published by Belt Magazine on June 11, 2020.

Nearly ten years before the killing of George Floyd, officers from the Minneapolis Police Department were responsible for suffocating another Black man to death. This is his story.

I'll never forget the burn of hot tears rolling down my face as I watched the video of my little brother being murdered by the men in blue. It's a deeply rooted, unimaginable, soul-shattering pain that has changed my family forever. After years of court appearances and depositions I accepted the sad reality that a little black girl could never win justice against the brotherhood of blue.

    —Angela Smith, excerpted Facebook post, May 27, 2020

David Cornelius Smith loved the ocean. He could not swim, and he had never actually seen the ocean, any ocean, in person, but he loved it all the same. It wasn't until a summer sojourn to Florida, during what would be the final months of his life, that he at last had the opportunity to see the Atlantic's vast expanse for himself. When he first set foot on its shores, he went running and crashing into the water with his characteristic exuberance, oblivious to everything except the waves before him—including the cell phone in his pocket.

David's sister, Angela Smith, was not surprised by the sense of wonder and abandon with which David met the ocean. She was just three years older than David and had grown up witnessing her younger brother's boisterous displays of affection for all that he loved—and he loved, and was good at, many things. He enjoyed music, sports, and the arts. He played violin, basketball, and baseball; once drew the mascot for a school art competition; and wrote poetry that often turned into raps. (He would ask Angela to sing the hooks.) David was charismatic and kindhearted and, as his sister put it, "the kind of smart that didn't have to study." He had a way with people that made them feel important and heard. More than anything, David, whose nickname was Pumpkin, loved his family and wanted to be a good example for his five younger siblings, and for the children he hoped to have himself one day.

David, Angela, and their siblings were primarily reared by their single mother, Diane Smith, on the South Side of Peoria, Illinois, a city that sits about halfway between Chicago and St. Louis on the Illinois River. Peoria's South Side is marked by the same types of socioeconomic disadvantage that structure most majority-Black cities and communities throughout the industrial Midwest, including a poverty rate of nearly 50 percent and an unemployment rate around 20 percent. In recent years, Peoria has been found to have the sixth-highest rate of Black-white residential segregation and the highest rate of school segregation in the nation, and these disparities have remained essentially unchanged for the past forty years.

I know Peoria's South Side intimately, as it is where I also grew up, and though I now live in north Minneapolis, it is the place I continue to call home. It is also where Angela and I met and became good friends while students at Trewyn Middle School. I never got to know David personally, in part because Angela and I largely lost touch after she graduated from high school a year early, but when she told me David felt that he had to leave Peoria, I recognized the feeling from my own young adulthood. To be clear, David's leave-taking was never meant to be an act of abandonment. He wanted to improve his financial circumstances so that he could eventually return home and help take care of his family. Like so many young and idealistic Black men before him, he dreamed of buying his mother a house and moving her out of the hood.

And so he moved to Minnesota.

David applied to the Job Corps and, after being accepted into the Twin Cities program, picked up, at the age of seventeen, and moved north. He spent three years in the Job Corps and decided to remain in the area upon graduation because he was convinced there were still more opportunities for him in Minnesota than in Peoria. He moved into his own apartment, established a relationship with a long-term girlfriend, and enrolled at Minneapolis Community and Technical College, where he took classes in business and political science. He also developed a relationship with a mentor at Penumbra Theatre who helped him engage his love of acting, and he even tried his hand at modeling (because, as Angela put it, "People told him he was cute!"). According to Angela, David believed that a person could become anything they wanted in the Twin Cities, and he regularly tried to convince her that she should move there as well.

Still, David began to struggle. What the family understood to be major depression was eventually diagnosed as bipolar disorder. The diagnosis remains controversial for David's family, some of whom were concerned that racial bias, not uncommon in the mental health profession, and David's lack of access to appropriate resources might have contributed to a misdiagnosis. Yet, whatever their misgivings, David's family helped him get the care he needed, which included maintaining a regular diet and exercise regimen to help better manage his symptoms. That regimen is the reason he was in the downtown Minneapolis YMCA on the afternoon of September 9, 2010.

According to most media accounts of the incident, the Minneapolis Police Department (MPD) was summoned because David, who is typically described in these accounts as being "mentally ill" or potentially under the influence of drugs or alcohol, was disturbing patrons in and around the sixth-floor gym. It is not entirely clear what the exact behavior was that was supposedly disturbing patrons. Most accounts of the incident offer up vague assessments that David was "acting bizarrely" or being "disruptive," while one account suggests that he was walking around shirtless and mumbling, that he threw a basketball into a kickball class, and that he "scared" a thirteen-year-old boy. According to Angela's understanding of the incident, the only "disturbing" behavior committed by David was that he was talking to himself while shooting jump shots in the gym.

In any event, MPD officers Timothy Gorman and Timothy Callahan arrived and attempted to subdue David and remove him from the facility. As far as Angela knows, no one from the YMCA had approached David prior to calling the police, and given that he was a paid member of the club, he resisted the officers' attempts to make him leave. In the ensuing struggle, the officers used a Taser on David multiple times, knocking him to the floor. They turned him face down and Gorman pressed his knees into David's back while Callahan restrained the bottom portion of his body, using a tactic known as "prone restraint," which restricts a person's ability to take in oxygen. The two officers held David down for more than four minutes, and when they finally released him, he was no longer breathing. Though paramedics eventually restarted his heart via CPR, David never regained consciousness. He remained in a coma until being taken off life support approximately a week later. David Cornelius Smith was declared dead on September 17, 2010. He was twenty-eight years old.

David was killed before body-worn cameras were in widespread use by law enforcement and cell phone footage documenting police encounters was commonplace, but the Taser used by the officers had a camera affixed to it and Callahan had clipped to his uniform a small pen camera that he had purchased independently. Video of the incident was eventually made public. On one of the recordings, Callahan can be heard talking to his wife soon after the incident, telling her that he wouldn't be home for a while because "I think me and Jimi killed a guy."

The Hennepin County Medical Examiner's Office found that David died of mechanical asphyxia caused by prone restraint and ruled his death a homicide. Gorman and Callahan were temporarily put on paid administrative leave, but they were back on the job within the month. Despite the video footage and the fact that Gorman had a documented history of misconduct complaints, both officers were ultimately cleared of any criminal wrongdoing by a Hennepin County grand jury.

The Smith family sued the City of Minneapolis, alleging excessive force and using the video as evidence. In 2013, nearly three years after David's death, they negotiated a settlement of $3.075 million, more than half of which went directly to attorney fees. Angela said that her family decided to proceed with the settlement after realizing that if they took the case to trial it could drag on for years, and that even then they knew they likely would never—could never—be made whole or get the justice they desired. The entire ordeal had already taken a tremendous toll on all of them, and they wanted to do what they could to pick up the pieces and heal as a family. So they settled the case, and David's mother used part of the money to purchase a new home—the one David had once dreamed of buying her.

The settlement also included an agreement that MPD officers would receive additional training on restraint tactics as a result of David's death. This agreement, which provided that systemic changes would be made within the MPD, was of critical importance to the family. It provided solace that even if the officers who killed David would never be held responsible, and even if the settlement money would never bring David back, they could at least help ensure that no other family would have to go through the terror of their experience. Though MPD would eventually claim that the agreed-upon trainings had been provided, George Floyd's killing by way of the same tactic that killed David led Angela and her family to question whether and to what extent the trainings had actually taken place or whether policies or practices had ever been established to improve how police officers deal with individuals suspected of having substance abuse disorders or mental health conditions.

The death of George Floyd on May 25, 2020, was a gut punch for Angela. When she watched the video of Floyd—pleading and struggling for air as Derek Chauvin knelt on his neck for nearly nine minutes, as three other officers aided in the offense, as outraged bystanders documented their brutality—she couldn't help but see her brother lying on a gymnasium floor ten years earlier, alone. What had her brother's story been if not a cautionary tale? What had she and her family fought for if not to prevent this very thing? As David's younger brother Louis Brown put it during an interview shortly following Floyd's death: "My brother's death was supposed to save Mr. Floyd's life."

The Smith family understood firsthand the confusion, pain, and rage that the Floyd family was likely experiencing. They understood how overwhelmed and perhaps even dismayed the family might be by the crush of cameras and commentators and reporters who showed up in the immediate aftermath looking for an interview, a sound bite, an explanation—something, anything, *everything*. "We didn't have the ability to communicate through our broken hearts," Angela sobbed.

In the end, Angela felt that having been suddenly thrust into a circumstance they neither asked for nor were prepared to contend with, she and her family were unable to fully express the beauty and complexity of David. They knew that the stigma attached to mental illness and housing insecurity, especially as it relates to Black people, meant that many would not understand the significance of David's death, both to the people who knew and cared for him and to the movements for racial and socioeconomic justice and against police brutality. And they knew that the terms being used to describe David were insufficient to explain the realities of his life—like the fact that David might not have had a stable address, but he was living with a friend and in constant communication with his family. Like the fact that, despite reports of a substance abuse problem, no alcohol or drugs other than cold medicine were found in his system at the time of his death. Like the fact that he was actively working, even until the final moments of his life, to stabilize his mental health. Like the fact that he had left the South Side of Peoria for the Twin Cities because he aspired to do all that young Black people from the hood are frequently told to do in order to "make it out."

Like the fact that he loved the ocean.

Minneapolis, MN
January 15, 2021

Terrion L. Williamson is an associate professor of African American and African studies and American studies at the University of Minnesota, where she also serves as the director of the Black Midwest Initiative. She is the author of *Scandalize My Name: Black Feminist Practice and the Making of Black Social Life* and the editor of *Black in the Middle: An Anthology of the Black Midwest.*

On the Precarity of "Safety"

A Black Mother Contemplates What It Means to Defund the Police

Shannon Gibney

This essay was first published as "A Black Mother Contemplates What It Means to Defund the Police . . . and for the Future She Envisions for Her Son" for the Twin Cities PBS Originals series in December 2020. The essay includes an epilogue from January 7, 2021.

I remember once, many years ago, watching a boyfriend run down a dimly lit street in downtown Minneapolis, a small package under his arm for the FedEx office on the next block. I sat in the car watching and waiting for him, unprepared for the sudden rigidity of my spine, the hole in my stomach. My eyes peered anxiously at passersby he raced past, waiting for someone—a white woman in a suit and heels, a cop coming out of the corner store—to grab him or knock him down suddenly, unhinged by the spectacle of his freely moving body. I hadn't known until that exact moment what it meant to love a body that the politic built a nation around controlling and, in fact, destroying. These days, loving my Black tween son, I have a new and constant intimacy with the experience.

As we settle into the era of post–George Floyd, post-protest, hundreds of institutional commitments to "anti-racist" initiatives, defunding the police movements and their inevitable backlash, rising crime rates, and incremental policy change to dismantle the Minneapolis Police Department (MPD), I look at my son, an affectionate, funny, caring, deeply engaged ten-year-old, and I wonder what his choices will be to push toward change. Of course, I also wonder about the costs.

Boisey wants to be involved. I have raised him that way and that is who he is anyway, but as an adult, a student of history, and a Black citizen myself, I know all too well how white people and white institutions so often plant the burden of social change on the backs of the most vulnerable. You push for the change that everyone says must happen, everyone says they want, and in doing so you become "The Problem" in the organization, the school, the community. Having been "The Problem" my whole life, I want more for Boisey. And yet, I know that nothing changes unless people change it. And the people who usually have to make it happen are those who are most at risk from the system. It's a conundrum I haven't worked out in my mind or heart. No Black parent has.

Yet here we are.

In late 2020 the Minneapolis City Council voted to cut the MPD budget for the first time in twenty years. The $8 million from the proposed cut was to be redirected to fund a new mobile mental health team and community-based violence prevention programs, and property damage and parking calls will be moved to other city departments. But it was a battle, even for these small victories. The number of police officers was not cut, despite pressure, and the establishment mayor threatened to veto the whole budget. The MPD still has a total budget of $171 million and little to no accountability measures in place. This is the pace of institutional change in a city that is still majority white—liberal, but not liberal enough to alter the racial power dynamics in any significant way. This is the culture of a place with some of the worst racial disparities in income, homeownership and housing access, incarceration, employment, education, and health care in the nation. This is, for all intents and purposes, the place I have chosen to call home. It is the place I am raising my family. The place whose opportunities and contradictions I struggle with every day. And as my son grows more and more into the Black man he is destined to become, he will too.

The thing that depresses me about this inevitably long fight is not the exhaustingly slow pace of bureaucratic change but the distance between my racial reality and that of some of my white friends and neighbors. Though they may only say it privately to other white folks and city employees as they contemplate an increase in shootings, carjackings, drug use, and petty crime in our neighborhoods during a pandemic, many of them really do feel safer *in their bodies* with more police, continued police funding, and little accountability. This is something so far away from my daily lived experience in my own body, and caretaking my son's, that it is almost unfathomable. The durability of racist practices within institutions, even and especially those that identify as "anti-racist," is depressing as well.

What is hopeful, though, is that the term "defunding the police" is now firmly ensconced in the American lexicon—something I could not have dreamed of even a year ago. Many people don't agree with the *concept* of defunding the police, but they nevertheless have to consider it in the wider public discourse as a possible strategy to ending police violence. We can't bring anything into being that we can't imagine, and we can't deeply imagine what we can't articulate. Words matter.

What gives me the most hope, however, is my son. We live about thirteen blocks from where George Floyd was killed, and when I suggested that he and his sister and I go down to the memorial at Thirty-Eighth and Chicago this summer to pay our respects and be with the people, he was initially reluctant. And I understood: Why would you want to go to the spot where a man was killed in cold blood? But we went, and he marveled at the murals and artwork of all kinds on the streets and buildings, approached two men drumming to discover how they were doing it, kibitzed with some kids in the street.

"Nothing will happen to those cops who killed him," Boisey told me after he learned of the murder. My first thought was that I was raising him right. He understands that the function of policing and the criminal "justice" system in this country is to keep white people and those owning property (mostly white people) safe, and to surveil, contain, and destroy Black and Brown folks. Paradoxically, this knowledge, difficult as it may be, will help keep him safer as he matures. My second thought was that I have to keep on showing and exploring all the various ways of fighting. And that sometimes loving and fighting are the same thing.

Epilogue: January 7, 2021

The MPD has killed again, as we knew they would. Once again, the victim was a Black man: twenty-three-year-old Dolal Idd, a Somali American who lived with his family in Eden Prairie, a suburb of Minneapolis. And this time the murder took place even closer to home: at the Holiday gas station at Thirty-Sixth Street and Cedar Avenue, barely three blocks from our house and across the street from Boisey's father's apartment. I do not keep hard things from my children, as I know it won't serve them now or as they age, so I made it a point to talk to Boisey about the tragedy as soon as I heard about it. I said that the details of the case were still muddled, but that it appeared that the police approached Idd on a traffic stop, he shot at them, and they returned fire, killing him. I said that Idd had been involved with guns in the past, and that the police were probably investigating him for something related to that when the encounter turned deadly. My son turned to me, his eyes damp but resolute, and said simply, "That's no reason to kill him." I nodded solemnly and told him he was right.

What is striking is not that these murders keep happening but that there is so little change in how they are narrated publicly, with the underlying assumption that a guilty body is a Black one. For our family, it feels like they are closing in, each one coming nearer to home. The only way they will stop is by a collective cultural racial reimagining of who is seen as "human" and who is seen as "dangerous." At ten, my son has dug in his heels for the long, bloody battle. And I, his mother, will do anything to protect him from the real danger that waits.

Minneapolis, MN
January 7, 2021

Shannon Gibney is a writer, an educator, an activist, and the author of *See No Color* and *Dream Country*, young adult novels that won Minnesota Book Awards in 2016 and 2019. Her new novel, *Botched*, explores themes of transracial adoption through speculative memoir. A Bush Artist and McKnight Writing Fellow, Gibney teaches writing at Minneapolis College.

Finding Myself in a Racialized World

A Personal Story of Being Black and Immigrant in Minnesota

Ibrahim Hirsi

I saw the back of the shirtless white man riding his bicycle at the intersection of Twenty-Eighth Street and Lyndale Avenue in Uptown Minneapolis, but I couldn't make out exactly what he said. It was a warm summer evening in 2019, and Uptown was buzzing with people and activity. I stood at the intersection with my two nieces, Zuhur and Hannan, and nephew, Said, waiting for the red traffic light to turn green. If I couldn't hear the bicyclist, Hannan, who was a couple feet away, heard the six words he uttered: "Get out of the way, niggers!" I was squatted down, tightening my shoelaces and chatting with Zuhur, when Hannan asked, "Did you hear what he said?" Before I could say anything, the fourteen-year-old answered her own question—repeating those words with dismay. By then, the bicyclist had vanished into the evening rush.

What came next was even more difficult to deal with: Zuhur, at age seven, wanted to know the meaning of "nigger," which she had just heard for the first time. I was unprepared to talk about race and racism with these youngsters, feeling it was unnecessary to burden them with the pain and emotions that come with discussing these weighty topics. Besides, I was elated that they had decided to vacation in Minnesota—which I've called home since 2005—and wanted them to enjoy some memorable experiences in their brief stay before returning to Melbourne, Australia. For that reason we had gone that evening to Milkjam Creamery, a popular ice cream shop in Uptown. Yet here I was—ostensibly in one of the most progressive cities in the United States—trying to figure out the best way to explain this horrible experience to a child.

For me, the bicyclist's bigoted remark was hardly a one-off incident.

I've dealt with similar episodes over the sixteen years I've lived in the North Star State. When I think about my journey to racial awakening and what it means to be Black and immigrant in Minnesota, it is clear that my experience as a local journalist in the Twin Cities and my ongoing investigation as a history PhD student at the University of Minnesota have helped me see two opposing sides of the story of Minnesota: one supports and tolerates Black people, and the other demonizes and criminalizes them.

Finding Myself in a Racialized Society

On May 25, 2020, a year after our unfortunate encounter with the bicyclist, George Floyd took his last breath under the knee of a uniformed police officer in south Minneapolis. The killing not only ignited nationwide protests and spurred renewed debate on race and racism, it also brought the decades-old plight of Black people in Minnesota into full view. In addition to a large community of African Americans, the state houses more than 142,000 African-born immigrants and refugees, many of whom have become naturalized US citizens. The majority of this population came from Somalia, Ethiopia, Kenya, Liberia, and Nigeria during the 1990s and 2000s. Though most of these new Americans live in the Twin Cities, where they've established vibrant communities, many have put down roots in small towns and rural areas across the state, including Austin, Faribault, Mankato, Marshall, Moorhead, Rochester, St. Cloud, and Willmar. Many are low-wage employees in public schools, health care facilities, manufacturing companies, and meat-processing factories.

In May 2005, my family and I joined this growing population. Our first home was a roach-infested two-bedroom apartment in an old three-story building—tucked between Blaisdell and Nicollet Avenues—in Minneapolis's Whittier neighborhood. We were new refugees, with no rental history and only a little income from the federally funded resettlement office, and it was the only place we could afford to rent. Barely a few weeks after my arrival, I came face-to-face with Minnesota's persisting racial income disparity. I noticed that the other tenants were mostly African Americans, Somali Americans, and Mexican Americans who held low-wage jobs in the construction, manufacturing, and transportation industries. *How did these Americans come to live in the same building as broke refugees who had just arrived in Minnesota?* I wondered. *And where do the well-dressed white professionals whom I come across at the education and social service centers—where I go to take school placement exams and apply for identification cards—raise their families?* It would take me many years to discover the answers.

Just a stone's throw from our apartment stood Calvary Baptist Church, which was established in 1883. On January 16, 2006, the church played Martin Luther King Jr. speeches to commemorate and celebrate the life and legacy of the civil rights icon. This was my first MLK Day in the United States. It was also the first time I heard King's captivating voice, even though I had read his "I Have a Dream" speech for an English class in Nairobi, Kenya, where I lived before moving to Minnesota. It was part of a collection of essays and speeches we read for an assignment. But the teacher didn't provide any context on the era in which the speech was delivered or its significance. So I moved on to other readings without fully grasping why King had a dream that one day "little black boys and black girls will be able to join hands with little white boys and white girls as sisters and brothers." I thought it was a peculiar dream to have.

On that MLK Day, sitting in that apartment's living room, I listened to those same words wrapped in King's actual voice as they resounded through the church's speakers. This time, I was certain that King's dream had come true. Look at all those white teenage boys and girls hanging with Black teenage boys and girls at the local strip malls! Look at those interracial couples raising families together in movies and in real life! America had, indeed, moved beyond those dark days King painted during the civil rights era—or so I thought.

Gradually, through books and through life, I became more aware of race and American racism. Back in my native Somalia, especially in the Mogadishu neighborhoods where I lived, race was almost never a thing. With the exception of ostracizing minority groups for belonging to clans "inferior" to the majority ones that trace their lineages to Arab tribes, Somalis tend to see themselves as a people who share one language, culture, and religion. Or at least that has been the dominant national narrative, and today nationalists and politicians depict the people of this eastern African nation as homogeneous.

In reality, though, Somalia's ethnic makeup doesn't boast that perceived uniformity. While the Darod, Hawiye, Isaq, and Dir—the four main tribes—constitute 85 percent of the population, the rest includes formerly enslaved people who were imported from such places as Mozambique and Malawi as well as Arab and Indian merchants who established permanent homes in the coastal regions of Somalia. These minorities now share culture, language, and religion with the dominant ethnic groups, though their physical features remain distinctive. In this minority category are also the Gaboye, Tumal, and Yibir. Unlike the former enslaved people and Asian migrants, however, this group shares the physical features of the dominant ethnic Somalis. But they have become outcasts, in part because of their occupations—as leatherworkers, blacksmiths, hunters, and tanners—which have placed them outside the elite pastoral lifestyle of the dominant clans.

Despite their racial and ethnic diversity, Somalis often accentuate their clan differences at home and their nationality abroad. So it's no surprise that there had never been serious discussions on race in my family. The only necessary identity that existed in our minds was nationality. In other words, we did not see people through the lens of race but through the specific nation-states to which they belonged. One, for instance, is a Somali. Or a German. Or a Brazilian. Or an American. Indeed, the practice of racial demarcations that has taken hold in many parts of the world was—and still remains—unfamiliar in Somalia.

But when I arrived in Minnesota, it wasn't just the cold weather with which I needed to come to terms. I also had to find my place in this racialized world—to learn to thrive in a society where the color of my skin is synonymous with crime. It didn't take me long to notice that race in America is, in the words of British Nigerian writer Sarah Manyika, "a defining element of personal identity." For instance, almost every application I filled out sought information about my race. If I had viewed myself as Somali before coming to the United States, I had to become Black or African American here. I came to understand that in the United States, it's not the place of our birth or the language we speak that forms our identities but the color of our skin and the texture of our hair. This peculiar race obsession in the United States led me to understand that the dream of Martin Luther King Jr. remains unfulfilled. Indeed, it wasn't the urge to have white bodies and Black bodies in the same room that animated King's concerns, but the inequalities and racism that have persisted in the United States for centuries.

As I progressed through high school—and later through college—and read about the history of race and racism in the United States, I became more aware of the advantages and disadvantages associated with race in this country. That knowledge helped me understand that the conspicuous racial compartmentalization in today's society is tied to the lingering legacy of slavery, imperialism, and the Jim Crow laws. In Minnesota, for example, it's not difficult to see the ever-widening disparities between whites and people of color. As *Minnesota Reformer* reporter Rilyn Eischens notes, the state "boasts of its quality of life, but conditions aren't so ideal for all residents—the North Star state's racial disparities in education, income and housing are among the worst in the nation."

These lessons taught me that America's racial structure doesn't merely place its citizens into separate categories. It also determines their fate and future. James Baldwin, in *The Fire Next Time*, explained to his fifteen-year-old nephew what this means for Black Americans: "You were born where you were born and faced the future that you faced because you were black and *for no other reason*. The limits of your ambition were, thus, expected to be set forever. You were born into a society which spelled out with brutal clarity, and in as many ways as possible, that you were a worthless human being." Though Baldwin wrote these words more than half a century ago, white America continues to view Blacks as worthless people whose lives do not matter.

Between 2015 and 2020, Minnesota police departments shot dead at least five Black men, including Jamar Clark, Philando Castile, George Floyd, and Dolal Idd. On December 30, 2020, Idd, at age twenty-three, was shot and killed by Minneapolis police officers. Instead of telling his parents about the killing, the Hennepin County Sheriff's Office raided his family's house in Eden Prairie at 2:00 AM. As I watched the scenes unfold in the twenty-eight-minute body-cam footage, I felt as if I were witnessing a US military operation taking place in Baghdad. More than a dozen officers in military gear and with long guns descended on the family during a search warrant execution. It wasn't until after the search that the police told Idd's parents that their son was dead. Speaking to the *Sahan Journal*'s Mukhtar Ibrahim, Idd's father, Bayle Adod Gelle, said, "Imagine your son getting killed, and then getting a visit from those who killed him and they terrorize you in your home?" This was what Baldwin meant when he told his nephew that Black people are viewed as "worthless human being[s]" in America.

The Two Sides of the Minnesota Story

Over the sixteen years I've lived in Minnesota, my experience, as a Black immigrant, has been generally positive. Three months after I arrived in Minneapolis, I began at Wellstone International High School, where my teachers, most of whom were white, nurtured me and believed in my potential. Soon after they noticed my passion for writing and storytelling, they began to provide me the support and guidance I needed to meet my career aspirations. They even went out of their way to connect me with opportunities and professionals outside the school. My English teacher Kathy Runchey, for instance, introduced me to a local program, ThreeSixty Journalism, which later inspired me to pursue a bachelor's degree in journalism at the University of Minnesota. My history and social studies teacher Carol Dallman helped me secure a spot at the *Wedge* newspaper as a contributing columnist before I even knew what it meant to be a columnist. Daniel Hertz, the school counselor, helped me apply for colleges and scholarships and encouraged me to continue writing through my high school years.

To this day, Hertz remains my friend and mentor. He, Runchey, and Dallman are just a few of a large group of white Minnesotans who have supported me over the years and continue to play a role in my journey to build a fulfilling career in journalism and academia. They've become like a family to me. And Minnesota, for all its flaws, has become home. It's given me many things that my birth country of Somalia could not. It's in Minnesota where I completed my high school education and earned an undergraduate degree; where I built a dream career as a journalist; and where I now pursue a PhD in modern US history, with a focus on immigration and the Black diaspora. It's in Minnesota, too, where I got my first internship and my first job, where I bought my first car and learned how to drive.

Indeed, Minnesota is a place where many Black immigrants—and their children—have made their marks. They're teachers. Engineers. Entrepreneurs. Doctors. Mental health practitioners. Community leaders. Many of them hold important elected positions in federal, state, and local governments across Minnesota. Among them is Ilhan Omar, the Somali American who was elected in 2018 to the US House of Representatives and became the first Black woman to represent the state in Congress. In 2019 Liberian American Mike Elliott was sworn in as mayor of Brooklyn Center. In 2020 Esther Agbaje, a Nigerian American, was elected to the Minnesota House of Representatives. In the same year, Oballa Oballa, an Ethiopian American, became the first elected Black city council member in Austin, Minnesota. These politicians are among over a dozen Black immigrant elected officials across the state, representing not just their own communities but also large segments of white constituents. Of course, their success is mainly due to their ability to lead and to mobilize voters. But it's also a testament to Minnesota's progressive reputation and acceptance of people from diverse racial backgrounds.

That, however, is just one side of the Minnesota story, one that's earned the state its elusive reputation as exceptional. Behind this exceptionalism curtain lies racism, Islamophobia, xenophobia, and anti-Blackness. It's not a coincidence that the Twin Cities, according to the financial news outlet 24/7 Wall St., ranked as the fourth-worst metropolitan area in the nation for Black people. In a 2019 report, "The Worst Cities for Black Americans," Evan Comen noted:

> While white residents of the Twin Cities metro area are better off than white Americans nationwide in a number of measures, the area's black population is worse off by several metrics compared to the black population nationwide. The typical white household in Minneapolis, for example, earns $78,706 a year, over $17,000 more than the $61,363 national figure. Meanwhile, the typical black household in Minneapolis earns $34,174 a year, 43.4% of the median for white household[s] and $4,000 less than the median among black households nationwide. Similarly, while 95.9% of white adults in Minneapolis have a high school diploma—the largest share of any city in the country—just 82.2% of black adults in the metro area do, below the 84.9% national black high school attainment rate.

Even with the increased number of Black immigrants and refugees who have arrived in Minnesota over the past three decades, the state remains 80 percent white. The Black population comprises only seven percent of the state's overall residents.

Perhaps because there are so few Blacks in Minnesota, they stand out wherever they are in the state, especially in places outside the Twin Cities. They attract unwanted attention from white residents and law enforcement, who view them as suspicious. Prior to starting my PhD program in 2018, I lived in St. Louis Park, a suburb about seven minutes west of Minneapolis. One day as I pulled into the parking lot of the building where I lived, a white female resident saw me coming and rushed into her car, where she rolled up the windows and stared at me. More than once, on my way to or from my apartment, I noticed people quickly changing pace when they saw me, some of them rushing back to their rooms, others holding tightly to their belongings. But it was not just in St. Louis Park where I experienced these things. It happens almost everywhere in the state. I cannot count how many times I have been followed around in stores, treated as a potential criminal. My only response these days is to walk out and spend my money elsewhere.

For a Black man in Minnesota, driving is more terrifying. I've probably been stopped about seven times over the past fifteen years. Even though this number might not seem high given the amount of time I've lived here, it's a lot when the officers, for the most part, had no obvious reasons to pull me over. One night, in St. Louis Park, an officer pulled me over and asked if I understood why he had stopped me. I said I didn't know. He responded that it was because I wasn't driving in a straight line. Of course I had been, but I decided not to argue—so I could live another day. Similar incidents happened in Edina and Burnsville, and each time I prepared my driver's license and insurance card, rolled down the window, and put both hands on the steering wheel, mindful of all the innocent Black men whose lives were taken following a mere traffic stop.

At the Uptown intersection where we stood that warm summer evening, Zuhur held my little finger. The light turned green, and we began to cross the road. She looked up at me and asked the question one more time: "What does 'nigger' mean?" I knew that to explain the word would require explaining the long history of race and racism in the United States. Zuhur is a curious child, smart, and mature beyond her age. She could certainly have handled a history lesson on racism. But I felt it wasn't the right time and place to talk about it. So I gently told her that it's a "bad word" and that she didn't need to worry about it. A few weeks later, Zuhur and her siblings returned to Melbourne, but the incident and Zuhur's profound question have never left my mind.

Minneapolis, MN
January 5, 2021

Ibrahim Hirsi is a PhD student in history at the University of Minnesota. His research interests include immigration, race, and the Black diaspora. Prior to graduate school, Hirsi was a reporter for various news outlets in the Twin Cities, where he covered immigration, race, and class.

May 29, 2020: We Are Not Okay

Enid Logan

We are not okay. Minneapolis–St. Paul is not okay. America is not okay.

I woke up today, May 29, 2020, still shell-shocked and traumatized. Last night I watched on CNN as the Midway neighborhood in St. Paul—immediately adjacent to us—was set ablaze. Rocked by tear gas, peaceful protesters, violent protesters, vandals, police, rocks, bricks, shattered glass, smoke and fire. Our local CVS, Target, and Cub Foods, our neighboring schools, gas stations, and grocery stores are shuttered or destroyed. I watched this scene unfolding for hours last night, only two miles away, while hearing sirens scream and police helicopters churn endlessly overhead.

I teach on race and racism at the University of Minnesota. And just the other week I was reflecting with satisfaction on how well I felt the semester had turned out despite the world being turned upside down by COVID-19—how I felt we had been able to build on the really strong foundation established in our weeks of in-person instruction, and what moving final projects my students had sent to me. But I don't have any such uplifting words of hope today, mostly just grief and outrage and shock.

Today is my tenth wedding anniversary. My husband is a St. Paul native, a St. Paul Public Schools high school teacher, and a longtime black political activist and writer. We are raising two *beautiful*, spirited, black boys, now finishing the first and third grades at home via their iPads during a pandemic. This morning the sun was peeking out from the clouds, and my boys woke up happy and unburdened . . . for now. They were pissed to learn that "our" Target has been looted, that the grocery store and the pharmacy are closed, and worst of all, that there is no internet. But hey, guess what? For the moment they're over it, because there are squirrels and cats to chase around and lots of wrestling with each other to get underway. There will be no homeschooling today.

For some reason, late last night, around 1:00 AM, after watching the Twin Cities go up in flames, I decided it was time for me to finish watching the video of George Floyd's murder. I had previously watched the first three minutes—sickened to the core, horrified, disgusted, and shocked—but stopped before he lost consciousness. Last night, however, as the city burned and images of the destruction were broadcast across America and the world, I played the video to the end. I watched, in incredulity and in horror, as the police CONTINUED to sit on Floyd's neck, long after he had ceased to struggle or even to move, after his body had gone limp, after he may well have been dead, yet they sat there and continued to punish and brutalize his body.

Maim and punish and kill, and kill and overkill again. Pressing down on his neck with the relentless MIGHT and WEIGHT of the state and the police, which appear nakedly now as an occupying, controlling force, crushing Floyd, extinguishing him, demolishing him, as they engage in rituals of punishment.

This is, it is unfortunate to say, the American way. Here the bodies of black and brown and indigenous people have been subjected for centuries to regimes of torture, punishment, control, and display. It is as though the might of white American manhood must be continually verified through these displays of conquest and rituals of torture. Indigenous bodies were first slain, captured, contained, and displayed as trophies in order to secure and justify the taking of the land that would become the United States. The University of Minnesota, a place that I have grown to love and where I began my career as a sociologist of race fifteen years ago, sits on Dakota land, a land that continues to be occupied by those who survived and remain, as well as the ghosts of those who were starved or driven off.

The tortured and broken bodies of black men and women also haunt this place, Our America. We are reminded again, so brutally with Floyd's death, and that of Breonna Taylor, and Ahmaud Arbery, and Philando Castile, and Jamar Clark, and Sandra Bland, and Freddie Gray, that the organizing imperative of black racialization in the United States is the permanent dispossession of the black body. Sometimes I feel the rhetoric that black lives "matter" misses the point, as not only are black lives treated as *expendable* in our America, but the *rituals* of *actively* expending and expiring our lives, of beating and suffocating and locking up and hanging and breaking and maiming our bodies, are ones that must seemingly be carried out again and again.

The violence against black and brown and indigenous people is also enacted daily in the form of massive structural inequities, routinely tolerated and enforced by our political leaders, and naturalized as somehow inevitable or just. It seems at times that there is certainly no reform that can fix this. The whole system must be abolished. It must all be burnt down to the ground.

Watching the city around me burn last night on the national news, as the sirens screamed and the helicopters roared overhead, was terrifying. And it all produced profoundly mixed and heightened emotions. I didn't know if I was more immediately concerned about the fires burning around us and the overwhelming rage and grief and frustration now set ablaze, or about the potential danger to my boys and to my husband and to me, as black people, posed by the police and the calling in of the National Guard.

The Minneapolis Police Department Third Precinct was also set on fire at around 10:30 PM last night. No police or fire trucks were sent to the area as the building—a symbol of brutalization and impunity—burned. And I have just received news that Derek Chauvin, the officer seen kneeling, minute after minute after minute, on George Floyd's neck, has been arrested.

This is a start. But the Twin Cities—a progressive metro area in a progressive state—is now known nationally and *internationally* for the recent deaths, at the hands of the police, of numerous black people going about their daily lives. This is a stain that cannot be erased. There will be no end to the ritual enactment of black and brown and indigenous death in America until we recognize that that is our national inheritance. And there will be no end to the grief and anger that these rituals inspire. We have had enough.

St. Paul, MN
May 29, 2020

Enid Logan is an associate professor and associate chair of the Department of Sociology at the University of Minnesota and the chair of the department's committee on diversity and equity. Logan writes and teaches on race and racism in the contemporary United States, focusing on the constructs of blackness and indigeneity.

Brown Minnesota

M. Bianet Castellanos

What is the value of Latino/a/x lives in Minnesota? I open with this question because it is ever present in my mind these days. It is sparked by the murders of George Floyd, Philando Castile, and so many others. By ongoing settler violence on Dakota homelands. By the violence against the transgender community as a I raise a transgender child. By the disproportionate impact of the pandemic on Latino/a/x communities. As I write this essay, my brother is fighting for his life against COVID-19, and the Latino/a/x communities where I grew up in California are so overwhelmed that hospitals are rationing oxygen and health care. These sparks prompt me to consider what it means to be Brown, Chicana, and Mexicana in the Midwest. As such, I share the following stories—one on police brutality and personal loss, and another on helping my children navigate racial and gender identities—because both have shaped my understanding of race and how to meaningfully address these disparities in Minnesota.

Jesús and Mr. Phil

When I moved to Minnesota in 2005 to join the faculty in American studies at the University of Minnesota, my dark brown body immediately felt out of place because almost everyone I encountered was white. Even after I became involved with Latino/a/x communities, I missed the everydayness of being brown in California, with its thriving Mexican American and immigrant communities, where I heard Spanish spoken everywhere. It wasn't until my children began kindergarten at Adams Spanish Immersion Elementary School in St. Paul that I felt a familiar sense of place—the halls were teeming with students of color and the cadence of my mother tongue was joyfully shouted on the playground.

I had grown up bilingual, and I wished to give my children the same opportunity. Yet this desire was superseded by my children's difficulties with the traditional classroom. Ben and Lucía struggled with selective mutism—a fear of speaking in social settings, which rendered them completely silent in school. It took them the entire year to trust their teachers enough to speak to them. Changing classrooms every year can exacerbate this condition. For first grade, I transferred Ben and Lucía to J. J. Hill Montessori, where project-based learning, multiage classrooms, and working with the same teacher for several years made it possible for my kids to thrive and speak. There we met Mr. Phil (Philando Castile). He was quiet, thoughtful, and kind, and he greeted my kids warmly at breakfast each morning. My family was devastated when he was murdered in the summer of 2016 by a St. Anthony police officer during a traffic stop.

For me, Mr. Phil's death recalled the trauma of another death that took place exactly one year prior. Minnesota resident, queer scholar, and social justice activist Jesús Estrada-Pérez had died tragically in police custody in Nebraska. Jesús was my graduate advisee and a friend. While on a road trip, he ran into trouble. Pure negligence led to his death. His life did not matter to the officers who detained him, but his life mattered to me, to his family, to his friends. Hundreds of people came out to protest and show their love on a muggy summer day.

Explaining these senseless acts to my children was heartrending. Ben and Lucía demanded to know how the police could commit these atrocities. They struggle to understand why BIPOC people are constantly at risk of losing their lives. As a parent, my job is to make my kids feel safe, but in the face of ongoing police brutality in Minnesota this task becomes nearly impossible.

Protest has been one way for us to cope and to push for change in Minnesota. To honor Mr. Phil, we marched. Since protest can take many forms, we also joined the J. J. Hill community to make art and share healing stories about Mr. Phil. To honor Jesús, I curated the *Remembrance* exhibit with Jessica Lopez Lyman at the Katherine Nash Gallery. In tribute to Jesús's research on gay Chicano art, we invited six artists (Rubén Esparza, Rigo Maldonado, Luciano Martinez, Miguel Angel Reyes, Joey Terrill, and Lalo Ugalde) from California, along with local artists Oskar Ly, Junauda Petrus, and Maria Cristina Tavera, to celebrate the power of art as a tool for social justice. Our conversations about the AIDS movement, the 2016 massacre in Orlando's Pulse nightclub, and police brutality forms part of a collective effort to change how we think about race in Minnesota and the United States.

Minnesota Whiteness

Racial violence in Minnesota is directly connected to the state's infamous achievement gap. The state has long been lauded for its excellent education system—if you are white. For Latino/a/x, Black, and Native American students, Minnesota is one of the worst places to be educated. For my children, these educational inequities are associated with whiteness. When Lucía was three years old, she came home from preschool lamenting that she wasn't blond-haired and blue-eyed like her classmates. Although her father is white, she has brown skin and black hair like me. Since I was raised in farmworker communities in California's San Joaquin Valley where anti-immigrant sentiment and white power have a strong foothold, I understood how shame can corrode a person's sense of self and cultural pride. What helped me counteract these negative stereotypes was watching Mexican American broadcasters on Canal 21 and Spanish programming on Univision. Seeing Latinos in positions of power made it possible for me to imagine otherwise. I wasn't able to re-create these conditions in Minnesota, so I decided to take my children with me on a sabbatical in Mexico in 2015. There my kids would be surrounded by people who looked like them and held leadership positions as teachers, politicians, and artists. After living in Mexico, Lucía confided that she wanted to be "brown" like me when she grew up.

Donald Trump's election in 2016 undermined these efforts. My kids worried about being deported. Lucía turned her frightened eyes to me and declared that she wished she was "blond and rich" so Trump wouldn't deport her. My son held similar fears even though he could pass for white because he inherited his father's lighter skin and hair color. That summer he gravely stated, "When I grow up, I want to be like Dad." I was puzzled by what he meant. "I want to be American," he explained. When I reminded him that I was American, he looked at me sadly and said, "Not like Dad. I don't want Trump to deport me." I was heartbroken and wondered: if we had lived in California, could I have prevented these traumas?

Queer Minnesota

One aspect of Minnesota that has been lifesaving is its queer community. In 2015, when Ben was six years old, he came out as transgender. As a toddler, he began to articulate his sense of self. He rejected feminine clothing and pointed out that he liked boy toys and clothes. By age four, he wished he was a boy and conveyed his discontent with his name. He renamed himself "PJ" after Prince John in Disney's *Robin Hood*, his favorite film. We encouraged him to name himself, but we gently prodded him to rethink naming himself after the prince who is legendary for stealing from the poor. After watching *Star Wars: The Force Awakens,* Ben renamed himself "Kai"—an abbreviation of Kylo Ren. We called him Kai at home. After reconsidering the name due to its association with the dark side, Ben finally settled on "Benjamin Alex" as his new name. I was especially pleased because, although he didn't know it, "Benjamin" was one of my favorite names. The J. J. Hill community rallied behind Ben. The school changed his name on all its paperwork and created its first LGTBQ+ student support group.

We were fortunate to have an LGBTQ+ community that educated us on how best to support Ben. My friend and colleague Kale Fajardo was open with Ben about being transgender. Before he came out, Ben obsessively searched the internet for experiences of other trans kids. At the time only a handful of books narrated these stories. Yet online videos told stories of kids who had been rejected by their families, friends, and neighbors. I didn't want Ben to associate being trans with abjection, so we had many conversations about how this wasn't his reality. He was loved and embraced by his friends, teachers, and family members. This is not to say that Ben has not experienced transphobia, but those are Ben's stories to share, not mine. Dr. Elizabeth Murray, Ben's developmental pediatrician, reminded us that although narratives of rejection and deviance circulate widely, we actually know very little of what it's like to grow up transgender.

The 2013 Minnesota Student Survey, conducted by the Minnesota Department of Health, is helping to shift our understanding. However, this survey is primarily made up of responses by white students. For Ben, being Latinx (the "x" marks his queerness) in Minnesota means coming to terms with racism, sexism, transphobia. But he is fortunate to have an LGBTQ+ community advocating for him. I may worry about raising Brown kids in Minnesota, but raising a trans kid in Minnesota has been a blessing.

Local Solutions

There is no easy solution to the racial inequities that plague Minnesota. My personal efforts to address these issues have been concentrated on Latino/a/x communities and the achievement gap. Because Minnesota has the worst high school graduation rates for Latinos/as/x in the nation, I have spent the past four years serving on the board of El Colegio High School, a bilingual, bicultural public high school in south Minneapolis located less than a mile from Cup Foods—the site of George Floyd's murder by Minneapolis police. Founded in 2000, El Colegio builds upon the talents of bilingual, bicultural students and their families to provide the academic rigor, leadership skills, college and career preparation, and community connections necessary to become lifelong leaders and change agents. El Colegio is doing an outstanding job of educating and preparing Latinx students for a bilingual, bicultural world. It is the only high school in the state of Minnesota committed to this mission. Half of the student population is over the age of eighteen, while ten percent of our youth are homeless or highly mobile. El Colegio has made great strides in Latinx graduation rates and postsecondary opportunities. For the past several years, one hundred percent of graduating seniors have been accepted to a post-secondary institution.

El Colegio is not only a high school; it also anchors our community. It has become a sanctuary for Latinx communities facing anti-immigrant sentiment, police violence, and the loss of jobs and loved ones due to a pandemic. During the protests against George Floyd's murder, El Colegio responded to the devastation by becoming a hub for food donations and redistribution to Little Earth, Pimento, and other pop-up food shelves. To serve our students' families and the Latinx community, El Colegio staff and youth partnered with nonprofit organizations to create a free grocery store that served more than ten thousand people. I joined other masked volunteers to bag groceries, baby food, diapers, and hand sanitizer. With the pandemic, the need has been so great that these youth organized Mercado El Colegio to continue distributing food and school supplies. According to Katie Groh de Aviña, El Colegio's director, "while hundreds of people would be waiting outside, our youth would go and talk to them, and hand out different informational literature about Black Lives Matter movement, and how we (as Latinos/as/x) can combat anti-blackness in our own community." In October, El Colegio and its partners began serving hot prepared meals two nights a week. By the end of December, 1,754 meals had been provided to community members. As El Colegio's youth remind us, the value of Latinx lives is intimately connected to BIPOC, immigrant, and queer communities in Minnesota.

These vignettes capture the challenges of being Brown and an immigrant in Minnesota. To thrive in a settler-colonial state built on racial violence and Indigenous dispossession means mobilizing for racial and social justice in big and small ways. Through my work with El Colegio, I am helping to decolonize our schools so our students can thrive. As a mother, I hold frank conversations with my kids on racial capitalism and police violence. They accompany me to protests and cultural events where they see activism at work. By teaching my kids to be proud of who they are, I nurture their ability to define themselves beyond the oppressive labels imposed on them. As a professor, I organize events and teach classes that critically examine the sociocultural, economic, and legal barriers that define race, class, and gender in the United States. These efforts and more are needed to envision a Minnesota radically altered. *¡Que siga la lucha!*

St. Paul, MN
January 7, 2021

M. Bianet Castellanos is professor and chair of the Department of American Studies at the University of Minnesota. She is the author of *Indigenous Dispossession: Housing and Maya Indebtedness in Mexico* and *A Return to Servitude: Maya Migration and the Tourist Trade in Cancún.*

Beyond Shadowboxing

Reflections on the Matrix of Race in the
Post-Floyd Era of Racial Protest

Jermaine Singleton

This essay was originally published in the September 2020 issue of Stillpoint:
A Magazine in the Eye of the Storm.

Once again, CNN is on a twenty-four-hour coverage loop. My attention toggles between work and civic unrest in HD. Another Black person dies at the hands of a police officer; however, there is something distinctly different this time: the murder was captured on video from multiple angles by bystanders. The video features Minneapolis police officer Derek Chauvin slowly choking the life out of George Floyd with a knee pressed against his neck. Just before Floyd's brain is deprived of oxygen, he cries out to his deceased mother for rescue. Yet another confirmation of criminal justice corruption, the mass circulation of the video was the equivalent of a match dropped into a tinderbox of a million unresolved racial grievances. Throw a global pandemic and white nationalists eager to make political use of the civic unrest into the equation and, alas, the nation is swept further into the multifarious matrix of race.

Race is intersectional (working in concert with other categories of social difference like gender and class), a social construction, a social institution, subject to change—and race implicates us all as agents of its survival. We all live in this fabricated ecosystem. For some it's a space of comfort nestled in real or imagined possibilities, while others are plagued by poverty, guilt, or relentless alienation. Its trappings are material and psychical, claiming us all, to varying degrees, in acknowledged and unreciprocated ways. I venture to argue that a vast majority of the

58 percent of US citizens under the impression that race relations are poor (as reported by a 2019 Pew study), even those on the front lines of resistance and social change, don't see the ways they are implicated in George Floyd's murder.

Far-right beneficiaries of the mechanisms of capitalism, the working poor, political moderates, and queer academics of color alike, we have all signed—in hope, in the need to belong, in blood, tears of resistance, or sweat equity—the social contract that devalues Black life systematically. Recently, the scales have fallen from the eyes of most US citizens, who now note the ways racism takes on discrete, procedural, and tactical forms through color blindness, the war on drugs, and neoliberal ideology and policy. The neoliberal pivot that took root shortly after the civil rights movement of the 1960s merged anti-racism and racism seamlessly. Yes, you read that right: the neoliberal rally around privatization, financial solvency, and competition maintains established racial hierarchies without reference to race or racism. For example, the neoliberal regime co-opted the cultural climate that was widely in support of desegregation to incentivize gentrification. A suite of tax breaks and subsidies for housing previously owned by displaced people of color made it possible for urban newcomers to convert undervalued, racialized spaces into generational wealth at the expense of Black families under the race-neutral cover of free-market capitalism.

We've entered a new era of critical race consciousness and accountability. It is no longer a secret: the struggle against educational disparities in the United States will have no sustainable traction as long as our racialized system of property continues to distribute generational wealth unevenly along racial lines. What's more, the national push to "defund the police" in response to the murder of George Floyd at the hands of Derek Chauvin is a strategic attempt to redirect the supposedly "race-neutral" flows of free-market capitalism away from what we've come to know as "the prison industrial complex."

Critical race consciousness and accountability has even hit late-night TV! Let's consider Trevor Noah's poignant remarks on the situation: "If you felt uneasy watching that Target being looted, try to imagine how it must feel for Black Americans when they watch themselves being looted every single day. Police in America are looting Black bodies. . . . Society is a contract that we sign as human beings with each other . . . and the contract is only as strong as the people who abide by it. . . . There is no contract if the law and people in power don't uphold their end of it."

Noah points to something implied that cannot be noted enough: the core aim of the Black Lives Matter movement is to close all gaps between our stated values and our lived realities, within and beyond the criminal justice system. For some, the terms "systemic racism" and "intersectionality" are mere buzzwords bandied about in exchange for a quick "woke" credit toward a personal or institutional life on the anti-racist side of history. Others are eager to push past the empty rhetoric and symbolism toward anti-racist shifts in policy and procedure.

The project to align the form and function of US citizenship has been in the works for quite some time. Indeed, the work of dismantling existing structures of privilege and injustice toward equal opportunity and outcomes has made considerable progress. Anti-racism scholars, teachers, cultural activists, and protesters around the globe are now equipped with a working knowledge of the ways everyday silence and "business as usual" subject the most vulnerable among us to death and disempowerment at the hands of law and capital. Moving beyond knowledge of the workings of the matrix of race to the work of dismantling systemic racism is a tall order, however, particularly in the face of the 42 percent of US citizens who don't seem to think racism is a matter of large concern for the nation. How do we fashion a new civil rights movement attentive to the revised structures of social and political power that secure life and death unevenly across racial and class lines? What's more, how do we do this work in ways that are mindful of the fear- and resentment-based tactics that keep our latest installment of the matrix of race in orbit?

I invite you to look just beyond the haze of rhetorical plays equating protestors with looters into the handiwork of the "Boogaloo Bois," a dispersed movement of radicalized antigovernment guns-rights activists— some of them white supremacists—suspected of attempting to ignite a second Civil War. Here, the shadow work that underpins the matrix of race in our contemporary moment takes on a distinct shape: our national tendency to quickly weaponize Black resistance or politicize it on a sliding scale according to its capacity for brand promotion and capital production.

Let me explain. In *The Erotic Life of Racism*, Sharon Patricia Holland invokes Michael Jackson's nod to what she calls the "ontological might" of race that is "too high to get over, too low to get under." We can never fully account for—and thus remediate—the forces of racial inequity when we politicize racial pain and grievance to the point of turning them into commodities that eclipse everyday Black humanity. Somewhere between the consciousness-raising Procter & Gamble advertisements, the NFL's newfound respect for Colin Kaepernick's stance on criminal justice reform, and the Black faces lost among the droves of white millennials and Generation Xers standing in solidarity with the Black Lives Matter movement, actual Black lives shimmer in and out of view. What's the point of gratuitous looting and vandalism after the call to "defund the police" has resulted in steps, however initial, toward criminal justice reform? Are the looters and vandals transferring the aftershock of the accumulative weight of ongoing racial inequities galvanized by the twin pandemics of racism and COVID-19 back onto the capitalist superstructure without remorse? Are they justified in doing so? Regardless, this method of protest poses countless barriers to substantive social change. All of this shadow work widens the existing ideological divide to the point of political paralysis. This is the perfect storm for the forces of structural inequity to affect aggrieved individuals and communities disproportionately without accountability and correction.

Meanwhile, in another precinct of the matrix of race, the *Star Tribune*, the upper Midwest's beacon of liberal journalism, offered a hot take on the first night of protest riots after the murder of George Floyd, selling the image of Black rage to the public. The front page featured the image of the faceless body of a Black man hulking in a pose of rage in front of an AutoZone engulfed in flames, a building damaged initially by a white supremacist who later became known as "the umbrella man." The nation has become so numb to the Black pain and grievance it manufactures that even the most conscientious photojournalist is hard-pressed to avoid appropriating figurations of Blackness in the service of pre-existing racial bias.

Racial grievance all too often functions as an elastic good. Unlike water and insulin, the value of racial grievance changes significantly across rhetorical and situational contexts. Racial grievance receives wider and extended airplay when packaged for the economic or political gain of an exterior entity. Notions like "inclusive excellence" furnish administrators and executives profitable opportunities to "talk in circles," embracing model minorities without offending conservative donors and clients. Meanwhile, polarization grows, with opposing interpretations of racial grievance, in degree and kind, alive and well. In these contexts, the ways systemic racism plays out against Black lives and opportunities fall on deaf ears. This is not an accident; it's contrived and crafted. We rarely listen to the grievances of marginalized people or, even worse, merely issue robotic nods of adherence when they share their grievances.

Every time a CNN camera pans across this strikingly diverse wave of protesters united in anti-racism, I'm cautiously optimistic. On one hand, I'm swept by hope for the alignment of the form and function of US citizenship. On the other, I'm reminded of the ways racial grievance, particularly when it hits the mainstream, is appropriated in the service of the existing racial hierarchy and the pervasive capitalist superstructure. There is a disparity between the declared public aims of neoliberalism (well-being of all) and its actual consequences (the restoration of class power). As David Harvey explains in *A Brief History of Neoliberalism*, neoliberal ideology and policy falsely assume a level playing field, consolidate upper-class power, and favor the solvency of financial institutions over the well-being of the general population or environmental quality.

In the neoliberal racial state, to which we in the United States belong, collective forms of opposition that emerge in response to such disenfranchisement are racialized, weaponized, and met with a host of policing tactics (chiefly, coercive legislation, incarceration, surveillance, and propaganda). The brand of Black-pain-appropriation engaged by the Boogaloo movement emboldened the politics of racial resentment and indifference against the Black Lives Matter movement by igniting all of these policing tactics at once.

The looting and arson, some of which was organized and initiated by the Boogaloo Bois in communities where people of color live and work, operated strategically within and against the grievances of minoritized communities across the nation. While the image of protestors united in multicultural bands against systemic racism across the nation sets the notion of a "racial divide" off-kilter, the infiltration of this spirit of social change—from setting buildings on fire gratuitously to provoking combustible situations between protestors and officers from the sidelines—by those with an endgame to exacerbate racial and political polarization will have lasting material effects. If we take the riots following the murder of Dr. Martin Luther King Jr. and the beating of Rodney King as historical precedents, efforts to rebuild the ravaged economic infrastructures will be met with political inertia and systemic disinvestments of all stripes. The full return will take decades. Certainly, as Michael Jackson proclaimed, "we're stuck in the middle."

Now more than ever, we must balance aspiration with acute realism. Our protest chants and cultural activism must carry the spirit of what Joseph Winters calls "melancholic hope," embracing and counteracting the incomplete struggle for racial justice. As we forge forward, we must question the efficacy of protest strategies that fold "Black burdens of proof" into "white benefits of the doubt" by placing white bodies on the front lines to protect Black lives. Why must our white allies stand on the front lines of racial protests in preservation of Black lives in order for the resistance to gain political traction? In all of its well-meaning expediency, this mode of social protest indirectly divests officers of the responsibility to see Black lives as subjects of political agency and autonomy.

I must admit: there is a small region of my mind that thinks "Black Lives Matter" so much these days because the moral authority of the white heteropatriarchy Derek Chauvin embodies is on a global witness stand. Are we mourning the loss of the moral authority of white heteropatriarchy in blackface? Or are we mourning the loss of the moral authority of the criminal justice system Derek Chauvin represents by proxy? Sustainable progress beyond what, on the surface, appears to be an intractable problem at the intersection of racism and the criminal justice system may rest in our willingness to mourn all three. If today's antiracism protesters are asking the nation to mourn the loss of the moral authority of white heteropatriarchy and the criminal justice system as they mourn the loss of George Floyd, this significantly alters the transformative value of this inflection point of civil unrest. It would signal our collective capacity to connect the dots between cause and effect, highlighting the enduring psychic attachments embedded within our institutional structures pursuant to policing them.

Until the publication of Michelle Alexander's *The New Jim Crow: Mass Incarceration in the Age of Colorblindness*, the neoliberal culture of surveillance and incarceration that targets Black life flew under the radar because it operated covertly. Policing and incarcerating "people of poor choice" for profit is a systemic maneuver—from providing cash incentives to police officers for populating privately owned prisons with people from Black communities to the corporate use of prison labor to avoid paying a minimum wage and health insurance—that has plagued poor communities of color disproportionately since President Richard Nixon's "war on drugs."

Redefining the prevailing definition of criminality is in order. Perhaps what might be more transformative than uncovering Chauvin's racist motives, given the shadow work of the matrix of race discussed above, is to point to its more insidious institutional corollaries. The persistence of structural racial bias, which is fed by the recycled discussions regarding the motives and intent of racist *individuals*, is, in large part, responsible for the fact that we've yet to standardize a set of policies and practices that balance the preservation of life and citizenship with efforts to protect public safety.

Earnest attempts to account for and ameliorate racial grievances fall flat when they fail to intersect with personal as well as institutional sacrifice and accountability. Somewhere between those who are armed to the teeth without an ethics of accountability and those who are the most vulnerable among us without equal protection under the law lie the masses of the relatively privileged who keep these poles in orbit. We must beg the question that dismantles comfort: is there an actionable alternative to placing a "Black Lives Matter" sign on the lawn or in the window?

While walking in my neighborhood, I stumbled upon a call to action painted on a boarded-up building that may possibly hold the key to disrupting racism's shadow work: "Love your Black Brother." This mandate is simple to understand, radical, and rife with promise. Targeted and sustained disruption of our racial economy requires all of those occupying the magical middle to share their boxes of social, financial, and existential privilege or promise with Black and marginalized individuals and families. However outlandish and extreme, this is the mark of radical protest.

Radical protest of this sort requires courage amid the mushrooming of rituals of resistance against social change. The recent return of what Billie Holiday called "strange fruit"—that is, lynched Black bodies hanging from trees in 2020—throughout the United States shortly after Mayor Muriel Bowser named the two-block-long section of Sixteenth Street NW in Washington, DC, "Black Lives Matter Plaza" should not be a surprise to those who understand the disciplining function of the lynching ritual. In addition to the social control of Black life, the ritual works through fear and intimidation to undermine cross-racial alliances. It does so while reinforcing the long-standing equation between whiteness and power. Just as the pendulum of the US presidency swung in extreme from the election of Barack Obama in 2008 to the election of Donald Trump in 2016, post-Floyd-era strides in coalition building are pushing the conservative forces of inequity in the United States back to their ancestral roots of racial policing.

Race-baiting rituals abound. How do we turn this tinderbox into shared boxes of financial and social safety? Is it even possible to do so in the face of the economic insecurity wrought by the COVID-19 pandemic? There are so many available points of intervention.

Tantamount to "Loving your Black Brother," one of the most radical forms of protest in which people of color working on and off the front lines of social change can engage is a hearty regime of self-care. Valiant intentions and commitments to social change are no match for the virulence of indifference to and criminal retaliation against the fight for access and accountability structures designed to secure equity of outcomes. While none of us living today invented the matrix of race, our actions and inaction implicate us in the fortification of its contours and trapdoors. With nowhere to run and nowhere to hide, all of this endangers mental health. Therefore, we must convert the destructive affect underpinning racial despair and rage into our motivational desires for a more perfect union. As Audre Lorde urged in her essay "Poetry Is Not a Luxury," this begins with claiming the destructive affect and giving it a channel for productive, outward expression.

In addition, with the necessary affective channels in place, one can carve out time to design and embed social change structures into the institutions to which we belong. Translating social justice mission statements into deeds of social change, given the porous boundary between private money and institutional budgets, is a trapeze feat. It's time to imagine what radical institutional change might look like within the context of these constraints. Diversity learning at colleges and universities that fails to translate into student-led civic engagement initiatives that prioritize equity of outcomes should be redesigned to do so. Academics might draw on their academic freedom more strategically, linking civic engagement and responsibility to their approaches to teaching and learning.

I also propose supplementing "intersectional inquiry and praxis," the examination of the mutually constitutive oppressions on the individual (racism, sexism, ableism, transphobia, ageism, economic inequality, etc.), with what I call "interstitial inquiry and praxis," a framework for understanding and addressing the overlapping and divergent impacts of the forces of oppression within and across communities. Accounts of the uneven, overlapping, and contradictory impacts of the forces of inequity and oppression are more attuned to collaboration; they circumvent the divisive identity politics upon which the racial matrix relies. Addressing the digital gap is another piece of low-hanging social change fruit all too often left on the vine. What's needed are more social change agents and allies teaching students to enlist advanced digital communications tools and strategies to promote cross-cultural understanding, sustainable community partnerships, and *ethical and just* decision-making against the multifaceted workings of power at community, institutional, and policy levels.

The video featuring George Floyd's murder and the covert forms of racialization that persist as the nation unites in protest against the tragedy is a sobering reality. Nevertheless, the video has opened a wormhole out of the racial matrix. In closing, we must beg one more hard question: who benefits from symbolic gestures of solidarity designed to restore the peace that needs to be disturbed? Even as the Boogaloo anarchists assimilate the mass protest into the mechanism of racial hatred and civil unrest, we must push past the pulls of window dressing and racial fatigue toward business as *unusual*.

Minneapolis, MN
September 1, 2020

Jermaine Singleton is professor of English at Hamline University. He is the author of *Cultural Melancholy: Readings of Race, Impossible Mourning, and Ritual*. He is currently completing a book project that explores the intersections of racism, anti-racism, and neoliberalism.

Minneapolis Rise Up 2020
Black Lives and Whiteness Unveiled

Rose M. Brewer

Radical artist and civil rights activist Bernice Johnson Reagon invoked the civil rights movement as the "borning struggle" of that time. We are in the borning struggle of our time in the wake of the Floyd rebellion. The fight for Black lives continues in Minneapolis and globally following the May 25, 2020, police killing of George Floyd, which shattered the liberal image of Minneapolis. Since the murder of George Floyd, tens of thousands of people in the United States have been involved in the struggle for racial justice against some aspect of the system. The mantra of "Black Lives Matter" has echoed nationally and internationally. The cries to stop police violence and the fights for a living wage, workers' rights, housing, and education have been at the center of the demands. The fight for political change is at the heart of the resistance to anti-Black racism in a world where Black lives are systematically and intentionally targeted for demise.

With the right-wing white nationalism exemplified by the Boogaloo Bois, Proud Boys, and other white supremacists appearing in the midst of the Twin Cities protests, Black community members asserted that this malevolent white presence was not new. Most significantly, hidden behind this vulgar display of white supremacy is the reality of systemic racism inhabiting the Minnesota terrain.

It's now January 2021, eight months since the police murder of George Floyd, since Minnesota became the epicenter of protests and resistance. The Floyd killing catalyzed protests locally, nationally, and globally—sparking action as far away as Johannesburg, Tokyo, London, Paris, and many other places. This activism draws upon the long tradition of Black struggle in the United States and in Minnesota. It is grounded in a history that too often is rendered invisible. We have to dig deep and ask how it has come to this. There is police murder on the one hand and Black uprising on the other. The question compels us to examine the underpinnings of a state and a city whose face is white and liberal. Underneath, however, a complicated race, class, and gender dynamic is in play. The liberal veneer hides powerful economic and racial realities. The true fight for racial and social justice requires lifting the veneer.

Contradictions of Liberal Minnesota: Lifting the Veneer

I have been struck by the disjuncture between word and deed in this state. I call it not disrupting the comfort zone. For the violence of the racial status quo to be unearthed requires moving out of the racial comfort zone. This means actually breaking out of racial privilege. It plays out concretely in who is seen and who is believed. For example, think of the salesperson who smiles but provides better service to the white customer slightly behind you. Whose comfort matters in this situation? As a Black woman, I've experienced this more than once in a number of Minneapolis establishments. A rawer example occurred while I was shopping for toys when my son was young. He was so excited. When we exited the shop, we heard loud shouts and saw security chasing us, demanding that we stop, demanding a receipt. I wanted to know why. Some clerk had alerted security, saying that she thought not all items were paid for. I was livid. I was acutely aware of my son, the dismay on his face. I produced the receipt; of course all items were accounted for.

White racial privilege is not an individual question. It is an act of bonding, an act of white recognition. Lifting the veneer demands breaking that bond. This moves beyond tending to so-called white fragility. White privilege is embedded in a structure of relationships. The demand must be for whites to understand that their privilege is not negotiated as individual acts but as collective actions. White privilege is transformed fundamentally through collective actions. The system will not transform itself. This must come from all of us, and the white racial bond must be severed. This is a critical principle I teach in my course on public policy, "The Power of Bottom-Up Change."

Our work is cut out for us. What must be built is a tough, robust movement aligning multiple complexities. These are the deep relationalities of race, class, gender, and sexualities. At the center of the rise up are the courageous, the forgotten, those who are most deeply impacted by police violence, and those suffering from economic, political, and social dispossession. But the stars are aligning. During the period of the Floyd rebellion, people in a thousand places and more have said no to police killings and deeply rooted structural inequality and the voraciousness of racial capitalism. Let's put my assertion in the context of policing in the state.

Policing the Black Body in Minnesota

There is a long history of police violence in Minneapolis, St. Paul, and their suburbs. In terms of the broader history of Minnesota, war and militarism were foundational to its establishment as a state in 1858. From the white settler colonialism that initiated the state with the removal of the Dakota people onward, policing has been shaped by these structural realities. More concretely, by the 1920s and 1930s there was an identifiable Klan presence in the Minneapolis Police Department. In the current period, built on the legacies and ongoing practices of white supremacism and built in the protection of the property of capital, structural inequalities are woven into the very fabric of police violence against Black communities in Minneapolis.

In the last thirty years, the Minneapolis police have killed multiple Black and brown people, in addition to being responsible for many other instances of so-called collateral damage to Black lives. There was Tycel Nelson, a Black teenager shot and killed by Minneapolis police in 1990. There was the 1990 "raid gone wrong," in which members of the Minneapolis police SWAT team killed Lillian Weiss and Lloyd Smalley during a no-knock drug raid. And the more recent murders of Terrance Franklin in 2013 and Jamar Clark in 2015. Philando Castile was killed in 2016 in the St. Paul suburb of Falcon Heights.

Ideologies of racial inferiority and superiority have long been embedded in Minnesota social practices if not always in law. Black Minnesotans have been in a continual struggle against systemic racism in the state. From the 1910s to nearly 1950, blatant restrictive covenants kept Black Minnesotans from living in white neighborhoods in Minneapolis, including the very south Minneapolis neighborhood in which George Floyd died. For decades, African American students were unable to live on campus at the University of Minnesota, an institution that obtained a loan from a slave owner to keep it afloat in its early years. Currently a multiracial collation of students is pressing for repair given this history. For example, they are demanding the removal from University of Minnesota buildings of all names of segregationists and those who practiced anti-Semitism, but the university's regents have voted not to do so and instead recommended continuing to "study" the issue.

George Floyd, a Counterfeit Twenty-Dollar Bill, and the Lost Minnesota Dream

I was struck by the fact that a Cup Foods employee had called the Minneapolis police because they believed George Floyd passed a fake twenty-dollar bill. The high level of Black poverty in Minneapolis rippled through my brain. How many times had I driven past this Thirty-Eighth Street store that became a crime scene? A Black man lost his life at the knee of the police here. The role of policing in catalyzing Black death is a long-standing narrative of the interrelationship between economic dispossession and policing.

Indeed, Black workers have continually been excluded from well-paid construction, electrical, unionized, and professional work. Jobs, wages, and economic access are bifurcated by race or denied altogether, leaving low pay or no work for Black folks. This is a Black tax on a population too often locked out. Though Minnesota has prided itself on having a small group of well-paid "Black elites" in the corporations that dominate the landscape of the Twin Cities, Black Minnesotans have long protested the inequitable economic conditions faced by their community as a whole. When the 1967 Black uprising occurred on Plymouth Avenue on the north side of Minneapolis in the heat of summer, those involved in the uprising expressed ills similar to those at the heart of the current protests. The 1967 uprising emerged in the context of the Black Power shift from civil rights to self-determination and expressed ideological and class tensions that are familiar to today's activists.

I wasn't in Minnesota at the time but was involved in undergraduate student struggles. We had been deeply influenced by the Black Power movement. Those involved in the urban rebellions of the late 1960s were looking for fundamental racial transformation. The politics of the period were fraught with difficulty, and the historical fissures ran deep. The political terrain required treading a delicate line between incorporation into the system and social transformation. This dialectic was firmly in play during the 1967 Minneapolis rise up.

Economic dispossession continued to play out over the decades, with capitalism and racism inextricably linked in the state. Little Black wealth is being built in the Twin Cities. Black homeowners were especially hard hit in the 2007–8 recession, particularly from predatory lending practices by banks such as Wells Fargo. In Minneapolis, the Black homeownership rate is 29 percent, one of the lowest in the nation; white homeownership in Minneapolis is 75 percent. As is the case nationally, the divide between Black wealth and white wealth is large. The system of racial capitalism builds into its logic the need to protect property and keep some Minnesotans "safe."

The call to defund the police is embedded in this history, in a theory and practice of change. The core idea is to invest in human needs—education, living wages, health care—germinating the seeds of a society without police. The idea is rooted in community safety defined as an ethic of care. This idea is foundational to Black feminist thought. Indeed, the protesters in Minneapolis skewed heavily young and female. In fact, the leaders of the Black Lives Matter movement include many women and individuals who are gender nonconforming, and the movement draws upon Black feminist praxis. Moreover, a powerful Black feminist intervention today places front and center the theory of intersectionality, articulating the deep interrelatedness of gender/sexuality, race, and class in Black liberation. The Black queer radical feminist intervention asserts that systems of inequality are deeply connected with one another. The simultaneity of oppression is core to this frame. Thus gender/sexuality was inserted in the center of methods for analyzing race and class. The Black queer activists in the Floyd uprising centered this analysis of intersectionality and state violence.

Radical Black feminism is important here for understanding youth protest in Minneapolis. Some of these young people were queer Black feminists who cut their activist teeth after the police killing of Jamar Clark in 2015. They took over the Fourth Police Precinct in north Minneapolis, which had once been a community center, and demanded that it be returned to its original purpose: a center for the community. I was there on a number of occasions. It moved me that an ethic of care so central to radical Black feminism was being deployed by these young activists. This early mutual aid effort was deepened during the Floyd uprising. The lessons had been learned that care for the community and the demand for social change were intertwined.

This ethic of care, of course, is connected to the demand to defund the police. The argument for defunding police asserts that state violence inheres in the very fiber of US society, interwoven with the protection of private property for profit and its contemporary expression in police violence, mass incarceration, war, and militarism. Twenty-first-century anti-Black racism means holding in check or removing a population of people who are deemed a threat to the status quo and who thus are locked out of opportunities in education, employment, housing, and health. When deep levels of disrespect and inhumanity are business as usual, the demand and the struggle must be for radical, transformational social change. Black Lives Matter challenges the fundamental reality of anti-Black racism in the United States.

The key question is this: what will it take for fundamental change to happen in the city of Minneapolis and beyond? I've been in these Twin Cities long enough, struggled continuously enough, to share the deep sorrow the community feels because of the police murder of George Floyd. That's the spirit calling for justice, but there is also the material reality of the ground shifting, the cry for human rights, the need for housing, food, health, and education. The hard knot is this: power. What can we do about a system of power behind the face of the police, intertwined with deeply rooted racial inequalities? The response is resistance.

In closing, today signals a crucial period of renewed political contention by African Americans, but the impetus and context for it began long before the death of George Floyd at the hands of the police in Minneapolis, Minnesota. The radical impulses that inform this era of Black life are drawn from the long history of the Black freedom struggle: self-determination and social transformation. These enduring songs of freedom were asserted in Minneapolis during the Floyd rebellion. White Minnesota and the nation must have the courage to summon a deep ethic of accountability.

I live the life of a scholar activist. I work closely with struggles on the ground. I've built deep relations with youth in the struggle. This dynamic differs from being locked in the academy. It means that we work intergenerationally. I share the history of the Black radical tradition and the history of my own activism through workshops, shared research, and protest. Most recently, I conducted a Black radical tradition workshop with a group of youth involved in the Floyd rebellion. I will continue to work in solidarity with people from multiple generations until rebellions are no longer needed and Black people are truly free.

Minneapolis, MN
January 23, 2021

Rose M. Brewer is an activist scholar and Morse-Alumni Distinguished Teaching Professor of African American and African studies at the University of Minnesota. She publishes widely on gender, race, class, and social change. Brewer is a College of Liberal Arts Dean's Medalist, Academy of Distinguished Teachers inductee, and American Sociological Association Teaching award recipient.

The State Is Not Our Friend

Brian D. Lozenski

How you gonna say, "We will delay full consideration of . . . full attention to issues of diversity and equity" and expect to be not havin' cops kneel on people's necks with impunity, and the rest of these dumbasses clutchin' their pearls like they never saw these snuff films before? was what I wanted to say on the Zoom call. Instead, I said something like, "You can't center diversity and equity if it is not the starting point of the entire educational project. It can't be an afterthought."

Whatever. Neither response was sufficient.

The Zoom call, with the comments disabled, led by the disembodied white man who wouldn't shut up, was emblematic of education in Minnesota. As I sat back in my chair at the kitchen table, I told myself to just breathe. It wasn't worth getting worked up by the state's Department of Education obfuscating their culpability in the killing of Jamar . . . I mean Philando . . . I mean George . . .

Being on a Zoom call in late December 2020 with ninety other Minnesotans commenting on the first draft of the revised Minnesota Social Studies Standards—where "we will delay full consideration of . . . full attention to issues of diversity and equity" was actually written in black and white—was not what I would call activism. Yet there I was along with others in my community, pleading to have Black studies (among the many ignored ethnic studies disciplines) taught to children across the state. Is this how far we've come? Marcus Garvey's Universal Negro Improvement Association declared Negro children be taught Negro history in school as a fundamental human right back in 1920, a century ago. Students at the University of Minnesota took over Morrill Hall demanding an Afro Studies Department in 1969, fifty-two years ago. The embattled department exists at the U—underfunded, stepped over, and denied its legacy as the conscience of the institution, but it still exists. Augsburg University is starting a Critical Race and Ethnicity Studies Department in the coming years, again thanks to student demand.

The Minneapolis Public Schools board recently voted to make an ethnic studies graduation requirement, after half-heartedly rolling out a handful of elective classes in some high schools across the city eight years ago. St. Paul Public Schools is trying to set up an ethnic studies class that may or may not be required for all students. Mind you, these requirements are only about taking a single class, not restructuring the entire curriculum around the subjectivity of communities of color. To my knowledge, no other districts in Minnesota have any required ethnic studies education.

In the 1897 book *Suicide: A Study in Sociology*, the French sociologist Émile Durkheim wrote, "education is only the image and reflection of society. It imitates and reproduces the latter . . . ; it does not create it." Minnesota is a case study in the realization of this sentiment. It is a constant struggle to remind myself of the illusion in which we're trapped. The Minnesota Department of Education is a bureaucracy deployed by the nation-state (hereafter called the "State") to manage its violent work in the realm of education. Black studies is anathema to the State because it undermines the legitimacy of the United States as a force for good in the world. This is not a novel idea. Critical educational theorists across time and geography have made clear the controlling force of State-run (what's typically referred to as "public") education. Part of the subterfuge of the State has been to conflate *public* education with State-administered education funded through tax dollars. Through this logic the State *is* the public. Thus, schools are run in a manner that benefits the State and its authority, often at the expense of the people who attend the schools—the real public. We should not be ready to concede publicness to the State. In reality, we exist in multiple publics, desiring different worlds but all contending with the State for resources and access to materials needed to survive and thrive. We are taught to rationalize school success as a marker for those deserving of economic resources. Here, schools serve as mechanisms for the State to continue to reproduce the social hierarchy of the publics.

If we juxtapose what is taught in compulsory, State-run, State-funded schools to what was taught in the Freedom Schools of the 1960s, for instance, it is easy to see that the purpose of each is distinct. The work of State schools, using organizations like the Minnesota Department of Education (MDE), is to adhere generations of youth to the idea that the country is functioning effectively in its democratic rhetoric, and that the injustices we see are simply mistakes that can be rectified by kindhearted people. This rhetoric is filtered through the lens of what MDE calls "college, career, and civic life readiness." In other words, it emphasizes disciplining youth into pathways that continue to perpetuate a linear status quo of "proper" life in the United States, where college attendance and then work become the modes through which civic life is possible and attainable. Here, "civic life" is devoid of the Black freedom struggle. It is exemplified by the responsibilities of the citizen (i.e., "ask not what your country can do for you—ask what you can do for your country"), while ignoring the debts the nation owes to various communities.

The Freedom Schools formed by organizations like the Student Nonviolent Coordinating Committee (SNCC) in states across the southern United States were designed as free alternative schools for Black communities. They were formed in response to the inadequate outcomes of the 1954 *Brown v. Board* Supreme Court decision that outlawed racial segregation in schools by law but not in practice. Freedom Schools centered political education that would prepare youth to agitate the State through organizing and protest. They also allowed for Black studies and preparation for the violent responses of the State to political agitation. Now, I ask the reader, which of these, State-run schools or Freedom Schools, is public education?

Nearly a century ago, educational theorist and a founder of Black studies Carter G. Woodson recognized this dilemma. Woodson saw the circular logic of State-run education that produced the hubris we see today in mostly white (and some BIPOC) education officials who continue to think they can predict with certainty the life paths of any child at any given time. This is the hubris of college, career, and civic life readiness. The structure rationalizes itself by ensuring that those who succeed demonstrate their faith to the parameters they were given. They are not asked to think critically about the nature of the State, and thus are put in positions of leadership to perpetuate its existence. Woodson also saw the circular effect on Black folks, whom he described as being more miseducated the further they went through this system. The outcome for educated Black folks was to look down upon where they have come from, yet be positioned as leaders of "lesser" Black folks.

In his classic text *The Mis-Education of the Negro*, Woodson wrote, "The same educational process which inspires and stimulates the oppressor with the thought that he is everything and has accomplished everything worth while, depresses and crushes at the same time the spark of genius in the Negro by making him feel that his race does not amount to much and never will measure up to the standards of other peoples. The Negro thus educated is a hopeless liability of the race."

The structures of education in Minnesota are designed to crush the outrage *sparked* by the killing of George Floyd. The outrage is the mark of genius in the public that recognizes State violence for what it is—a necessary function of the State and not an anomaly.

The French philosopher Michel Foucault acutely described this necessary violence of the State. Breaking it down to its most basic sense, Foucault suggested that the sovereign State seeks to exercise control over life and death of its subjects—those we call citizens and/or residents—specifically by determining who is vulnerable to preventable death. "The power to make live and let die" is how the modern nation-state has come to exercise this conception. Sometimes the State literally kills through the death penalty or police violence, but these are the extremes of State violence. More mundane practices happen through "letting" people die based on lack of access to health care, the vulnerabilities of poverty, forcing people to risk their lives for material necessities, or targeted surveillance by police. According to Woodson, educational dispossession is also a mechanism by which the State "lets" people die. Woodson reminds us that personhood and history are inextricably linked.

In fact, as a doctoral student at Harvard around 1910, Woodson found the inception of his life's work by challenging one of his "distinguished" professors, Edward Channing, who claimed that the Negro had no history. When Woodson retorted that "no people lack history," Channing challenged Woodson to prove him wrong. This example may sound ridiculous today, but the State's educational structures and the dispossession of history from Black youth are effectively repeating this scenario every day in nearly every classroom. Black communities are being mocked and asked to prove the State wrong by studying their history outside of school buildings.

Black communities have been engaged in these self-education projects since we were brought to this continent. Whether by firelight in the woods, gathering out of sight in churches and barns, developing our own schools, designing our own curricula, building information-sharing networks and educators' unions, or, today, creating our own webcasts, we have always educated ourselves. However, the amount of time and energy we have spent fighting the State to also educate us is incalculable. The State has made the slightest of concessions over time. Black children receive watered-down narratives of civil rights heroes and inventors. Black History Month celebrations open up a tiny window to acknowledge that Black people have such a thing. As Africana studies scholar Yannick Marshall noted in *The Black Myths Podcast*, "the past always absolves the present." We can look to the most violent forms of Black curricular dispossession, such as history textbooks that described Black people as mentally inferior, as a way to see the erasure of Black studies today as some form of progress: "At least we're not degrading you anymore." But to understand State schools as engaging in a project of anti-Black violence is a more accurate and effective way to situate ourselves moving forward.

My exhaustion on the Zoom call with the Minnesota Department of Education was not coincidental or accidental or novel. It was simply an indication of a social order operating effectively—a parlor trick of the State. Our contemporary battles in "public" education are mediocre. The demands we are making are diluted versions of battles lost to history. We are pleading to institutions that are in the business of developing actors and accomplices to State murder and silent bystanders, begging for concessions from those whose puny imaginations are bound up by their very histories. Let's not forget that the officers who killed George Floyd, the district attorneys who would not prosecute Jamar Clark's killers, and the judges who presided over and failed to bring justice to Philando Castile's killer were all holders of multiple degrees from Minnesota's educational institutions. We are not dealing in metaphor.

In his 1972 book *No Name in the Street*, James Baldwin shed light on this social arrangement through his juxtaposition of justice and liberty. It is the eternal struggle Baldwin faced in his recognition of the contradiction of his Blackness and his Americanness. He recognized a similar struggle in the fabric of the colonial relationship between France and Algeria. Baldwin wrote, "It is power, not justice, which keeps rearranging the map, and the Algerians were not fighting the French for justice (of which, indeed, they must have had their fill by that time) but for the power to determine their own destinies." Baldwin's framing of justice is about some perception of fairness within a prearranged set of power relations. Justice is merely about a tolerable arrangement on a map that someone or something with more power gets to arrange. It is the struggle of Black people in the United States to perpetually fight for "civil rights." It is in every colonial arrangement where someone else is able to define our identity and the borders of our existence. And it is in the way the Minnesota Department of Education constructs education for Black youth. We have betrayed the struggle handed to us by our ancestors by fighting on terms of justice rather than on terms of liberty, self-determination, and power.

What would it mean to reframe our struggle through the lens of education for liberation rather than social justice; to determine our destinies rather than be ranked against the standards of whiteness—white language, white history, white subjectivity? How do people go about changing the mode through which a struggle is waged, instead of merely fighting about the positions of pieces on the chessboard? These are the questions that confront us as much today as when Baldwin penned his interpretation, perhaps even more so. My recognition of the futility of engaging power over Zoom, with the comments disabled, led by the disembodied white man, could be seen as a data point in a much larger study of power. The progressive illusions of the twenty-first century are the gains Black communities have made in terms of access to the power structure. If that access cannot translate, for instance, into Black children learning Black history as Garvey demanded a century ago, then what is it actually worth?

Mounds View, MN
January 4, 2021

Brian D. Lozenski is an associate professor of urban and multicultural education in the Educational Studies Department at Macalester College in St. Paul, Minnesota. His research explores the intersections of critical participatory action research, Black intellectual traditions in education, and cultural sustainability.

"End White Supremacy"

From Black Lives Matter to the Toppling of the Columbus Statue: A Testimonio from San Pablo

Gabriela Spears-Rico

As an Indigena born in Michoacán and raised in California, I never thought I would be living in Minnesota, far from my homeland and the Chumash coasts that raised me. My marriage to an Indigenous Minnesotan brought me here. Love brought me here, and love keeps me here, even in the midst of racial and viral pandemics. I have learned how to navigate the temporality of Mni Sota Makoce and the challenges and beauty of its seasons. I have community and family here, and I've gotten to know the Dakota people who steward this land. My partner and I consciously decided to raise our daughter here, in the Dakota territory that her fifth great-grandfather—her great-great-great-great-great-grandfather—Standing Buffalo called home. From this geographical position, away from Michoacán (my own "place of the fishermen"), I chose to teach my daughter Miskikwe to rematriate the space with her presence.

In 1863, upon the end of the US–Dakota War, my daughter's fourth great-grandmother Many Tracks was marched out of Mni Sota by white soldiers. She was ten years old. According to my daughter's third great-grandfather John Barry, Many Tracks was removed to Fort Sully "along with other peaceable Sioux for safety." And while I sometimes fear for our safety while living with white supremacy in this very racialized space, we stay. We stay despite the looks of disapproval we get in stores from older white Minnesotans. We stay regardless of the microaggressions I've experienced as a very brown woman while working for long-established Minnesotan institutions. We stay despite public assaults on Native identity by museum exhibitions and theatrical productions that display settler narratives. We stay even though I don't feel safe driving through Trump country to get to my partner's homeland (Red Lake). We stay even though my daughter and my husband are outlaws on their own lands due to an outdated law that bans Dakota people from being in Mni Sota. We remain in hopes that our daughter Miskikwe will wage war against the white settler violence that traffics in the erasure of Indigenous people (she is entangled in these conflicts by virtue of belonging to a tribal nation here). And, as a displaced Mexican Indigenous migrant, I will stand by her side. Every time. I will stay for her and for Latinxs and for my Black brothers and sisters to continue challenging the racism that hides behind the veil of Minnesota nice.

Having been raised in a community of Mexican migrant farmworkers and the white "aggies" who underpaid us in Nipomo, California, I grew up navigating rigidly divided class and racial lines. As a child, I understood the insults hurled at my parents because I spoke English and they did not. I learned to live with the disgusted looks of white people, our landlords' snide comments, the accusations of gringos in the laundromat who called us thieves. I learned to hold back tears upon hearing my folks referred to as "strawberry pickers" or "dirty Mexicans" by my teachers. In my brown skin, with my Indigenous face and short stature, I am no stranger to racism, nor am I a stranger to the dissent that emerges organically from experiencing racist violence. It was knowing the realities of poverty and racial exploitation and witnessing my mother walk out of the fields yelling "Huelga!" alongside her compañeros that led me to organize in high school and in college.

I came to Chicana consciousness in the midst of Proposition 187, a xenophobic initiative approved by California voters in 1994 that would have deprived immigrants of access to medical care and public education had it not immediately been found unconstitutional, and Proposition 227, a xenophobic initiative that passed in 1998, which eliminated bilingual education in California public schools until it was reversed by Proposition 58 in 2006. I started leading chapters of Movimiento Estudiantil Chicana/o de Aztlán (MEChA) to fight this overwhelming xenophobic climate in our state that targeted immigrant students like me. College helped contextualize and grow my rebellion because it gave me the opportunity to meet and organize with students of color from various backgrounds.

Leading MEChA at Stanford allowed me to form ties with the leaders of other groups for students of color. We formed the Students of Color

Coalition and campaigned for community center funding, got people of color elected to executive positions in the student government for the first time in the university's history, and rallied against Proposition 21, an initiative passed by Californians in the year 2000 that required adult trials for juveniles fourteen years of age and older and increased punishment for crimes committed by youth. We viewed this proposition as an acceleration of the school-to-prison pipeline.

My journey to becoming an experienced and conscientious organizer was purposeful. Having not grown up around many Black people, I was interested in learning about Black struggles due to the close alliances that Mexican American and African American communities had during the civil rights movement. I enrolled in Black studies courses and I lived in Ujamaa, Stanford's African American–themed dorm. Learning that racism operated through a Black-White binary by exerting the most violence on Black bodies led me to become invested in fighting for Black humanity through the struggle to end police brutality. After Amadou Diallo's murder in New York City in 1999, my friends and I took over Stanford's White Plaza and marched through Palo Alto. As a graduate student at Cal Berkeley, I participated in the Oscar Grant protests in Oakland and met formidable activist Alicia Garza, who would go on to cofound Black Lives Matter.

Trayvon Martin's murderer had been pardoned by a grand jury shortly after I arrived in Minneapolis in 2013. Angry and disillusioned, my husband and I attended the protest on July 16 in Minneapolis. As a recently hired academic adviser for the Martin Luther King Jr. Program at the University of Minnesota, I helped organize and facilitate a campus-wide conversation on how Trayvon's killing impacted our students of color. I believed that working for the MLK Program, which was established following the Black-led Morrill Hall takeover, also required of me a commitment to Dr. King's legacy as a staff person. Being an advocate for students of color is still a personal priority now that I serve the university as an assistant professor. Thus, when I witnessed on social media George Floyd's gruesome murder at the hands of Minneapolis police, the people I worried about were my students, because I knew that, like twenty-something me, they would be on the front lines, standing up for Black humanity, during a critical moment in our country's history.

May 26, 2020, was a regular Tuesday in my daily pandemic routine. I was wrapping up a fellowship year and woke up early to write before my daughter's homeschooling schedule began. As customary, I checked my Facebook feed for familial and national news updates. I noticed one post from a local Chicana activist affiliated with the Brown Berets: a video of a Black man being held on the ground by a white police officer with a knee on his neck. I noticed the city: Minneapolis. And the date: yesterday. This atrocity happened yesterday in our proximity, in the city my husband was born in, blocks away from where his family still lives in his childhood home. Used to bearing witness to police killings of Black men on social media, I knew this was another horrendous murder that somebody had videotaped. But watching even a clip of this video sat differently. The multiple officers. The mockery of bright daylight. The smug look on this white man's face. The sunglasses he casually adjusted while killing a man. The victim's cries for his mama. The nine-minute length. The knee on the neck. With a similar reaction to the snuff videos taped by Mexican drug cartels that I've encountered in my research, I stood up from my chair in horror. I couldn't contain the emotions that bubbled from the pit of my stomach; I ran to my bathroom to vomit.

My husband woke upon hearing me retch. "What's wrong?" he asked. "MPD killed a Black man at Cup," I cried. Cup. He knew exactly where that was. He went into that store as a teenager to buy snacks. We had gone into the store together before. I had gone in there once when we first moved to town to buy a microwavable hamburger that made me so sick, we swore to never shop there again. "Do you remember the burger I ate there?" I asked Chester. "I think I'm throwing it up all over again, years later." We held each other for a few minutes, both of us shaking.

I returned to the computer and called my sister in Oakland while scrolling through my friends' commentary and reactions. By this time, my sister, a professional organizer, had seen the video. "What do I do?" I asked her. I shared my plans to attend the day's march. "Look, Gabby," she said to me, "your partner is severely immunocompromised. And, as the head of household and a mother, you have to assess the risks you're willing to take. This is going to get rightfully confrontational. This is going to be as big as Rodney King. Stay home for now and see how you can support as the situation evolves."

Having lived through the 1992 Los Angeles uprisings in Southern California, my sister knew that referencing them would trigger memories of worrying about our family and friends in LA while consuming violent footage of the riots as children. I stayed home that day after Floyd's murder, glued to the news and my phone, texting all my friends who I suspected would head to the front lines. My vulnerable mother-in-law lived near ground zero; my former students, colleagues of mine, and my brothers-in-law took to the streets. By the third day, I was at George

Floyd Square demanding justice with First Nations United (FNU), an organization started by my husband's family. We met and kept in touch with neighbors we had never spoken to before. Everything in our lived reality changed.

Upon hearing that protesters had taken over stores on Lake Street, we realized that the push for justice would escalate, and we didn't falter from openly supporting the protests. We sent money to the bail fund and lent our labor to mutual aid efforts. We held Zoom meetings with our neighbors and family members to express our position and garner further support. I called my relatives to have conversations about anti-Blackness. I talked to my dad about why I felt the burning of Wells Fargo near Lake Street was justifiable considering the historical connections between white wealth and enslaved labor. As a former migrant farmworker who'd been sprayed with pesticides and denied wages, he grasped my position.

On May 28, the dissent reached my St. Paul neighborhood. Stores we frequented were broken into and burned to the ground. There was a standoff at our neighborhood Target that made us turn around from a shopping trip. A gas station blocks from us had its windows busted and was shut down. We had to explain to our child that we were watching the news more to make sure that everything was okay with her uncles, who were out patrolling with FNU to protect Native-owned buildings. Upon hearing from our contacts on the ground that white supremacists were en route, we packed go bags with immediate necessities and informed our relatives at Red Lake to expect us should we have to abandon our home.

By May 29, white supremacist organizations made their appearance in visible numbers in the Twin Cities. People in my diverse lower-middle-class neighborhood received racist notes threatening arson against their homes for having Black Lives Matter signs on their lawns and in their windows. "Your home burns next," the notes read. Proud Boys in Hawaiian shirts were also spotted in vehicles displaying white supremacist adornments while missing license plates. On May 30, the Klu Klux Klan was spotted meeting at a park two miles away from us, and the National Guard was deployed to our neighborhood. We slept intermittently, taking turns while one of us kept watch. Our white neighbors organized a patrol to protect families of color, but knowing that as an Indigenous family we could be targets, for the first time in our lives we armed ourselves. My brother-in-law dropped off hunting rifles before taking his family to the reservation as night descended. My husband, an army veteran, gave me a two-hour training on how to shoot a rifle that felt too heavy for my frame. Thinking back to my ethnic studies classes and my strong stance against gun violence, I felt numb from shock and grief as I held the cold, hard weapon.

As an American Indian–Latino household, our biggest nightmare was that we'd one day have to wield weapons to protect our daughter from white mob violence. And we were as afraid of the militarization of our community as we were of the white gangs that stormed our cities. Keeping in touch with friends at ground zero, it was intense to realize that we were not alone as first-time weapon wielders. An artist Chicana/o couple we knew patrolled a gas station in their neighborhood with baseball bats. They were afraid that outside arsonists would target the gas station just as outsiders had burned down other gas stations, putting folks in danger in nearby barrios, which had been evacuated in previous days. My people, Mexican immigrants, stood outside of their businesses keeping vigil all night to ensure their mom-and-pop shops would still be standing in the morning. My husband and I took turns patrolling our block and securing the perimeter as men with gas cans were reported on the neighborhood text thread. Everything was topsy-turvy, and I felt like I was watching it all from above, outside of my body.

As we were being terrorized, the police violence against Black and Brown bodies ramped up. On May 31, the date that marked my fortieth birthday, I watched WCCO in disbelief as the National Guard used tear gas and rubber bullets to clear the streets of protestors. It was intense to witness these events that questioned Black and Brown humanity while I was just miles away, and while my students, friends, and colleagues of color were in the crowd taking fire. I cried constantly and had to call upon the strongest in my family to keep me grounded. I hardly watched national coverage, though I knew that uprisings had erupted in numerous other cities. I had to stay focused on what was happening locally. I had to call my folks daily to check on them and ask how I could assist their needs.

The most affected within my circle was one of my former students, a Chicano who always smiled in my class but rarely discussed his personal beliefs. I never realized how committed or politicized he was until I found myself checking in and worrying about him daily. "Are you going out today?" was the morning message I would send him. He was a constant presence at ground zero until he was hit with rubber bullets in sensitive areas of his body for not dispersing from a crowd fast enough. I led efforts within my network to raise funds to cover his hospital bills. It was important to me that my colleagues and I offered concrete support to those on the front lines beyond releasing departmental solidarity statements condemning George Floyd's killing.

I navigated all of this while also mourning George, thinking of the two degrees of separation he'd had from me while working as a security guard at a Latino nightclub. Some of my friends and family had met him in passing at El Nuevo Rodeo, and he was always kind and friendly to Boricuas and Mexicans. George's cries for his mama are all I heard many nights as I fell asleep. It is the most primordial cry we have as human beings—the same cries my baby expressed as an infant when hungering for my breast, the same cries I shouted when I was separated from my mother at an early age.

To release some of my grief and rage, I smudged and helped prepare medicine bundles for my community, all along thinking of Floyd and his family, upset that in the new decade we are still fighting for the humanity of my own Chicano and Indigenous brothers, of Black people, of Black men like Jamar Clark, George Floyd, and Philando Castile. I found solace in a poster my daughter had scribbled and helped me place at George Floyd Square—a sign that read "Solidaridad con la Comunidad Afro-Americana." The poster was photographed by friends who tagged us on social media. Images of the poster gave my daughter a sense of pride. Perhaps this will be a lesson she will remember. Maybe her generation will fight more effectively than us because we're teaching her that it doesn't have to be this way in her homeland; that she can imagine and fight for a more healing and decolonized Minnesota.

On June 10, our FNU collaborator, Mike Forcia, called for the removal of the Christopher Columbus statue in St. Paul. I attended the protest to show my support for this act and share my outrage that a monument to genocide was still standing on the capitol grounds despite years of American Indians expressing their objections through established channels. Being present at the statue's toppling allowed me to openly mourn and heal, even if just a bit, after weeks of unrest over the killing of George Floyd. As I took my spot in the round dance celebrating Columbus hitting the ground, tears welled in my eyes from the radical solidarity I witnessed. Black, Brown, Asian, and white people partook in the protest. Reflecting on the significance of this Indigenous-led public declaration of humanity, I looked up to see a huge banner near the fallen statue. "End White Supremacy" it read, and I remembered that this was the goal that the entire two weeks of revolution, struggle, and fires was aimed at accomplishing. Sitting with this epiphany, I held between my hands a piece of the rope that moments earlier had brought down the statue. I thought about the future. Millions of people organized and protested to demand the end of white supremacy after George Floyd's murder. I would take this piece of rope home to my daughter as a symbol that together, as Indigenous people and people of color, we can spark revolution and take on the mightiest of topplings.

St. Paul, MN
January 21, 2021

Gabriela Spears-Rico is an assistant professor of Chicano-Latino studies and American Indian studies at the University of Minnesota. She has a PhD in ethnic studies from the University of California, Berkeley, and is a Mellon Fellow and a Woodrow Wilson Fellow. Her scholarship appears in Chicano studies and Indigenous studies publications. She is also a poet.

"Beyond the Borders of the State"

Being Native in Minnesota

Katrina Phillips

I have lived in Minnesota half my life. I grew up in rural northern Wisconsin about half an hour southeast of Duluth, moved to Minneapolis for college, and have yet to live anywhere else besides these two states. I'm also a citizen of the Red Cliff Band of Lake Superior Ojibwe, and our reservation, created through an 1854 treaty, sits on the south shore of Lake Superior near the famed Apostle Islands. The Midwest as a whole—and particularly my two home states—has long considered itself a bastion of racial equality. Yet the memory of an elementary school classmate lying to me, telling me that the bus driver didn't allow Indians on her bus, is forever burned in my brain. My ethnic ambiguity means that supposedly well-meaning Minnesotans speak to me in bumbling Spanish or follow me off a bus to ask if I'm Mediterranean.

On the Saturday after George Floyd's murder—and after yet another day of protests that turned to violence at night—I took my six-year-old son down to Pow Wow Grounds/All My Relations, a coffee shop and art gallery in Minneapolis's American Indian Cultural Corridor. They'd posted a call for donations and volunteers, and I wanted to show my son what Indigenous community organization looked like. On the drive, we talked about George Floyd, racism, and why so many people are sad and mad and frustrated. I'd been dreading this conversation, but like so many other parents in Minnesota, I had to explain to our beautiful, funny, smart—and brown—son that he and his little brother might encounter people who'd treat them differently based on the color of their skin or because they're Native.

As I talked to my son, the fact that I had to teach him the same things I teach my college students took my breath away. While my courses on Native history cover broad geographic and temporal ranges, the US–Dakota War plays a pivotal part in my early Native history class. In the fall of 1862, as the Civil War raged and threatened to tear the country apart, Minnesota governor Alexander Ramsey called a special session of the state's legislature. Frustrated by a lack of government-promised annuities and faced with stingy traders who refused to extend credit, Dakota people in the southern part of the state had taken up arms in order to feed their families and force the government to act. Ramsey called for retribution in his speech to the legislature, insisting that "the Sioux Indians of Minnesota must be exterminated or driven forever beyond the borders of the state." The battles of the US–Dakota War ended within a few weeks, but the government's response to Dakota resistance has left deep scars across the state. A military tribunal condemned more than three hundred Dakota men to die, but President Abraham Lincoln—just a few weeks out from delivering the Emancipation Proclamation—felt that number was too high.

On the day after Christmas in 1862, thirty-eight Dakota men were simultaneously hanged in Mankato in what remains the largest mass execution in the history of the United States. The surviving Dakota were imprisoned at either Fort Snelling or Davenport, Iowa, through the winter. In February 1863, the US Congress passed legislation that abrogated all treaties the United States had signed with the Dakota. A subsequent bill removed the Dakota from their ancestral lands. Ho-Chunk people living in southern Minnesota were also forcibly removed from their lands. They hadn't been involved in the war, but historian Peter DeCarlo contends that colonists wanted the Ho-Chunks' prime agricultural land. Ojibwe people in northern Minnesota also resisted the government's impositions in the early 1860s, and the state narrowly avoided another Indian war.

As a historian, I shouldn't be surprised by the ways in which the events of the past rise up to meet us, to greet us, or to haunt us. But I am. Minnesota serves as a microcosm of racial tensions and entanglements, from the early-nineteenth-century treaties with Native nations and the practice of slavery at Fort Snelling to suburban Edina's experimentation with redlining and the 1970s development of American Indian survival schools in Minneapolis and St. Paul. In the week following George Floyd's murder at the hands of a Minneapolis police officer, I wrote a piece for the *Washington Post*, "Longtime Police Brutality Drove American Indians to Join the George Floyd Protests," that connected the presence of

Native protestors to the 1950s federal policies that led to the growth of Minneapolis's Native population. This growing population, coupled with increased police brutality, pushed Native activists to create the American Indian Movement (AIM) in 1968. As the national and international spotlight turned a sharp eye toward Minneapolis in the summer of 2020, I wrote about the historic and contemporary experiences of Black and Native people in Minnesota. Using Fort Snelling as the centerpiece, I traced the connected histories of racism and violence against Black and Native people. I wrote about the Indigenous history of what's now Minneapolis, turning toward the more recent efforts of Native activists around the push to reclaim the name Bde Maka Ska and the toppling of the Christopher Columbus statue in St. Paul.

This piece should have been an easy one to write. I know the history, I've done the research and the analysis, and I've been writing about different facets of it for years. The kicker with this one, though, is that I can't just focus on the history anymore. I've spent years trying to convince myself that my encounters with racism in Minnesota have been purely accidental. I've tried to paint them as anomalies, not as indications of broader systemic and structural issues. I've wrestled with how—and when—to teach my sons how to protect themselves from the words and actions that might come their way. But George Floyd's death was the match that lit the tinder as protests sprang up around the world and as statues celebrating colonizers and oppressors came tumbling down.

My son and I pulled into the parking lot at Pow Wow Grounds/All My Relations. We had packed grocery bags with donations, and they asked if we could stay to help sort things. They'd turned the art gallery into the drop zone, and propped-open doors greeted a near-constant stream of people. A group of men, some of whom wore AIM shirts and jackets, stood in the parking lot. Some volunteers brought a bag or two of food, water, and supplies, and others brought truckloads. Some stayed to help; others just dropped by on their way. One woman brought in several armloads of fire extinguishers—she'd purchased all she could find at a local hardware store. A couple brought some tents and sleeping bags in addition to a carload of food and water.

My son showed people where to set their donations, and he proudly carried jars of peanut butter and jelly, boxes of pancake mix, bags of fruits and veggies, and loaves of bread to their designated spots. A team of volunteers put together what we called "snack packs"—brown paper grocery bags with ready-to-eat food so the folks who headed out for the night patrols could just grab a bag and go. The night patrols mirrored the

1960s AIM patrols that protected community members from potential police brutality, but now the people on patrol were intent on protecting their communities, their businesses, their organizations, and their homes from the nightly destruction that had started accompanying the protests. Others began preparing bags of food to drop off for elders who, like many others, were cut off from access to critical resources.

When we left a few hours later, I apologized because we couldn't stay longer. The woman in charge grinned and shrugged her shoulders. "We all have our place in a riot," she said, "and ours is here." Here—a place that so many of us love but that rarely loves us back. A place that holds Bdote, the center of the Dakota creation story. A place that holds Ojibwe history, Dakota history, Ho-Chunk history, and the histories of other Native nations. I'm reminded of Patrick Wolfe's thesis on settler colonialism, a form of colonialism that works to replace the original population of the now-colonized territory with a new society of its own settlers. At the crux of his argument in "Settler Colonialism and the Elimination of the Native" is what he deems the "logic of elimination," meaning the ways in which settler colonialism "destroys to replace."

"Land is life," Wolfe argues, "or, at least, land is necessary for life. Thus contests for land can be—indeed, often are—contests for life." For those of us who have called or still call Mni Sota Makoce our home, Indigenous history is deeply embedded in how we experience the land where the waters reflect the clouds.

Maple Grove, MN
December 23, 2020

Katrina Phillips (Red Cliff Ojibwe) is assistant professor of Native history at Macalester College. Her first book, *Staging Indigeneity: Salvage Tourism and the Performance of Native American History*, examines the role of Native history in regional tourism endeavors. Her second book will center Red Cliff activism, environmentalism, and tourism.

Rediscovering My Purpose
The Politics of Race, Access, and Change

Brittany Lewis

Act I

My mother's goal in life was to move our family out of the Phillips neighborhood that lies adjacent to downtown Minneapolis and to a new opportunity in the suburbs. This new opportunity in Eagan, Minnesota, included having our garage spray-painted and finding the word "nigger" etched into my locker at school. That day, I left school early and walked home to tell my parents, "I'm not going back." We left the suburbs and moved back to the city, ultimately settling on Minneapolis's north side.

My mother's desire to be closer to the resources she never had is not an uncommon story. There are many Black folks who are disillusioned by the experiences they've had growing up without adequate resources, but leaving those spaces and entering more affluent ones can be traumatizing for their children, who are forced to endure racial trauma in the pursuit of access and privilege that a close proximity to whiteness is assumed to yield.

Act II

When I came out as a queer Black girl, my family abandoned me. In their place, a loving Black woman with little means took me in. Behind yet determined, I was the first student from my high school to go to Macalester College. Once there, I got a tutor and was told that I had moxie and was someone with enough cleverness, skill, and determination to face anything. While an undergrad, I became keenly aware of the systemic nature of poverty and how my life experiences had been shaped by people in power and the data they used to create policies aimed at controlling my existence. Most of the research about Black women frames us as objects of study or the causes of urban poverty. I decided that I wanted to create research that builds power within the community and provides equitable policy solutions.

At the age of twenty-eight, I would earn a doctorate degree in gender, women, and sexuality studies with a focus on urban housing policy and racialized gendered resistance, while mothering two children and becoming a first-time author. Society would have predicted a different outcome for me. Instead, I became a respected thought leader and scholar, bringing hundreds of low-wealth families across the region to the decision-making table through collaborative research. Although I have been honored by receiving scholarly awards and offers for tenure-track positions, these never defined my vision of success. Rather, my success is rooted in reimagining how data influences public policy and in becoming a leader who works with the community as my collaborators.

Act III

According to the US Census, 1.68 percent of Americans over the age of twenty-five have a doctorate degree. Of that 1.68 percent, less than 2 percent are Black women like myself. On average, it takes eight years to complete a doctorate degree; I completed mine in six. The realities of Black urban poverty, informed by my own experience as a young girl, necessitated that I develop an urgent and unwavering commitment to fight for myself and other Black women, whom national statistics tell us are leading all other women in labor force participation but who are forced into the low-wage sector. In addition, we are disproportionately impacted by evictions and faced with retiring with an average of a hundred dollars of wealth.

Despite my own convictions, I struggled to maintain my sense of purpose as a graduate student, quickly learning that the academy did not love me or my perspective and voice. I found many of the classroom settings to be hostile and would get into arguments with my professors. Most of these arguments were related to my questioning of how the course material, which was highly theoretical, could lend any relevant perspective to the lives of our nation's most impoverished community members. I was also forced to engage in debates with predominantly white graduate students who were simply trying to prove their own intellectual prowess by participating in bouts of intellectual masturbation without any conscious politics. I don't think they liked me very much. However, when I learned that my grades were on the line I decided to temper my approach, understanding the performative function of the academy, the classroom, and the ruses of whiteness. Like many of my graduate peers, I got caught up in the notion that there was only one way to do something. I learned later that this was how the PhD process was designed. It was not designed for Black women who wanted to create real, tangible change.

The professors who first taught me to value and honor my knowledge as a Black woman were Rachel Raimist and Duchess Harris at Macalester College. I will never forget bringing my firstborn with me to office hours, changing diapers and talking feminist politics with Professor Raimist, or bringing my daughter to my senior seminar, where Professor Harris talked about Black public intellectuals. I will also never forget what black feminist scholar bell hooks told me when I met her at the National Women's Studies Association Conference in San Juan, Puerto Rico. hooks advised me not to allow the conservative politics of the tenure process to overshadow my commitment to making my work accessible to the community I loved. She also warned me that the academy makes you forget why you pursued an advanced degree in the first place, pushing many women of color into depression and disillusionment.

In the spring of 2016, I left my teaching position at Bowdoin College after one semester, filed for divorce, and moved back to the Twin Cities, unsatisfied that my research was reaching only a privileged few. Since the communities I aimed to serve were not benefiting, I felt I was not living up to my purpose as a leader.

Act IV

In June 2016 I began my first non-tenure-track position as a research associate at the Center for Urban and Regional Affairs at the University of Minnesota, a move that many academic colleagues criticized. In less than three years, with coaching and the expansion of my network, I became a senior research associate in charge of the center's large-scale research agenda. I reframed the center's research model using community-centered action research and an equitable policy framework. For the first time, the center was no longer claiming a false objectivity about the data it was producing but was standing on concrete policy implementation recommendations.

As we worked, I guided the center in producing collaborative action research with the support of local influencers and empowered community participants using data to implement policy solutions. During my first year, I completed a study on gentrification, the findings of which were used by regional planners to build equitable development plans. In my second year, I completed an in-depth study of evictions in north Minneapolis, and these findings were used as direct testimony at the Minnesota State Legislature and in a Minnesota Supreme Court case that expanded tenants' rights. This study also informed a local funder's decision to pay for the redesign of the Hennepin County Emergency Assistance Program and to fund a pilot program that would eliminate the county requirement for shelter guests to pay to stay. In my third year, I was invited to be an expert witness on a federal class action lawsuit on behalf of plaintiffs who were sexually harassed by their landlords before being evicted. I also consulted with the Minneapolis City Council as it developed renters' protection ordinances.

Act V

Low-income communities of color are never in the room when research studies or reports that will impact them are being designed and written. This is the case even in a state like Minnesota, which is constantly honored for its progressive politics while data shows the most detrimental racial gaps in the nation. The outcomes usually don't favor communities. These studies tend to blame communities for the circumstances they are in, absolving local power brokers and erasing histories of disinvestment from responsibility for redistribution of resources. In reality, community-engagement strategies matter as much as the data collected and can work to disrupt uneven landscapes of power.

In 2020, in the aftermath of the murder of George Floyd, Dr. Joi Lewis and I received an invitation from the Department of Human Rights—the organization investigating the Minneapolis Police Department—and the Pohlad Foundation—an organization known for philanthropic giving in the areas of homelessness and housing—to cochair the Time of Reckoning, Healing, Listening, and Action task force. We held a series of quarterly community action and healing justice sessions that culminated in five Black-led town hall events and a final policy action roundtable focused on the criminal justice system and its collateral consequences.

We see this process as an opportunity for true "radical re-imagining" of what is possible within our collective efforts to advance racial justice. The community sets the agenda with the support of the cochairs and acts as lead facilitators to ensure that the ethical values of Black-led social change—transparency, accountability, healing justice, and community-centered practice—guide the creation of a policy action agenda that is intersectional.

The four pillars that structure our work—reckoning, healing justice, listening, and action—aim to support Black-led social change. *Reckoning* requires that we face oppression-induced historic trauma created by harmful criminal justice system practices and their collateral consequences. *Healing justice* asks us to embrace our need for radical self-care and social justice as we confront our traumatic histories and the present manifestations of those traumas in our communities. *Listening* invites us to develop shared meaning and understanding for the purposes of identifying the steps that we all must take to create the systemic change so desperately needed. *Action* transforms our shared understandings into the concrete strategies needed long term to transform the current criminal justice system into something that actually leads to safe communities.

Act VI

Black Minnesotans are far too accustomed to outside government leaders, researchers, and community-engagement practitioners demonstrating their political will through the use of equity-based language without producing any meaningful public policy or tangible results that directly impact our daily lives. The type of large-scale change I aim to create through my work requires building partnerships with the community. I want not to simply pull up a seat at the existing public policy table but also to work in collaboration with the community to reimagine the ethics of public policy that they want to see created. Moving beyond equity-based rhetoric toward purposeful innovative policies in a state with some of the largest disparities between white and Black populations, we should never shy away from supporting community-articulated needs and actions. However, it is a reality that I know all too well.

Minneapolis, MN
January 12, 2021

Brittany Lewis is the CEO/founder of Research in Action and a senior research associate at the Center for Urban and Regional Affairs at the University of Minnesota Humphrey School of Public Affairs. In 2020, Lewis was honored with a Bush Foundation Fellowship award and was named one of the Top 100+ Leading Black Women by the Minnesota Black Chamber of Commerce.

George Floyd Was Murdered on Dakota Land

Kate Beane

George Floyd was murdered on Dakota land. Gasping for life and calling out for his mother, he was killed just one block from where my children attended preschool. Within a matter of hours, the words "I can't breathe" reverberated across our city as we demanded accountability for harms caused by officers in uniform who are supposed to protect us. American Indians were visible and ready to defend from the beginning, as our community members stood up (during the middle of a pandemic) to support our brothers and sisters in solidarity. We all knew that this moment of reckoning was one rooted in a shared history of being marginalized and victimized simply for being who we are. As the Indigenous people of this land, and as warriors, the fight to protect our homelands from white supremacy goes all the way back to first contact.

Damakota, I am Dakota, citizen of the Flandreau Santee Sioux (Dakota) Nation, which is in present-day South Dakota, but my family descends from those who were removed from Minnesota under the Dakota Removal Acts of 1863. This removal, though amended by the State of Minnesota in 2012, is still federal law today, in the year 2021. The Dakota Removal Acts were policies that removed Dakota people from our homeland following the war that was waged against the US government and settler colonists in 1862. This divisive war was a result of the US government's failure to distribute treaty annuities for food to starving Dakota families during a time of great need. I was taught by elders in my community that our relatives fought to remain Dakota (treaty stipulations at the time were requiring us to assimilate); I was taught that our Dakota relatives who fought in the war were patriots, and that without their struggle I would not be here today.

My siblings and I grew up visiting our kunsi (grandmother) Lillian on our reservation in South Dakota. She was born in Sisseton and raised at

Wakpa Ipaksan (Bend in the River), also known as Flandreau. Our home community was a place Kunsi loved, where she proudly resided until her passing at the monumental age of one hundred and one years. She told us stories about where we come from, and she often recalled how her own grandmother had fled Minnesota on horseback during the Dakota War. That these atrocities happened to our grandparents' grandparents speaks to how recent this history is, how close these events still sit with us, and illustrate why the emotions that come with learning about this history are still raw for so many of us.

My family had returned to reconnect with our Minnesota homelands when I was an adult. Currently, I reside just a few miles from where our ancestors lived before the war, and two miles from where George Floyd was killed on Thirty-Eighth Street and Chicago Avenue. Today there is a vibrant urban American Indian community in this city, the surrounding metro area, and suburbs, and we are proud to live here, but it is not an easy place to be Indigenous, or a person of color. Though as American Indian people we are often left out of statistics that speak to our existence, we are present, we have a voice, and we are resilient. The red American Indian Movement flags and the familiar drum and tune of the American Indian Movement song were present, often at the forefront, at every Black Lives Matter protest that followed in the days and months after George Floyd took his last breath. Minneapolis, known to us as Bdeota (Many Lakes), is the birthplace of the American Indian Movement (AIM), born out of the Red Power movement of the 1960s. In those early days, armed AIM patrols formed to canvass neighborhoods and protect American Indian community members from the widespread police brutality in the Phillips neighborhood of south Minneapolis. There is a rich history of protecting our own in this city, and though the city's roots are deeply embedded in the perpetuation of racial violence, our ongoing community stories that unite us as Indigenous and people of color also highlight our common call to action and shared resistance.

For over a hundred years we have sought a historical acknowledgment of our colonial past as a society and community here in Minnesota. Yet acknowledging the past often seems too far-fetched and too difficult in a place that struggles to confront the injustices of today. Far too often we find ourselves forced to engage in the task of explaining and translating our pain for those who do not see it or live it every day. When we speak of Mni Sota Makoce (the lands where the waters reflect the sky), we must ask ourselves, *who is the "we" in "us"*? That answer lies in our collective history and is something we must help determine for our descendants. As an educator, I try to model for my own children that these lands and all the beauty and strength within this place we call home do not just belong to those who have been in power for the last two hundred years. Yet it often feels as if we are required to craft our words of dissent so very carefully. We are warned about rocking the boat of an already sinking ship of racist rhetoric, this legacy of complacency and passiveness that is also sometimes referred to as "Minnesota nice."

Just a few years prior to Floyd's murder, my father, my twin sister, and I had worked alongside others to restore the Dakota name Bde Maka Ska (White Earth Lake) to the largest lake in the city of Minneapolis. Almost two hundred years ago this body of water had been bestowed the settler name of Calhoun by whites in honor of former vice president and South Carolina senator John C. Calhoun, who was an aggressive advocate for the expansion of slavery across the western states. Calhoun helped to create the Bureau of Indian Affairs (BIA) within the War Department, signaling American Indians as the enemy of westward expansion. He would go on to draft the original version of the Indian Removal Act, which was signed into law in Washington, DC, in 1830. The Indian Removal Act opened the door for removal treaties and ushered in policies and practices of tribal ethnic cleansing and genocide (such as the Cherokee Trail of Tears). Though Calhoun's legacy was honored for what at the time was deemed "in perpetuity" with the naming of this lake, he had most likely never even set foot here on Dakota lands. Yet it was here that he was and has been for so many years memorialized. Calhoun's contributions represent a mindset that was honored by those who founded this city and the state of Minnesota. Names of white men such as Ramsey, Sibley, and Hennepin permeate Minnesota's landscape, from street names to counties to schools where our children are not taught the actions of these men or the impacts of their actions on communities today. We live and breathe every day surrounded by the language, symbolism, and direct impacts of white supremacy.

Often, when the forced removals of Dakota people are taught in this state (if even taught at all), the story is that we somehow simply decided to relocate elsewhere. And in Minnesota, for many years it was as if people just forgot that we were ever here. The vanishing Indian trope became a reality—except that some of our relatives never left, or returned over time, facts lost on many who choose to not see our continued existence (and survival) today. It is no irony that our language has remained everywhere in the land we were banished from, in place-names from Winona to Wayzata (Waziyata, meaning "the north"), Owatonna to Minnetonka. Somehow it is fine for the colonizer to anglicize our language for places, reworking our Native words to fit their foreign tongues to the point that we can barely recognize these words as our own. Yet when we proposed that a place of historic integrity and significance to our own be called by its rightful Dakota name of Bde Maka Ska, we were labeled radical activists, and our credentials as professionals and leaders in our community were questioned.

Although critics of the name restoration often stated that our language was too hard to pronounce, the Dakota language is already seen throughout this state and region; Minnesota itself is a Dakota word. It thus becomes clear that it was *not* our precious language that made the name restoration a problem for others, but rather the fact that it was the result of a concerted effort by Dakota people to reclaim our rightful place within a state that often does not acknowledge us—or recognize our language as belonging to us. In spite (or perhaps because) of all this, the Bde Maka Ska name was federally restored in the summer of 2018, and this decision was upheld by the Minnesota Supreme Court in 2020.

Those who fight back against oppressive, exploitative actions by those in power have historically paid the ultimate price. Here in Bdeota (Minneapolis), there is a long history of suppressing or omitting the perspectives of those who do not fit a singular narrative. Often rolled into the term "absent narratives," our Native stories have nevertheless prevailed over time as we continue to know and tell them. The hard truth is that our ancestors were never absent; they were just ignored or expunged from the master narrative of American exceptionalism, this nation's and state's inauthentic feel-good story. This tactic is not new in any way; colonization has been imposed upon Indigenous peoples throughout the world for centuries.

The work that people of color put in to correcting the state narrative and reinserting our voices is exhausting. It is tiring to constantly fight or argue ourselves back into existence day in and day out. And while we have seen a recent shift in public interest and support, the struggle of trying to educate people about complex histories when the "average Minnesotan" (whatever that means) doesn't even know who we as Dakota people are in the first place is a monumental burden to carry. The notion that our families and communities were viewed by white missionaries as "doomed to extinction" continues to impact both our educational and our justice systems, systemically racist structures we are rallying against as the "unfinished business of colonization." And despite the attempts of many to silence and eradicate us, we persist. We are still here.

During the Bde Maka Ska renaming efforts, it quickly became clear that my family's organizing work to restore Dakota language at one of our ancestral village sites had also made us a target. My father received hate mail at home, and open threats appeared regularly against my father, sister, and me in the local newspaper's comment section and on social media. Those who opposed the name Bde Maka Ska created a GoFundMe campaign and spent over $20,000 to advertise their position in local newspapers, as they did on December 4, 2017, in the *Star Tribune* with an ad that read: "Please Save Lake Calhoun. The Dakota Tribe and extremist political activists are unwilling to live and let live. And now our iconic Lake Calhoun is about to be erased forever." It was maddening that a few wealthy racist individuals (one of whom lived along the lake and did not wish to be inconvenienced by a change of address form) could so publicly declare the lake's existence was in jeopardy because of our language's association with it. On our end, we spent a total of thirty dollars to boost event notifications for public hearings so that our community members could show up to voice their perspectives on the issue.

What I never understood about statements decrying *historical erasure*, as related to Bde Maka Ska, was that there was no empathy for us as *people* who had been erased, only for words and names created by others tied to a nostalgic memory of times past that didn't include us. We eventually realized that the opposition was driven by an irrational fear: that we were going to do to them what they did to us. This seems to be a consistent fear for the oppressor, that they will become the oppressed.

Despite, or perhaps because of, a history of trauma, we as Dakota people have survived, and as we reclaim our traditional ways and create spaces for new ones, we have prospered. The thing about trauma is, as much as it informs our identities, it does not define who we are—only we can do that. Interwoven throughout our most difficult and troubled histories are just as many (if not more) stories of resilience. Those who pass on our traditions, our children relearning our languages, and the very survival of those who persevered so that we could be here today speak to this. The inherent spiritual power of this land is also something that we Dakota people know much about, and we saw this strength rise from the ashes in our neighborhoods during the summer of 2020.

That summer my family was living near the Third Precinct, where the police officers who killed George Floyd were stationed. This precinct building, and much of our beloved neighborhood, became the epicenter of social unrest and led to our local grocery, pharmacy, and other retail stores, our neighborhood restaurants and local library, banks, and post office being burned to the ground. The smoke was so thick around our home that we could not open our windows and my children, only four and six years of age, and struggling to feel hopeful in the midst of the coronavirus pandemic, could not play outside. Their father, a former BIA tribal police officer, often went out to check on what was happening in the neighborhood. During the first days of protests, the news stations could provide only limited media coverage, stating that it was "too dangerous" to venture into our neighborhood. So the only way we could find out what was happening a few blocks away was to check for ourselves or search social media for live feeds.

At night my children were frightened by the loud noises, and I told them, out of motherly worry, that the shots they were hearing (the National Guard shooting at protesters) were "just fireworks." I pride myself in speaking the truth to my children, but in this instance I was nervous about showing any anxiety to them. Although in no way a similar situation, I couldn't help but wonder what my grandparents, just children at the time, were told by their mothers when they were living through the Dakota War. Now as a parent I was straddling a line of speaking the truth and protecting my children's delicate young hearts.

Just as our children often watched their mother, grandfather, and auntie speak out at local hearings as a way to protect them and their identity as Dakota wankanyeza (sacred beings or children), they watched their father, Hinhan, join community patrols that were protecting our neighborhoods and our community organizations in the days following Floyd's murder. Hinhan was born and raised in the lakeside community of Oglala, South Dakota, on the Pine Ridge reservation, which is where the spiritual reawakening of the American Indian Movement took place in the 1960s and '70s. He remembers growing up with movement leaders visiting around the kitchen table with his parents and grandparents. He also remembers being told stories by his father about the FBI coming to the door of his childhood home when he was just a baby, and the dangers of being a full blood traditional Lakota living on the Pine Ridge reservation in that era. Watching him leave our home with his rifle worried me, but I also understood that his training and his commitment to caring for his community, passed down by his parents, needed to be honored. This personal connection between his own community's history and what was happening in this city also helped me to witness and better understand the ways in which the American Indian Movement and other civil rights movements of our past continue on through this current movement. We learn from and gain strength from those who came before us, and we carry their legacy. Witnessing history is not easy; it can be terrifying.

Over the summer, the violence that erupted each night seemed to dissipate just as quickly by dawn each day. By morning those who resided in the suburbs would arrive in droves to help clean up. Out of an abundance of caution, my husband and I waited a few days to show our children the devastation of our neighborhood. Our youngest noticed the crews cleaning graffiti off the side of a building and stated, "Oh nice, look Mama, those wasicu are cleaning up the mess that they made." A little farther down the block, we witnessed the rubble of burned-down buildings. And just as I was feeling overwhelmed about her seeing what had been destroyed, she said excitedly, "Mama, everything that's old is new again!"

At that moment I realized that what we were living through was helping my daughter see the true strength and resilience of her land. She saw value in what was left after the buildings were gone, and as traumatic as it felt to me to experience the destruction of these structures around us, what was left in her eyes was Dakota makoce (lands), pure and simple. I understood then that my children were much more resilient than I had given them credit for. My daughter recognized her home, and thanks to the teachings of our community and of those who came before her, she knew she belonged here. Today my children also know that George Floyd belonged here with us too, and they will always remember his name and legacy as being tied to Minnesota. They will speak his name, they will remember this historic moment, and they will be all the better for knowing their truth.

Bdeota (Minneapolis), MN
February 2, 2021

Kate Beane (Flandreau Santee Dakota and Muskogee Creek) holds a BA in American Indian studies and a PhD in American studies from the University of Minnesota, Twin Cities. A Dartmouth College Charles A. Eastman Predoctoral Fellow and University of California, Santa Cruz President's Postdoctoral Fellow, she is currently the director of Native American Initiatives at the Minnesota Historical Society and teaches Dakota history at Minneapolis College.

Unsettled Mourning

Kong Pheng Pha

Fong Lee, 2006–2010

On an unusually warm day in October 2010, I arrive at the Justice for Fong Lee rally and press conference at Cityview Elementary School in north Minneapolis, the site where nineteen-year-old Hmong American Fong Lee was murdered in cold blood by Minneapolis police officer Jason Anderson on July 22, 2006. I am wearing black jeans and a black oversized hoodie to show solidarity with the Lee family. A crowd forms lopsided circles around a white canopy tent where the Lee family has just announced that they will be appealing to the US Supreme Court to hear Lee's case. A year earlier, a federal appeals court had upheld a federal jury decision that Anderson did not use excessive force when he brutally murdered Lee at the elementary school, even though security camera evidence revealed that Lee was unarmed and was running away from Officer Anderson.

As I scan the crowd, my vision blurred by the tears clogging my eyes, I see a multiracial group of protestors—Hmong, Black, Asian American, White—carrying signs with slogans that now feel strangely unexceptional. "Why take my uncle away from me? Is riding a bike a crime?" "Racism Kills!" "Stop Police + MPD Cover ups. Justice for Fong Lee." "I is Fong, Fong is I, I is one, Fong is us." As we snake around the red brick school building and explore the killing fields in which Lee died, each step conjures intense emotions for me as a twenty-one-year-old college student, close to Lee's age. In that moment, I am Fong Lee and Fong Lee is me.

In December 2010, the US Supreme Court announced that it would not hear Lee's case. I immediately expressed my anger on social media: "I am EXTREMELY saddened by the Supreme Court's decision to deny a hearing on Fong Lee's case. Justice will be served, whether that be 1 year later, 5 years later, 10 years later, or 20 years later."

It has been more than ten years since Lee was murdered, and we are still waiting for justice.

Hmong Americans have long been subjected to state terror, perhaps most famous being our entanglement with the US settler-imperial state in the 1960s and 1970s as proxy soldiers for the Central Intelligence Agency's unjust secret war in Laos. Hmong people became refugees after the war and were later resettled in the United States, mostly into urban ghettos, where we endured the brutalities of spatialized and socialized segregation, housing inequality, police terror, and disproportionate criminalization that Black and Brown people have been experiencing for centuries.

Official discourses would have us believe that Minnesota welcomed Southeast Asian refugees with open arms. This welfare state version of Hmong refugee resettlement hides the imperial origins of Hmong displacement and the economic marginalization, policing, and criminalization that we continue to experience as a stateless people.

Scholars Bao Lo, Pao Lee Vue, and Kari Smalkoski have demonstrated that Hmong American boys and men are indiscriminately subjected to policing and surveillance in ways similar to Black boys and men. In fact, Vue argues in his book *Assimilation and the Gendered Color Line: Hmong Case Studies of Hip-Hop and Import Racing* that "Hmong are racialized like Asian Americans, but also stratified like poor African Americans." As children of non-English-speaking refugees, Hmong American boys and men are stereotyped as gun-toting gang members who should be profiled, surveilled, punished, and ultimately killed. I was horrified— although not surprised—when these stereotypes manifested themselves in Hollywood in the form of Clint Eastwood's film *Gran Torino*. I also recall disproportionate surveillance and punishment in schools, like the time a teacher chastised a group of us nine- and ten-year-old Hmong American kids for speaking our native language in gym class and put us in time-out. In essence, our refugee status enables our racialization as perpetually foreign and outside the US nation-state. Thus, we are punished simply for existing—in my case, being put in time-out; in Lee's case, being murdered. Our very presence is also distorted as deviant to English speaking, to US citizenship, to whiteness itself.

The Justice for Fong Lee rally and press conference and the subsequent dismissal of Lee's case by the Supreme Court fundamentally changed me.

I left the rally vowing that I would always fight against white supremacy. I promised myself that I would become a scholar and writer so I could document our experiences with racism and policing, and also our agency and the variously complicated cross-racial solidarities that constitute the unique threads of our Hmong American lives.

Jamar Clark, 2015

I was living in north Minneapolis when Minneapolis police officers Mark Ringgenberg and Dustin Schwarze murdered Jamar Clark on November 15, 2015, near the Fourth Precinct police station. Demonstrations erupted across the city. The most intense protests occurred just three blocks from my home, right in front of the Fourth Precinct station on Plymouth Avenue, a fixture I drove past nearly every day. Black Lives Matter activists established an encampment for two weeks at the precinct. Protestors blocked Interstate 94, and forty-two people were arrested. Protestors hurled rocks and Molotov cocktails at police. Minneapolis police retaliated with chemicals and tear gas. Four white men intruded upon the encampment and shot five protestors. After nearly a month of protests, police in riot gear forcibly removed the encampment with no regard for the well-being of the protestors.

After Clark's murder, I became involved with the Minneapolis chapter of APIs 4 Black Lives. The official purpose of APIs 4 Black Lives is to work for "social justice in solidarity with Black Lives Matter–Minneapolis and St. Paul to address anti-blackness in Asian American communities, advance cross-community collaboration, and increase Asian American and Pacific Islander participation in political and racial justice issues." As a collective, we organized door knocking across north Minneapolis to raise consciousness about Black Lives Matter, policing, and Jamar Clark. We were intent on elevating our communities' voices and experiences without judgment. We were prepared to engage in conversations with residents who opposed Black Lives Matter. We understood that authentic grassroots social movement building must involve engagement with the most marginalized and disenfranchised communities on the ground. By undertaking the challenging work of engaging our own Asian American communities, we were playing our part in the revolution by bringing our communities along on a collective journey toward social justice.

The majority of Asian American residents of north Minneapolis are working-class Hmong and Vietnamese Americans. They speak English primarily as a second language, if at all. A Hmong- or Vietnamese-speaking door knocker was always present during the canvassing. Conversations with residents outside their homes informed us that many of them had indeed faced ruthless policing. In an article I coauthored with my colleague Eunha Jeong Wood, "On Police Abuse and Black Lives Matter: Talking Asian to Asian in North Minneapolis," we discussed the multitude of experiences Asian American residents in the area had with police, including racial profiling, unjust detainment, unreasonable searches, and drawing weapons on non-English-speaking elderly folks. In essence, Asian American residents understood that they were disproportionately subjected to policing because of their race, ethnicity, and English-language proficiency.

The majority of residents also revealed in our conversations that they were not affected by the protests at the Fourth Precinct but cited disturbances such as delayed traffic and helicopter noise. It is significant to note that these disruptions were produced not by the protestors but by law enforcement agents who were surveilling the protestors.

Asian Americans are not apolitical. The media portrays our communities as being passively swept up in social movements, or even as the victims of protests carried out by Black Lives Matter activists. However, the research and grassroots activism by APIs 4 Black Lives highlight the complex racialized experiences of Asian Americans in north Minneapolis and across the United States. Hmong and Vietnamese American experiences of policing remain invisible within dominant discourses of racism and white supremacy. The "model minority" stereotype is also utilized by legislators and American society at large to divide and conquer communities of color, particularly Blacks and Asian Americans. Yet, through conversations and critical community engagement, APIs 4 Black Lives divulged that our experiences of race, racism, and racialization are both unique and inherently linked to the ongoing Black Lives Matter movement.

So how does one talk about policing as integral to Asian American experiences and senses of belonging in the United States? We pivoted our frame of reference from one of allyship within Black Lives Matter and the police abolition movement to one focused on the policing that is fundamentally embedded in our own lives as Asian Americans. I intimately understand that policing is an essential element of Hmong American racialization and racialized experiences. By doing our part, APIs 4 Black Lives laid the groundwork for how to live and breathe in the revolution.

George Floyd, 2020

Memorial Day is designated as a day of mourning. I carefully observed Mom sitting on a bamboo stool prudently situated on the cement front porch of our north Minneapolis home as she burned spirit money and incense for her father, my maternal grandfather, Zang Lue Chang, who passed away years ago. She then burned some spirit money for my paternal uncle Xiong Pha, who had died tragically in a drunk driving accident some twenty years earlier at the age of twenty-one. Their departed souls will be impoverished in the afterlife for all of eternity if we forget their deaths. So, in Hmong American religious practices, we burn spirit money and incense to pay respects to their wandering souls, hoping they can be led to redemption and rebirth.

On this particular Memorial Day, May 25, 2020, four police officers arrived at Cup Foods on East Thirty-Eighth Street and Chicago Avenue in south Minneapolis on a complaint of a customer using a counterfeit bill to pay for some cigarettes. What transpired is now all too familiar. The police officer apprehended George Floyd and cemented his knee on Floyd's neck. *I can't breathe.* An image of Eric Garner's murder flashes across my mind. The apparition of Jamar Clark, murdered blocks away from my north Minneapolis home, floats before me.

One of the officers involved in Floyd's murder was Hmong American Tou Thao. Why did he have to be Hmong American, like me? We have been victims of police killings. But at that moment, a Hmong American police officer helped murder an innocent Black man. All I could do was cry. But was I mourning because of Floyd's death? Or was I mourning because Tou Thao was involved? My agonizing emotions were confusing even for me to recognize. I finally realized I was experiencing an unsettled state of mourning that I still cannot properly articulate.

Protests erupted all over the nation, unlike anything I'd witnessed before. Not even the Jamar Clark protests and encampments at the Fourth Precinct were this intense. Buildings were burned. Stores were ransacked. Police in riot gear retaliated with a vengeance to disfigure and dismember protestors. Smoke bombs turned south Minneapolis into a war zone. Rubber bullets blinded journalists. Tear gas choked protestors. Flash grenades disoriented onlookers acting as witnesses. Would the protests make their way to north Minneapolis?

I wrote on social media: "My city Minneapolis essentially burned overnight. Please pray for our city. I'm feeling such a deep and profound sense of despair, pain, and anger in ways I don't know how to articulate.

This rebellion and uprising will only intensify for as long as racism exists. I'm still trying to survive a global pandemic while resisting state-sanctioned terror (aka police). I'm feeling like I'm at full capacity."

The following days seem to go by slowly. May is finally over. Summer is here. We have reached the halfway point of 2020. I am walking along Chicago Avenue toward the memorial for George Floyd that has grown at the site of his murder. An ensemble of Indigenous dancers gathers in a circle. Spectators in masks surround the dancers, as do I, to bear witness to a performance that soothes our souls. A beautiful mural has been painted on the side of the building in front of which he was killed. His name is painted in yellow, figures of confidently raised fists painted in blue tucked within the letters. Floyd's portrait is painted in the middle, the names of other Black folks killed by police written behind him. *I can breathe now*—these words complete Floyd's memorial. I solemnly kneel before the mural amid the flowers that fill the sidewalk, tears clouding my vision once again. I do not utter a single word, only wishing I could reach out and caress Floyd's beautiful face with my bare hands and pull him into a deep embrace.

I walk farther along Chicago Avenue to bear witness to the devastation brought by the rebellion. A National Guard military vehicle whirrs past, four smiling guards in the back flashing a peace sign to me. I walk past two elderly men observing a burned-down Chinese restaurant. I peek inside a stretch of stores, seeing only burnt tables and chairs and unidentifiable objects. There is a moment of pause. The weight of injustice sinks into my feet.

Pulling these scenes from my memory is difficult and painful. Yet I think about the strong Hmong American community that has formed in the Twin Cities in the last forty-five years and our resilience in challenging the cruelties of war, displacement, segregation, policing, and racism to ultimately make a life for ourselves. In the long history of Hmong American refugee resettlement and community building, it was Hmong Americans ourselves who had to assemble the splinters of our displaced lives to build the vibrant community we are today. We are thriving despite efforts by the US settler-imperial state to fragment our lives. In a similar vein, it was the community who pieced together Floyd's life at the memorial. The community is all that we have and all that we need in these moments.

I return to Fong Lee again and again because he gives me purpose.

I return to Jamar Clark because he gives me hope. I return to George Floyd because he gives me inspiration. Their spirits enable me to escape my perpetual state of unsettled mourning. Like Black Americans, Indigenous people, and other people of color living in the US racial caste system, Hmong Americans are seen as a threat to the white racial order and thus must be killed in order to perpetuate the myth of men and boys of color being inherently criminal. These realities should be compelling enough for us to wholeheartedly say #BlackLivesMatter! Being a Hmong American at a time of heightened policing is terrifying, but bearing witness to the world-shattering revolution for Black lives is liberating.

Eau Claire, WI
December 28, 2020

Kong Pheng Pha is assistant professor of critical Hmong studies and women's, gender, and sexuality studies at the University of Wisconsin–Eau Claire, where he teaches courses on critical race, feminist, and queer theories. His current book project examines the racialized, gendered, and queer dimensions of Hmong culture and their implications on Hmong social and political life in the United States.

All the Stars Point North

Wendy Thompson Taiwo

You are a child who doesn't know
the four cardinal directions.
Your mother tells you to look up
as the evening's pastel colors
fall away to the muted
blue-blackness of night.
There is one star, the brightest.
It will stay with you. Always,
she says. *And tell you the way home.*
How she knows that you out of
all her born children will travel
the farthest away is a mystery.
But for now, you feel safe,
knowing there is a map built into
the sky, ready to lead you.

Mother is another name for star.
Don't believe me?
Ask the voice belonging to the
neck crushed by a knee:
8 minutes and 46 seconds.
Mama. Mama.
She heard him, and all the stars
fell to earth in an inferno of black
rage that shriveled up precincts
built like armories. Then the
white supremacists came and

smashed out the AutoZone,
deliberate in their framework.
There will never be enough
stars or Norths to free those who
dream of colonizing Mars.

Minnesota is a map of lakes,
over 10,000. All of which hold
many stars at night.
That one there points north
and rides on the tail of
the Little Dipper. It is the same
star they saw in Charleston
and Savannah:
Nanny, country born, abt. 5 feet,
light complexion with full eyes,
and a tendency to speak
short and surly; Zephire, age 50,
African born and wearing
a leather hat, fluent in broken
English and French; and
yellow John Mordy and Robert
who saw it too before they
were caught and jailed
in Baton Rouge.

In a cabin,
in a swamp,
on a quilt (that's a myth),
in a Quaker's plainspoken word
that's kept,
freedom is a flicker,
is a barred owl's call,
is a patch (that's a myth),
is a secret carried to the grave,
sworn and true,
of a family of four
traveling west then north.

<u>Below are three math problems. You will have thirty minutes
to answer them.</u>

1.
Imagine the northern sky as
a large clock.
At what time does the little hand,
connected to Polaris,
point to freedom?

2.
What if you aren't thirsty?
Is there another constellation
you can follow instead of
the drinking gourd,
spilling over with all those
GPS directions north in song?
Turn right at the dead trees.
Turn left where the river ends,
between two hills.
Remain in the right-hand lane
behind left foot, peg foot,
travelin' on.
Rerouting.

3.
It is January, around 9:00 PM,
and you look up and see
Orion's Belt in the face of
three bright stars:
Alnitak, Alnilam, and Mintaka.
Do you still pack your sack with
hardtack and a kitchen knife
and emancipate yourself?

No cheating.

Minnesota is a cartography,
is a constellation of black people
who left other Souths

to head north
to the Promised Land,
to a safer Chicago.
Once there, we all became
Dred's children: behind the walls
of a military fort there was
no need for chains when
frozen ice sheets inhibit escape.
And so we stay because
the master keeps us fed
(we reason).
(And then there's Harriet.)

From the Purple One:

Baby I'm a (star)
Might not know it now
Baby but I are, I'm a (star)
I don't want to stop, 'til I reach the top
Sing it (We are all a star!)

What is a star but an astronomical
object full of luminous plasma
held together by gravity?

What is a star but a black woman
rising in the dark?

She has many names: Sirius, Vega,
Alpha Centauri A, Mimosa.

In the event that she expands,
throwing her heavy mass and deep
knowledge, her life-sustaining
energy and labor—thank her later
for saving the world—into
space to be recycled as new stars,
her core becoming
a stellar remnant.
An astrophysicist corrects me

at a public talk:
Not a nothingness, but a white
dwarf, a neutron star, or, if she
happens to be massive,
a black hole.
By the time you see her, she may
already be dead.

I used to be afraid of such things:
not the literal gap of blackness,
but a region,
the heaviest gravity eating through
the walls and roof,
through imagination and dreams,
consuming without end.
Is this not an apt metaphor for
black being in America?
Coming for the last crumb after
all that was stolen?
Isn't this why they remain armed
and gerrymander the smallest
abandoned lot?

The boundary of a black hole from
which there is no escape is called
the event horizon.
For every black person,
that boundary is both
the Mason-Dixon Line and the
Middle Passage.
That boundary is both
the crime of scarcity and the
battering ram of the police.
That boundary is the barely visible
demarcation between being the
one black friend and the
black person a white person
knows (and will vouch for).
That boundary at work is where
someone felt the need to

minimize or report, then,
passing too close,
got shredded before being
swallowed whole.
Witnessing this marvelous event,
the office staff became
understandably fearful and, in
plotting against her, call her
many names of their own making:
sassy, fiery, ghetto, angry.

A falling star that enters earth's
atmosphere is called black boy joy.
A falling star that survives
atmospheric entry and touches
the earth's surface is called
black girl magic.

If you want to see the stars,
my childhood friend tells me,
you need to go up into
the mountains, away from the city
and all its light pollution.
There you will find stars like
memory, fuzzy Polaroids
taken right before
the shouting and crying.
Tactile, sensory things that once
occupied your small nervous
hands but no longer exist.
You will find galaxies like
genealogies of stars,
stellar remnants, gas, dust,
and dark matter: people you
knew and know and look like.
The Milky Way is a film of
all of them together,
in a kitchen somewhere,
smiling on that one occasion
before someone threw your uncle

out. See him falling,
a meteor spotted on
the eastern rim of the forest,
behind the trees.
    Turn west and find the parts of
    yourself that were torn away
    in grade school, the edges you
    were made to feel ashamed of,
    the bottom that a group of boys,
    then men, took, piece by piece,
    to sell as collector's items.
        Turn north and find yourself
        staring into the imprint of your
        grandmother's shoes, walked
        miles across the sky.
        You now see a path worn
        to freedom and your cue
        to put on the shoes.

Look up and trust
the thing that you see.

Wendy Thompson Taiwo is an assistant professor of African American studies at San José State University. Her research and teaching interests include Black migration to the Bay Area, Black women and mothering, race and the built environment, and Black visual expressions of social status and class.

Minneapolis to the Sea

Haibun* in Memory of George Floyd

Kale Bantigue Fajardo

Running to a Black Lives Matter playlist
blonde-tan medium-sized Chihueenie dog running in lead
cross Lake Street at 14th Ave S
Powderhorn Park, powdery snow
Sun, Oh Glorious Sun
A DIY sign nailed on a tree seems to direct the way
"We Remember Them," it reads:
"Dolal Idd
Sandra Bland
James Paredes
Oscar Grant
Elijah McClain
George Floyd
Breonna Taylor"

"I can't breathe." I can't
Breathe, snow angel, Black saint, breathe
M i n n e a p o l i s

---

*Haibun are a Japanese poetic form. They are associated with the Japanese Buddhist monk-poet Matsuo Bashō (1644–1694). They often begin with a prose poem and then a haiku, and they are often about traveling, the seasons, the elements, land- and waterscapes, and mindfulness/awareness. To learn about haibun, see "More than the Birds, Bees, and Trees: A Closer Look at Writing Haibun," https://poets.org/text/more-birds-bees-and-trees-closer-look-writing-haibun.

He moved here from Texas looking for work
Great Migrations repeating
Freeway(s) cut through historic Black neighborhood(s)
Laid off from work because of COVID pandemic
Tobacco is what he wanted

s l o w drag, inhale, b l o w . . .
fresh green leaves, canopy, trees
sit and rest a while

A viny plant's shadow traces
the right side of your face as
you sit on your balcony in Cabo Rojo, Borikén
Go to the memorial site more, you say
Things will become clearer
and you'll know what to write

Chicago Ave Love
Mississippi River flows
A r c h i p e l a g o s

When I first arrived in Minneapolis
from Oakland, 15 years ago
I googled "Trans" and "Filipino"
and found myself—
although, I was looking for community.
This place ain't easy, Y'all.

Garden for elders
Afro-Indigenous joy
anon,* papaya . . .

digital kissing
pandemic—climate emergency—attempted coup—civil/race war?
lovers

---

*Anon is a Spanish word for "sugar-apple or sweetsop" (*Annona squamosa*). The fruit
is indigenous to the tropical regions of the Americas and the Caribbean. In the
Philippines, we call this fruit *atis*. Spanish traders brought *anon/atis* to the Philippines via the Manila-Acapulco galleon trade (1565–1815.)

Sail, canoe the length of the Father of Waters
into the Gulf, into the Caribbean!
Immigrant Queer Trans Filipino/x joy!

Bathe in the ocean
the sea, circle the Earth, heal
ancestors . . . mothers

In one of our indigenous precolonial traditions,
those our ancestors lost
were placed in wooden canoes
and released into the sea
and into the infinity of the sky and universe

A boatman paddles
reading currents, shores, sky
Saltwater Freedom

Minneapolis, MN
January 15, 2021

Kale Bantigue Fajardo is an associate professor of American studies and Asian American studies at the University of Minnesota, Twin Cities. He is the author of *Filipino Crosscurrents: Oceanographies of Seafaring, Masculinities and Globalization*. He is also a coeditor of the *Island Studies Journal*.

Conclusion
Where Will We Be on May 25, 2022?

Walter R. Jacobs, Amy August,
and Wendy Thompson Taiwo

Sparked: George Floyd, Racism, and the Progressive Illusion was published one year after George Floyd's murder on May 25, 2020. Several of this volume's essays discuss the authors' whereabouts and reactions that day. In this concluding chapter, each of the book's editors discusses their memories of May 25, 2020, and outlines a hope for an aspect of racial dynamics in the United States of America on May 25, 2022, the second anniversary of George Floyd's murder.

Walt

My eighty-five-year-old father has vivid memories of hearing the news of Martin Luther King Jr.'s assassination, even though it was fifty-three years ago. He remembers where he was (the White House Inn in downtown Charlotte, North Carolina), what he was doing (finishing a late dinner with his White boss), and his initial reaction (it would be dangerous for a White man to be in downtown Charlotte, where a large crowd of angry Black people was gathering, so he asked the boss to go check on my mother, who was eight months pregnant with me at home in Raleigh, three hours away). His sister Evelyn also has strong memories of MLK's assassination. April 4, 1968, was a formative event for members of the Greatest Generation, especially for African Americans like Dad and Evelyn.

A date that members of my generational cohort—Generation X—have seared into our collective and individual consciousness is September 11, 2001. When the planes hit the World Trade Center in New York

City, I was having a leisurely breakfast at a friend's apartment in Minneapolis. The friend was not there, as he had recently moved into his girlfriend's house but had not yet terminated his apartment lease. My apartment had been plastered and painted the day before following a water leak from the unit upstairs, so I spent the night at the friend's place to escape the fumes. In those days I never checked the news until I got to my office on the University of Minnesota's Minneapolis campus, so when I arrived there about an hour after United Airlines Flight 175 crashed into the World Trade Center south tower, I was shocked when a former student relayed the news. I thought he was joking since the student was frequently flippant, but when my neighboring colleague ignored my "good morning" greeting at her office door while she was glued to her computer screen, I knew that something was up. It took twenty minutes or so for me to find a website that would load in heavy internet traffic, but after that I was also transfixed by the unfolding events.

Six years later, another tragedy occurred that formed memories I'll recall when, like my father, I'm in my eighties. At 6:05 PM on August 1, 2007, the Interstate 35W bridge across the Mississippi River in downtown Minneapolis collapsed, killing thirteen people. I was attending a screenwriting class several miles away in St. Paul. At our 7:00 break the instructor received and relayed news about the catastrophe, but we continued the class after a few students checked on relatives and learned that they were okay. I did not call my wife, as I knew she was at home and that she knew I was not anywhere near the bridge. Or so I thought until I got an earful when I returned home. Valerie: "Why didn't you check in?" Me: "You knew I was going to class in the opposite direction from the bridge." Valerie: "You expect me to remember that during a disaster this close to home?!" While not as far-reaching on the worldview-changing scale as September 11, 2001, the events of August 1, 2007, did alter some of my everyday practices.

May 25, 2020, may turn out to be another epochal day in the histories of Minneapolis, locally, and the United States of America, nationally. Indeed, the murder of George Floyd by a Minneapolis police officer and the subsequent global protests about police brutality and other injustices faced by Black people here and in other countries may lead to significant changes in race relations in the United States.

By this time, I was living in Oakland, California, and I did not hear the news of George Floyd's murder until May 26. In fact, I don't remember anything about my reaction to hearing the news. It's sad to say, but after so many recent murders of unarmed Black people in the United States, I probably was not surprised or shocked by that latest atrocity. The next day—May 27—I started to check in with friends in the Twin Cities about their wellness after learning that the police used tear gas, rubber bullets, and concussion grenades to disperse crowds at Minneapolis's Third Precinct police station and a nearby Target. I could vividly picture both sites, as my first house in Minneapolis was just one mile from there. On May 28 I posted a note on Facebook: "Yesterday while processing the tragic events in my spiritual hometown of Minneapolis with a friend who lived there for a few years, she noted that Minnesota is a 'wonderful wretched' place for Black people. There is a lot to love about the state (especially in the Twin Cities), but there are many very destructive disparities that are known but swept under the rug. Going forward, hopefully there can be more explicit discussion of the inequities and the creation of solutions to address them."

On May 29 I sent a note to the College of Social Sciences at San José State University, as outlined in the preface to this book.

In the aftermath of the protests, many colleges and universities have begun to have serious conversations about how to stop anti-Black racism in their institutions. As a Black college dean, it was inevitable that I was called upon to be one of the leaders in San José State University's efforts. I was happy to do so, especially given our university's long history of social justice activism; I knew that we would be serious about attempting to find long-term solutions, instead of putting out a public relations "Black Lives Matter!" statement that would quickly be forgotten when the news cycle shifted. SJSU's president initiated several conversations, and new folks were hired to assist us in this work.

On May 25, 2022, I hope that San José State University and other colleges and universities will have tangible adjustments in place. For instance, many Black faculty and other faculty of color currently engage in "public scholarship," the analysis of contemporary social problems that appears in nonacademic publications such as op-ed newspaper essays and nonprofit community reports. This type of work often does not get much credit in the faculty's performance evaluation, but it should. Recognizing and supporting this work will result in increased job security for the faculty and the production of more scholarship to address the many serious issues confronting communities around the world. I hope that by May 25, 2022, public scholarship will be highly valued and properly rewarded.

Amy

Like Walt, I did not hear about the murder of George Floyd immediately after it occurred. I was getting a paper in shape for submission to a journal and scrupulously avoiding the internet throughout the bulk of May 25, 2020. It wasn't until much later that evening, as I was scrolling through Twitter, that I came across dozens of reposts of the horrific video of his murder. Despite my own visceral response upon viewing it, I did not recognize its import right away. Over the next few days, statements of support and solidarity and condemnations of police violence were released rapid-fire from every administrative office at the University of Minnesota. But it wasn't until the twenty-seventh, when I was conducting an interview with a ninth grader about the impact of the coronavirus on kids, that I realized George Floyd's killing had the potential to prompt the most important racial reckoning since the 1960s civil rights movement.

Speaking candidly, my young interviewee told me of her frustration that, so often, kids hear only one side of the story. But her example wasn't about the pandemic; it was about George Floyd. So many of her friends had inherited prejudices from their parents—cops are bad; the people looting and rioting are bad—without getting enough information to think critically or see the whole, messy picture. After all, there are *some* good cops, and most of the protesters are peaceful, she pointed out. Speaking for her generation, she expressed faith in the ability of tomorrow's leaders to know the difference between right and wrong and to make good decisions, but only if they're educated about the issues.

By May 25, 2022, the second anniversary of George Floyd's murder, it is my hope that federal, state, and local agencies will have instituted policies that work to level the playing field for Black families and allow children of color to have the same opportunities as their white counterparts to ensure a more equitable start to their future paths. Given the racial inequalities in income and wealth, interventions to reduce child poverty are a good place to begin. Increasing assistance for the poor and implementing a plan like the one suggested by President Joe Biden in February 2021 to expand the federal child tax credit by turning it into a monthly cash payment for families with children, including families with the lowest incomes (who currently fail to receive the full benefit of the child tax credit), would begin to close Minnesota's persistent racial gap in income and wealth. Government subsidies to families for high-quality childcare would go a long way in helping parents—and especially mothers—get back to work outside the home if they so choose.

Raising wages and certification standards for day care providers and early childhood educators, and increasing funding for university programs that prepare young people to teach and care for children would help to attract talented newcomers to the field. Increasing the number and quality of childcare centers and preschools as well as the amount of support families receive to enroll their children in them would help Black families in particular, given the current gap in enrollment in high-quality educational programs.

Investing in universal preschool is a progressive policy because its greatest benefits accrue to children who are the most disadvantaged. Longitudinal studies show that attending a high-quality preschool leads to many positive outcomes throughout the life course. These include fewer teenage pregnancies and arrests, higher earnings, and greater likelihood of graduating high school, maintaining employment, and owning a home and a car. Even the children of parents who attended preschool as children will tend to benefit from their parents' participation, regardless of whether they attend preschool themselves.

Beyond ensuring that all families have access to high-quality preschool and educational opportunities for their children, I hope that by May 25, 2022, Minnesota will have enacted statewide policies to ensure that all Minnesota students are exposed to anti-racist pedagogy from the start. Given that prejudicial attitudes are deeply entrenched by adulthood, preschool programs are the ideal places to foster the development of positive intergroup attitudes, which begin to form during early elementary school. Children who attend preschool with a racially diverse group of students have more cross-race friendships and lower racial bias throughout elementary school, and kids whose preschools include classroom materials showcasing people from diverse backgrounds hold fewer racially biased attitudes. For these reasons, school districts should strive to ensure that classrooms are as diverse as possible. In addition, providing affordable, high-quality universal preschool with anti-racist curricula is an indispensable intervention for changing attitudes and eradicating prejudice and discrimination. It may even bring the hopes of my young interview respondent to fruition by equipping Generation Alpha with the tools necessary to create a more compassionate and just society.

Wendy

"Take sun people, put 'em in a land of snow"
—Andre Benjamin, in Goodie Mob's "Black Ice"

I was at my mother's house with my two children when news got out that the police had killed another Black man in Minnesota. In that instant, it did not matter that we were in California, a little over 1,900 miles away from the state where I endured the trauma of giving birth to my son surrounded by an all-white medical staff and where white people practice polite racism and the police are always armed and ready to fire. By leaving Minnesota in 2018 after multiple Black men had been murdered by the police and I had grown exhausted with the white reaction and response to institutional and interpersonal violence—which amounted to the best of white folks putting Black Lives Matter signs in their front yards—I thought we could catch our breaths. But while being home in the Bay Area could not be farther away from that video recording, layering it over the video of Philando Castile being shot to death by a police officer in the driver's seat of his car, Thurman Blevins being shot in the back in a Minneapolis alley while running away from the police, and several older Black folks being mauled by aggressive police dogs while going about their business constituted a mixtape of Black life in Minnesota. Immediately after hearing the news I called my husband to tell him, "They killed another Black man in Minnesota." But I could barely hear him. His voice, flat and small over the phone, was inaudible as my shock turned to grief and my grief to indecipherable rage. My children, for whom Minnesota continues to be synonymous with snow, would not recognize me for several days afterward.

If we hadn't left in 2018, I would have been in the streets.

If we hadn't left in 2018, I would have been in a car heading down East Lake Street.

If we hadn't left in 2018, I would have been a brick hurled at the Minneapolis Third Police Precinct.

If we hadn't left in 2018.

Since George Floyd's murder, I find myself presented with two questions: *Where do we want to be on the anniversary of the rebellion that grew from the intersection of East Thirty-Eighth and Chicago and spread across the nation and globe following the murder of George Floyd by the police? Who do we want to be going forward?*

Both questions demand an imagination beyond what we as Black people know and have always known: that there won't be anything close to the justice and accountability we seek in a country that is so deeply and consistently anti-Black. After four hundred years of watching, waiting, and living surrounded by our killers, every Black person has mastered the art of holding freedom in the same arms that we hold death. We also know that for many of us, death—natural, unsolved, premature, or by the hands of the police—is the one way we are able to taste the freedom that we are never afforded in life. (At least dead we don't have to worry about predatory loans, preschool-to-prison pipelines, driving while Black, or displacement.)

In the midst of COVID-19 disproportionately infecting and killing Black people, I find myself grappling with both of these questions that push me to consider the possibility of a different freedom in the face of repeatedly asking: *What is the cost of Black life in a country where and in a time that Black people have to remind every other non-Black person that our lives have value and should matter?* Just as we know that there will be another snowstorm in Minnesota requiring us to collectively dig out our cars and those of strangers from beautiful frozen drifts, we can also assume that there will be another shooting at the hands of the police. The reason hardly matters.

While driving. While jogging. While sleeping. While joyriding. While listening to music at a decibel and frequency above the sensory capacity of white people. While getting something to eat. While having a manic episode. While playing. While looking for help.

Even now as I make my home elsewhere, I am always thinking about my people in Minnesota and holding my breath for Black people everywhere. In the wake of such a prolonged, public, and viral execution, I wonder whether the killing of George Floyd will really change the conditions that inhibit Black life in this country. Is this "moment of reckoning" just a break in the series? A pause in the cycle? How can we be certain that the fire this time will burn away the deadwood and detritus and fuel new growth when the entirety of our lives, of our parents' lives, of our children's lives has been forged around the murder of Black people by the thing inside, behind, and above the law?

What is white supremacy besides a gun?

What is capitalism besides a food desert?

What is a white person's future besides a prison full of Black potential?

But what if we can grasp freedom and be free while alive in a nation that is so fully and heavily invested in theft, trauma, violence, and Black erasure? What if we can, in the wake of George Floyd's stolen life, have it all, everything our foremothers and othermothers and heroes and ancestors pocketed away and scrimped and hungered and struggled for? To find freedom this way requires one to dig deep into the speculative Black feminist tradition of imagining otherwise and otherworlds, knowing full well that we as Black people continue to live in the long afterlife of slavery, in the forever time of social death, and in a country that is consciously trapped in its own violent white settler colonial origin story.

We are alive in a country where every region is just another South. Yet, standing on the mountaintop of the nourishing practice of Black women's creativity and political organizing, we are high enough above to see the possible futures of this place as well as the opportunities we have to alter the way forward if we plan and act with justice, sustainability, wisdom, and abundance in our every step. We as Black people know there is magic everywhere, built into our survival, our songs, our DNA. There is life that stirs in the darkest corners. There is possibility, hope, joy. Even the moss told Harriet the direction north.

And in Minnesota, itself a unique state existing as part of the vascular system of northern midwestern cities where Scandinavian heritage hangs thick on stoic faces and progressive whiteness lives mostly in anti-racist book clubs, there is an entire ecology and constellation of tools and knowledge. In Minnesota there have long been maps to get us home, to keep us safe, to keep us together. Wasn't this where Dred met Harriet, waiting years to escape to freedom even when freedom was just beyond the wall? Just beyond a Supreme Court case?

All one has to do is ask what justice looks like to Black folks who still remember Rondo. Or ask what the future looks like for Black transplants from other regions and cities who are currently engulfed in Twin Cities first- and second-ring suburbs. Each answer is part of the blueprint to build better worlds, one that is starting in Minnesota. It is in Little Earth. It is in Frogtown. It is in Near North Minneapolis. It necessitates prioritizing the next generation's well-being and development starting with birth and ensuring quality health care. It teaches us that we are stewards of the land and that housing should be collective. It teaches us that communities are resources, and our most vulnerable neighborhoods are critical sources for mapping environmental and community futures.

It is the process from which we get homegrown Black leadership—we see you Melvin Carter, Andrea Jenkins, Phillipe Cunningham, and Jeremiah Ellison.

And it is the reminder that we are the ones we have been waiting for and truly all that we've got—in every census tract, in every ward, in every district, in every public housing project, in every lonely white suburb, in every office, at every East Thirty-Eighth and Chicago.

For Further Reading

Books

Alexander, Michelle. *The New Jim Crow: Mass Incarceration in the Age of Colorblindness*. New York: The New Press, 2012.

Baldwin, James. *The Fire Next Time*. New York: Vintage Books, 1993.

———. *No Name in the Street*. New York: Vintage Books, 2007.

Chavez, Leo R. *The Latino Threat: Constructing Immigrants, Citizens, and the Nation*. 2nd ed. Stanford, CA: Stanford University Press, 2013.

Choy, Catherine Ceniza. *Empire of Care: Nursing and Migration in Filipino American History*. Durham, NC: Duke University Press, 2003.

———. *Global Families: A History of Asian International Adoption in America*. New York: New York University Press, 2013.

Coates, Rodney D., Abby L. Ferber, and David L. Brunsma. *The Matrix of Race: Social Construction, Intersectionality, and Inequality*. Thousand Oaks, CA: SAGE Publications, 2017.

DeCarlo, Peter. *Fort Snelling at Bdote: A Brief History*. Newly annotated ed. St. Paul: Minnesota Historical Society Press, 2020.

Du Bois, W. E. B. *The Souls of Black Folks*. Chicago: A. C. McClurg, 1903.

Durkheim, Émile. *Suicide: A Study in Sociology*. 1897. New York: Free Press, 1951.

Eady, Cornelius. *Brutal Imagination: Poems*. New York: Penguin, 2001.

Galang, M. Evelina. *Screaming Monkeys: Critiques of Asian American Images*. Minneapolis, MN: Coffee House Press, 2003.

Glaude, Eddie S., Jr. *Begin Again: James Baldwin's America and Its Urgent Lessons for Our Own*. New York: Crown, 2020.

Hartman, Saidiya. *Lose Your Mother: A Journey Along the Atlantic Slave Route*. New York: Farrar, Straus and Giroux, 2007.

Harvey, David. *A Brief History of Neoliberalism*. Oxford: Oxford University Press, 2007.

Holland, Sharon Patricia. *The Erotic Life of Racism*. Durham, NC: Duke University Press, 2012.

Mitchell, Jasmine. *Imagining the Mulatta: Blackness in U.S. and Brazilian Media*. Urbana: University of Illinois Press, 2020.

Omi, Michael, and Howard Winant. *Racial Formation in the United States*. New York: Routledge, 2015.

Patterson, Orlando. *Slavery and Social Death: A Comparative Study*. Cambridge, MA: Harvard University Press, 2018.

Rankine, Claudia. *The White Card: A Play in One Act*. Minneapolis, MN: Graywolf Press, 2019.

Roediger, David R. *Working Toward Whiteness: How America's Immigrants Became White: The Strange Journey from Ellis Island to the Suburbs*. New York: Basic Books, 2018.

Shin, Sun Yung, ed. *A Good Time for the Truth: Race in Minnesota*. St. Paul: Minnesota Historical Society Press, 2016.

Vue, Pao Lee. *Assimilation and the Gendered Color Line: Hmong Case Studies of Hip-Hop and Import Racing*. El Paso, TX: LFB Scholarly Publishing, 2012.

Winters, Joseph Richard. *Hope Draped in Black: Race, Melancholy, and the Agony of Progress*. Durham, NC: Duke University Press, 2016.

Woodson, Carter G. *The Mis-Education of the Negro*. N.p.: Tribeca Books, 1933.

Academic Journal Articles, Book Chapters, and Research Reports

Bhabha, Homi. "Of Mimicry and Man: The Ambivalence of Colonial Discourse." Discipleship: A Special Issue on Psychoanalysis, *October* 28 (Spring 1984): 125–33.

Ellison, Ralph. "The Art of Fiction: An Interview." In *Shadow and Act*. New York: Vintage International, 1995.

"The Fiftieth Anniversary of the Kerner Commission Report." Special issue, *Russell Sage Foundation Journal of Social Sciences* 4, no. 6 (September 2018).

Gaias, Larissa M., Diana E. Gal, Tashia Abry, Michelle Taylor, and Kristen L. Granger. "Diversity Exposure in Preschool: Longitudinal Implications for Cross-Race Friendships and Racial Bias." *Journal of Applied Developmental Psychology* 59 (2018): 5–15.

Hanson, Brady, et al. "Invisible Youth: The Health of Lesbian, Gay, Bisexual, and Questioning Adolescents in Minnesota." Rainbow Health Initiative, October 2015. https://www.justushealth.org/sites/default/files/inline-files/Oct_23_MSS_Report.pdf.

Heckman, James J. "The Economics of Inequality: The Value of Early Childhood Education." *American Educator* 35, no. 1 (2011): 31–35.

Heckman, James J., and Ganesh Karapakula. "Intergenerational and Intragenerational Externalities of the Perry Preschool Project." National Bureau of Economic Research Working Paper no. 25889, May 2019. DOI: 10.3386/w25889.

Horowitz, Juliana Menasce, Anna Brown, and Kiana Cox. "Race in America 2019." Pew Research Center, April 9, 2019. https://www.pewsocialtrends.org/2019/04/09/race-in-america-2019/.

Jones, Camara Phyllis. "Confronting Institutionalized Racism." *Phylon* 50, no. 1–2 (2002): 7–22.

Kids Count Data Center. "Children Age 3 to 5 Enrolled in Nursery School, Preschool or Kindergarten, by Race and Ethnicity in Minnesota." Annie E. Casey Foundation, 2021. https://datacenter.kidscount.org/data/tables/

8045-children-age-3-to-5-enrolled-in-nursery-school-preschool-or
-kindergarten-by-race-and-ethnicity#detailed.

Lorde, Audre. "Poetry Is Not a Luxury." In *Sister Outsider: Essays and Speeches*. Berkeley: Crossing Press, 2007.

Manyika, Sarah. "Oyinbo." In *Problematizing Blackness: Self-Ethnographies by Black Immigrants to the United States*, edited by Percy C. Hintzen and Jean Muteba Rahier. New York: Routledge, 2003.

Minnesota Compass. "Planning District: Highland Neighborhood." 2015. https://www.mncompass.org/profiles/city/st-paul/highland-park.

———. "Planning District: Macalester-Groveland Neighborhood." 2015. https://www.mncompass.org/profiles/city/st-paul/macalester-groveland.

Myers, Samuel L., Jr. "Why Diversity Is a Smokescreen for Affirmative Action." *Change: The Magazine of Higher Learning* 29, no. 4 (July/August 1997): 25–32.

"Perry Preschool Project." High Scope, 2021. https://highscope.org/perry-preschool-project/.

Pha, Kong Pheng. "Doorknocking for Justice: Exploring Asian Dreams, Lives, and Issues Through Critical Conversations." American Asian Organizing Project, June 13, 2017. http://aaopmn.org/2017/06/13/__stpdoorknock4 justice/.

Rutland, Adam, and Melanie Killen. "A Developmental Science Approach to Reducing Prejudice and Social Exclusion: Intergroup Processes, Social-Cognitive Development, and Moral Reasoning." *Social Issues and Policy Review* 9, no. 1 (2015): 121–54.

Sarmiento, Thomas Xavier. "The Heartland of Empire: Queer Cultural Imaginaries of Filipinas/os in the Midwest." PhD diss., University of Minnesota, 2014. Digital Conservancy: https://conservancy.umn.edu/handle/11299/200264.

Singleton, Jermaine. "Out of the Hands of Others' Fantasies: Minority Mental Health in the Eye of Neoliberalism's Storm." *Stillpoint Magazine* 1 (2019). https://stillpointmag.org/articles/out-of-the-hands-of-others -fantasies/.

Wolfe, Patrick. "Settler Colonialism and the Elimination of the Native." *Journal of Genocide Research* 8, no. 4 (December 2006): 387–409. DOI :10.1080/14623520601056240.

Wood, Eunha Jeong, and Kong Pheng Pha. "On Police Abuse & Black Lives Matter: Talking Asian to Asian in North Minneapolis." American Asian Organizing Project, February 15, 2019. http://aaopmn.org/2019/02/15/ on-police-abuse-black-lives-matter-talking-asian-to-asian-in-north -minneapolis/.

Journalistic and Op-Ed Articles

Brown, Heather. "'The 'Minnesota Paradox': Why the State Has One of the Largest Racial Disparities." WCCO CBS Local Minnesota, June 23, 2020.

https://minnesota.cbslocal.com/2020/06/23/the-minnesota-paradox-why
-the-land-of-10000-lakes-has-one-of-the-largest-racial-disparities/.

Cassidy, John. "A Bold Proposal to Ease Child Poverty Is the Essence of
Bidenomics." *New Yorker,* January 26, 2021.

Coleman, Justine. "Texas Lt. Governor on Reopening State: 'There Are More
Important Things than Living.'" *The Hill*, April 21, 2020. http://thehill.com/
homenews/state-watch/493879-texas-lt-governor-on-reopening-state
-there-are-more-important-things.

Collins, Jon, and John Enger. "Beltrami Co. Becomes First in State to Reject
Refugee Resettlement." *MPR News*, January 8, 2020. https://www
.mprnews.org/story/2020/01/07/beltrami-co-rejects-refugee-resettlement.

Collins, Jon, and Riham Feshir. "Noor Sentenced to 12 1/2 Years in Death of
911 Caller Justine Ruszczyk." *MPR News*, June 7, 2019. https://www
.mprnews.org/story/2019/06/07/police-trial-shooting-justine-damond
-ruszczyk-australia-noor-sentence.

Comen, Evan. "Worst Cities for Black Americans." 24/7 Wall St., November 5,
2019. https://247wallst.com/special-report/2019/11/05/the-worst-cities
-for-black-americans-5/4/.

Cowan, Jill. "Why So Many Filipino Californians Are on the Front Lines." *New
York Times*, May 15, 2020.

Eischens, Rilyn. "Data Show Disparities Between Black and White Minnesotans in Education, Income, Criminal Justice Are Among the Worst in the
Nation." *Minnesota Reformer*, June 2020. https://minnesotareformer.com/
2020/06/08/data-show-disparities-between-black-and-white-minnesotas
-in-education-income-crimina-justice-are-among-the-worst-in-the-nation/.

Furst, Randy. "Family Awarded $3M in Man's Death." *Star Tribune* (Minneapo-
lis), May 25, 2013.

Furst, Randy, and Paul Walsh. "Floyd Family Sues City, Officers." *Star Tribune*
(Minneapolis), July 16, 2020.

Grant, Kristin. "The History and Complexities of Gift Giving." *Reporter*,
December 2, 2016. https://reporter.rit.edu/features/history-and
-complexities-gift-giving.

Hassan, Adeel. "Sandra Bland Video: What We Know." *New York Times,* May 7,
2019.

Hill, Evan, et al. "How George Floyd Was Killed in Custody." *New York Times*,
May 31, 2020.

Ibrahim, Mukhtar, and Jared Goyette. "Police Raided the Home of an Older
Somali Couple, Bound Their Wrists, and Yelled at Their Small Children.
Then the Police Told Them Their Son Was Shot Dead." *Sahan Journal*,
January 1, 2021. https://sahanjournal.com/police/minneapolis
-police-shooting-dolal-idd-family-home-bca/.

Ingraham, Christopher. "Racial Inequality in Minneapolis Is Among the Worst
in the Nation." *Washington Post*, May 30, 2020.

Jacobs, Walter R. "30 Years a Minnesotan." *Blackasotan*, June 15, 2016. https://
blackasotan.com/2016/06/15/30-years-a-minnesotan/.

Kenney, Dave. "'State That Works' Cover Offered a Minnesota Image That Doesn't Fit as Comfortably Today." *MinnPost*, August 13, 2013. https://www.minnpost.com/community-voices/2013/08/state-works-cover-offered-a-minnesota-image-doesnt-fit-comfortably-today/.

Korn, Melissa, and Shibani Mahtani. "Minnesota Police Officer Jeronimo Yanez Found Not Guilty on Manslaughter Charge." *Wall Street Journal*, June 17, 2017.

Lisi, Brian. "Campus Security Guard Admits He Accidentally Shot Himself After First Lying about Black Man in a Hoodie with 'Short Afro.'" *New York Daily News*, September 14, 2017.

Lopez, German, Christina Animashaun, and Javier Zarracina. "How America Has—and Hasn't—Changed since Martin Luther King Jr.'s Death, in 11 Charts: From Economic Well-Being to Criminal Justice Issues, Racial Inequality Is Still Very Real in America." *Vox*, April 4, 2018. www.vox.com/identities/2018/4/4/17189310/martin-luther-king-anniversary-race-inequality-racism.

Miller, Greg. "When Minneapolis Segregated." *CityLab*, January 8, 2020. https://www.bloomberg.com/news/articles/2020-01-08/mapping-the-segregation-of-minneapolis.

Orrick, Dave. "State Opens Wide-Ranging Probe of 10 Years of Minneapolis PD Race Relations." *St. Paul Pioneer Press*, June 2, 2020.

Pheifer, Pat. "St. Catherine University Security Officer Shot, Injured in St. Paul." *Star Tribune* (Minneapolis), September 13, 2017.

Phillips, Katrina. "Longtime Police Brutality Drove American Indians to Join the George Floyd Protests." *Washington Post*, June 6, 2020.

Raddatz, Kate. "College Guard Who Shot Himself, Blamed 'Black Man,' Released from Jail." *CBS Minnesota*, September 14, 2017. https://minnesota.cbslocal.com/video/3730739-college-guard-who-shot-himself-blamed-black-man-released-from-jail/.

Redmond, Leslie, interview by Michael Martin. "Minneapolis NAACP President on Why a City Ablaze Is 'A Long Time Coming.'" *All Things Considered*, NPR, May 30, 2020. https://www.npr.org/2020/05/30/866204366/minneapolis-naacp-president-on-why-a-city-ablaze-is-a-long-time-coming.

Siegel, Rachel. "A White Security Officer Told Police He Was Shot by a Black Man. Turns Out He'd Shot Himself." *Washington Post*, September 15, 2017.

Vitale, Alex. "Would Defunding the Police Make Us Safer?" *The Atlantic*, June 6, 2020. https://www.theatlantic.com/health/archive/2020/06/would-defunding-police-make-us-safer/612766/.

Xiong, Chao. "Ex-St. Catherine Guard Gets Probation for Making Up Story of Being Shot by a Black Man: Brent Ahlers Was Charged with Fabricating a Story of Being Shot by Black Man." *Star Tribune* (Minneapolis), December 18, 2017.

Xiong, Chao, and Paul Walsh. "NAACP Laments Wounded St. Kate's Security Officer Making up Story about Black Gunman." *Star Tribune* (Minneapolis), September 14 2017.

Podcasts, Videos, and Websites

Las Cafeteras. "Luna Lovers" music video. YouTube. https://www.youtube
.com/watch?v=NZGznPUC43k.

KRS-One. "Sound of da Police" music video. YouTube. https://www.youtube
.com/watch?v=9ZrAYxWPN6c.

Mapping Prejudice project. https://mappingprejudice.umn.edu.

Marshall, Yannick Giovanni. "Myth: Black People Died to Vote, Part 2." *The
Black Myths Podcast*. https://www.stitcher.com/show/the-black-myths
-podcast/episode/myth-black-people-died-to-vote-pt-2-w-dr-yannick
-giovanni-marshall-78177900.

Noah, Trevor. "George Floyd, Minneapolis Protests, Ahmaud Arbery & Amy
Cooper." YouTube. https://www.youtube.com/watch?v=v4amCfVbA_c.

Prince. "Uptown" music video. YouTube. https://www.youtube.com/
watch?v=ZiuSRQHLv88.

The Society Pages. https://thesocietypages.org.

"Wonderful/Wretched Memories of Racial Dynamics in the Twin Cities,
Minnesota" special feature in The Society Pages: https://thesocietypages
.org/specials/wonderful-wretched-memories-of-racial-dynamics-in
-the-twin-cities-minnesota/ and http://z.umn.edu/WWseries.

Reading Discussion Guide

Edgar Jesus Campos and Amy August

The essays in this book present a wide variety of perspectives on race and racism in Minnesota and the ways in which institutionalized racism and white supremacy permeate our lives and communities. To facilitate deeper, more robust conversations, we have provided the following questions to be addressed individually or in dialogue with others.

Questions

1. What does "Minnesota nice" mean to you? How does "Minnesota nice" operate as an agent that abets racial inequality? How does it contribute to the Minnesota Paradox and the state's substantial racial inequalities despite surface progressivism? Do you agree with the assessment that Minnesota is a "White Wakanda"? (The essays by Marcia Williams, Samuel L. Myers Jr., Taiyon J. Coleman, and David Todd Lawrence may spark some ideas.)

2. Ibrahim Hirsi reflects on race as being one of the primary organizing principles in American society, a stark contrast to his experiences in his native Somalia. Mi'Chael N. Wright recounts similar experiences of White people in Minnesota treating her race as salient in ways that had not occurred in California. In a sense, these authors' interactions with Minnesotans resocialized them to understand race in different and more problematic ways. Have you ever been in a different social context—while traveling, or even among different groups of people in your hometown—where race or ethnicity seemed to have a different significance than you were used to? What did you learn about the meaning of race or ethnicity among the members

of that community? What did you learn about your previous way of thinking about the meaning of race or ethnicity?

3. Black women authors Mi'Chael N. Wright, Terrion L. Williamson, Amber Joy Powell, Shannon Gibney, and Enid Logan each reflected on their intersectional and/or personal identities as women and how those identities are perceived in everyday society while navigating parenting or being in public "White" spaces. What are some of the particular challenges they faced? How do those challenges differ from those faced by White women? Why do you think they chose to call readers' attention to these issues?

4. Consider the specific fears faced by Black men and those who love them, which are described in the examples listed in question 3 as well as in the essays by Taiyon J. Coleman and Wendy Thompson Taiwo. Have you ever experienced fear of the police for yourself or for a loved one? In what ways is it similar to and different from the fears described in the essays? What steps did you take to keep yourself or your loved one safe?

5. Amber Joy Powell's essay reflects on how her values changed after she learned to see something familiar from someone else's perspective. Think critically about how you understand and rank your own values (e.g., freedom, safety, community, independence, interdependence, self-reliance, integrity, success, etc.). Does the complex picture of the social world presented in this book change how you understand these values or which ones are most important to you? Why and how did they change? If they didn't change, why do you think they did not?

6. In both Walter R. Jacobs's "Blackasotan Identity Lanes" and Thomas X. Sarmiento's "In Transit," physical travel around the Twin Cities provides an opportunity to reflect on the racial and social class geographies of the metro area. Both essays illustrate the multiple worlds that exist simultaneously for people who differ by race, class, gender, sexual orientation, ability status, and consequently privilege. What are some of the different worlds that you've encountered in Minnesota or in your own community? How is the space in which you are located defined, and how can you tell when you're leaving one

particular space and entering another? How does your identity and behavior change as you navigate different spaces?

7. When reading the essays, were you surprised at how the authors of color who are not Black processed the experiences and emotions of anti-Blackness? How does this processing by people of color who are not Black affect the discussion around anti-Blackness in the United States? Think of essays by M. Bianet Castellanos, Gabriela Spears-Rico, Katrina Phillips, Kong Pheng Pha, and Kale Bantigue Fajardo for examples.

   If you are a person of color who is not Black, do any of these essays reflect your own thoughts about racial inequalities toward the Black community and any community of color that is not your own? Why or why not?

8. Think about the images presented in the poetic responses in Wendy Thompson Taiwo's "All the Stars Point North" and Kale Bantigue Fajardo's "Minneapolis to the Sea." Which images were the most powerful or striking to you? What emotions did they conjure up? If you were writing a poem to express your own response to George Floyd's killing, what images might you include? What themes or ideas would you want your readers to take away from your poem?

9. After reading these essays, what do you feel are the most important ways in which Minnesota is wonderful and wretched? How has your understanding of the state's racial dynamics changed? What were the most important insights you gained from reading *Sparked*? What would you tell others about the book, particularly those who might be resistant to reading it?

10. In their essays, Brittany Lewis, Kate Beane, and Jerry and Sarah Shannon each provide examples of their involvement in the fight for social justice. They illustrate how social activism on the part of regular citizens can be effective. How are their forms of social activism influenced by their social identities (e.g., their race, gender, age, sexual orientation, socioeconomic status, etc.) and the privileges and constraints that accompany them? Given your social identity, what can you do to further the cause of racial justice?

Edgar Jesus Campos is a fifth-year PhD candidate in sociology at the University of Minnesota. He is an ethnographer and historical sociologist focused on the intertwining of sport, culture, and politics, and his current research focuses on the cultural politics of nationalism, modernity, and globalization of Latin American nations in the Olympic Movement.

Amy August is an assistant professor of sociology and the assistant director of the Institute for the Study of Sport, Society and Social Change at San José State University. She is an ethnographer focused on sport, education, family, and culture, and her current research compares the forms of cultural capital recognized and rewarded by preschool teachers and coaches.

The text of *Sparked* has been set in Chaparral Pro, a typeface designed by Carol Twombly. Chaparral combines the legibility of slab serif designs popularized in the nineteenth century with the grace of sixteenth-century roman book lettering.

Book design by Wendy Holdman